I0810319

IMAGES
of America

THE CASCO BAY ISLANDS

What is an Islander?

"One who lives on an island", states Webster, briefly. However, a more definitive explanation is, one who -

- hears the music in the swirl of breakers, cry of gulls, and sound of buoy bells.
- is proud of being quaint and keeps a hand on the past.
- values things in terms of beauty and comfort rather than shine and speed.
- decors a home with beachcombings.
- insists on using up the old before breaking in the new.
- counts wealth in terms of friendships. Is aware of the neighbors' needs and takes time to help.
- dines on baked beans 51 Saturday nights each year.
- bears a touch of hermit and craves the peace of solitude.
- prizes his individuality and finds it difficult to conform.
- cannot bear crowds and refuses to wait in lines.
- is related to other islanders.
- is stimulated by the scent of seaweed, salt air and burning driftwood.
- easily identifies trees, wildflowers, plants and birds.
- likes to walk for transportation, exercise or just to 'neighbor around'.
- sets a slower pace, but enjoys life along the way.
- lives a step away from the world - by choice. Whose activities are governed by the weather, water, and a boat schedule.

Ruth Sargent

IMAGES
of America

THE CASCO BAY ISLANDS

Ruth S. Sargent

ARCADIA
PUBLISHING

ISBN 978-0-7385-9709-6

Published by Arcadia Publishing
Charleston, South Carolina

Printed in the United States of America

For all general information contact Arcadia Publishing at:
Telephone 843-853-2070
Fax 843-853-0044
E-mail sales@arcadiapublishing.com
For customer service and orders:
Toll-Free 1-888-313-2665

Visit us on the Internet at www.arcadiapublishing.com

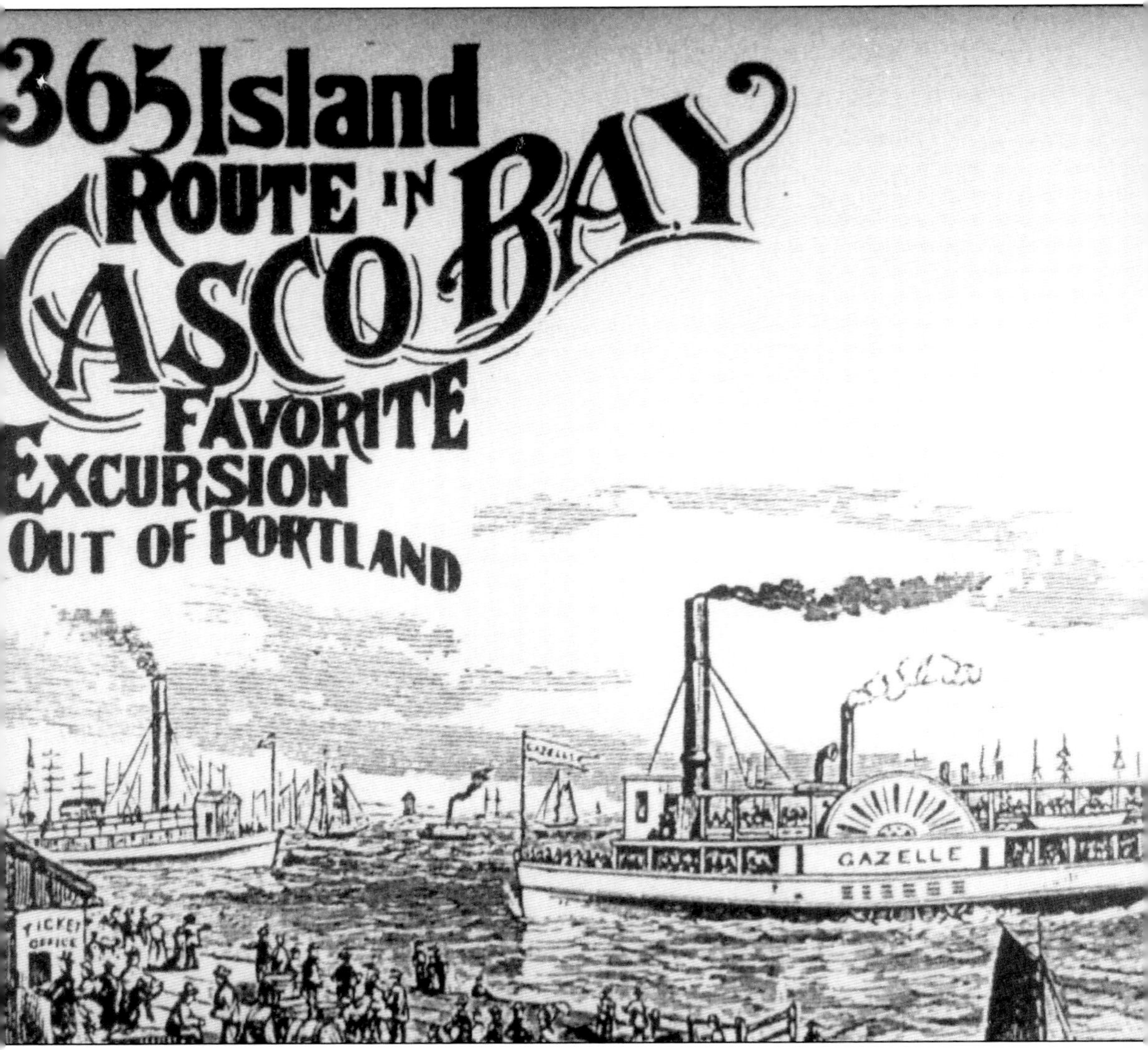

Contents

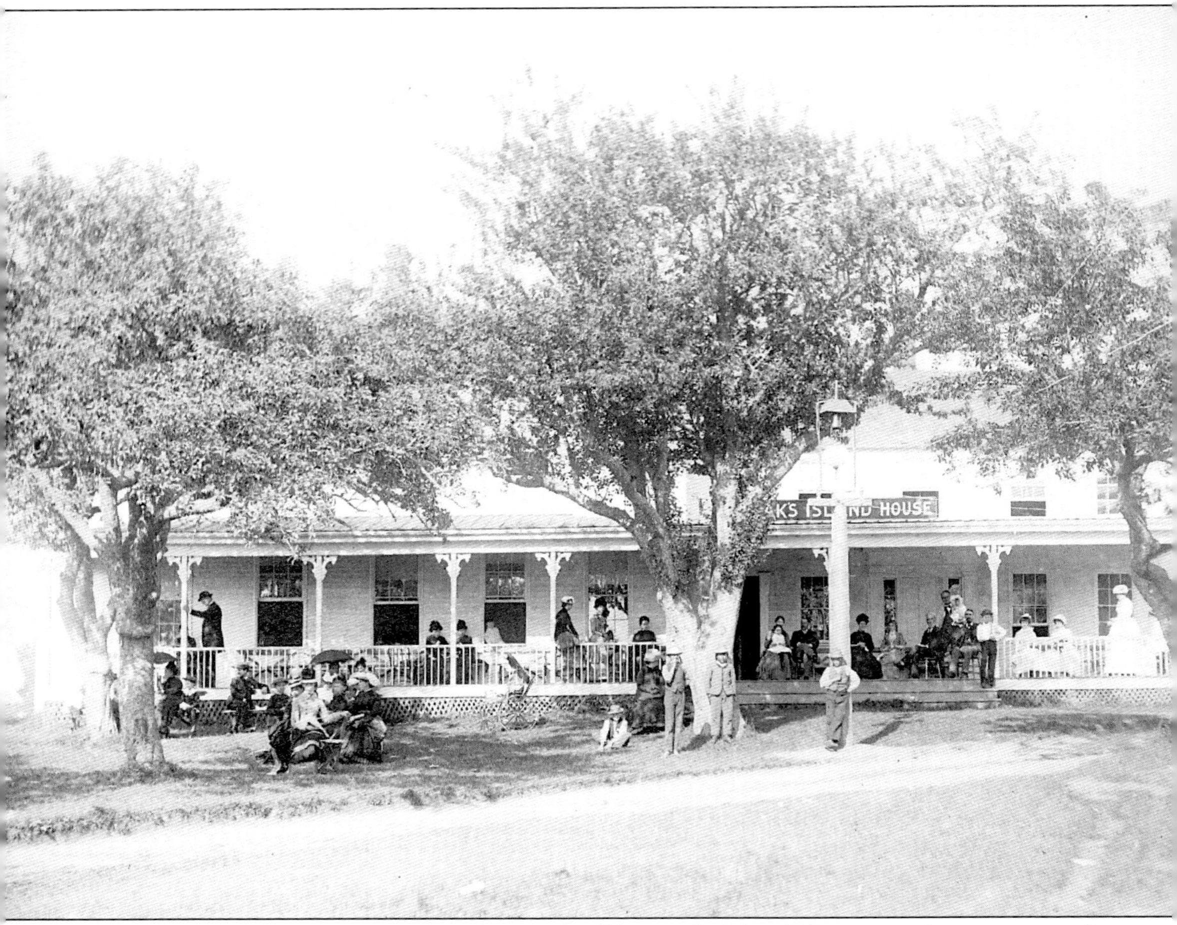

Guests and locals congregate on the porch of the Peaks Island House on what appears to be a very sultry summer day at the turn of the century.

Introduction

Along the southeastern edge of Maine, where the Atlantic Ocean surges against the land, lie the islands of Casco Bay. They face the open sea and watch the sunrise on one side, then later look back across the harbor to the mainland to see the sunset.

Romantics term them the Calendar Isles, claimimg there is one for each day of the year. But if a rock large enough to support one person at high tide is counted, can this number be acceptable? Noted historian Edward Elwell set the total much lower.

However, we are concerned only with those islands large enough to be measured in acres and capable of supporting a small community: Peaks, Cushing, Little Diamond, Great Diamond, Long, Chebeague, Cliff, and tiny House.

Scientists tell us that during the Ice Age these islands were the tips of mountain peaks. When the glaciers melted and the water receded, vegetation took root. It seems plausible, for ledge is a prominent factor throughout this group, especially along the shorelines.

Proofs have been found that four thousand years ago the Abenaki Native Americans ("People of the Dawn") spent their summers here. In 1614 the famed Captain John Smith sailed by and called it Aucocisco Bay ("Place of Rest"). This was shortened to Casco in the 1620s by the first settlers.

Ownership of the islands was challenged by the whites, and, after much bloodshed, they took over. Homes were built in the 1700s, followed by churches, cemeteries, schools, and sites for businesses. But the first essentials were boats and wharves. Unless those are available, no one can live on an island.

Eventually, a boat line had to be considered. Islanders needed regular, safe, and reliable transportation as well as all the materials necessary for survival. Things went well and the islands prospered. With the development of the railroad and trolley car systems on the mainland in the mid- to late nineteenth century visitors (later called tourists) began arriving to spend cool summers on the islands. Hotels were built, larger and larger in competition. Greenwood

Garden opened to provide entertainments. Gradually the fame of Casco Bay spread far and wide, even to Boston and New York!

By the early 1920s fresh water was being piped over from the mainland, electrical and telephone systems were organized, and fuel oil and gasoline were delivered along with the daily mail and the Portland newspapers. The islands were indeed the place to be—especially Peaks!

Everyone seemed to prosper and the islands were booming—until Henry Ford's invention came along. An auto could take you to the mountains, to the lakes, and to other places for vacations. The lure of the islands began to fade. Their heyday was over.

But after a lull of two decades, the islands were crowded again, this time in preparation for World War II. Barracks were raised, homes for servicemen's families built, and fortifications put in place. The islands were on guard! Thankfully island life is difficult to destroy. Family strengths held fast; few local people fled to the mainland for safety when the islands represented the security that they had always known. Everyone met the situation in their own way and did their part. Islanders are strong.

When this difficult era ended and peace returned, so did the "summer folk." The islands regained their strengths, and once again became secure in winter and a delight in summer. Old friends were welcomed back. It was almost like the old days that some folks could recall.

Just as the famed Maine poet Rachel Field warned, "If you have ever slept on an island, you'll never be quite the same." I hope that the pictures contained in this book bring alive some of your memories, or let you discover the magical feeling of island life!

One

Peaks Island Boats and Landings

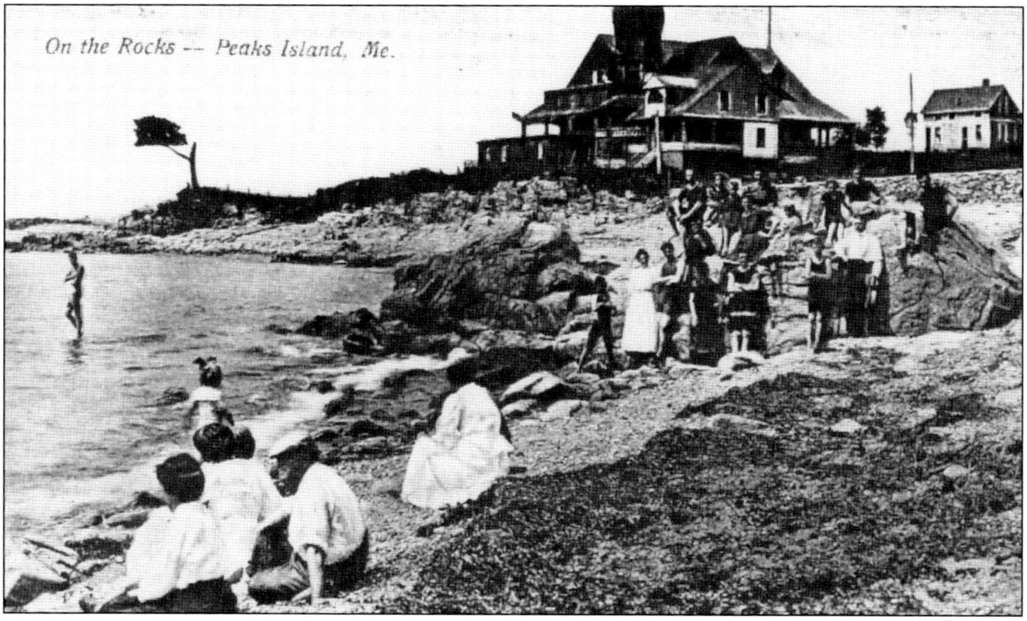

A group enjoying a hot day at a beach on Peaks Island.

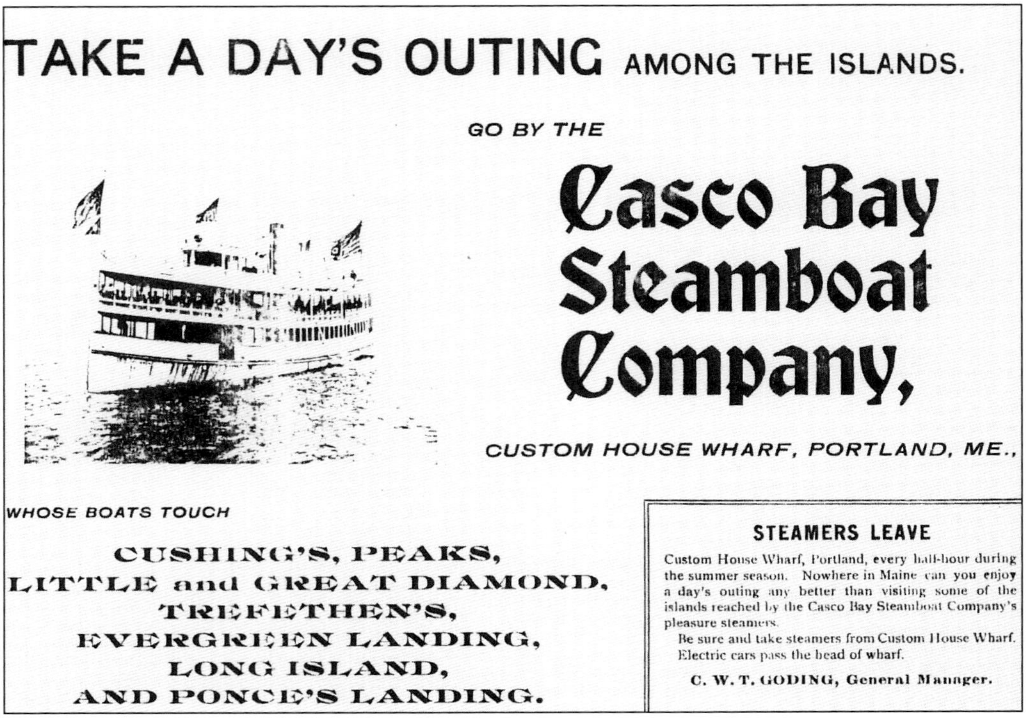
TAKE A DAY'S OUTING AMONG THE ISLANDS.
GO BY THE
Casco Bay Steamboat Company,
CUSTOM HOUSE WHARF, PORTLAND, ME.,
WHOSE BOATS TOUCH
CUSHING'S, PEAKS,
LITTLE and GREAT DIAMOND,
TREFETHEN'S,
EVERGREEN LANDING,
LONG ISLAND,
AND PONCE'S LANDING.
STEAMERS LEAVE
Custom House Wharf, Portland, every half-hour during the summer season. Nowhere in Maine can you enjoy a day's outing any better than visiting some of the islands reached by the Casco Bay Steamboat Company's pleasure steamers.
Be sure and take steamers from Custom House Wharf. Electric cars pass the head of wharf.
C. W. T. GODING, General Manager.

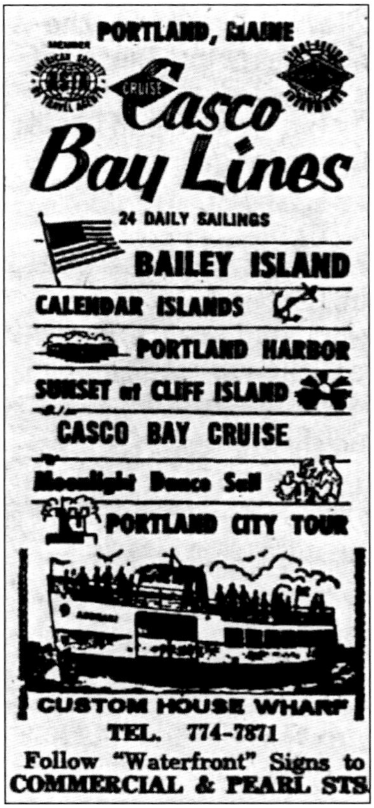
PORTLAND, MAINE
CRUISE
Casco Bay Lines
24 DAILY SAILINGS
BAILEY ISLAND
CALENDAR ISLANDS
PORTLAND HARBOR
SUNSET at CLIFF ISLAND
CASCO BAY CRUISE
Moonlight Dance Sail
PORTLAND CITY TOUR
CUSTOM HOUSE WHARF
TEL. 774-7871
Follow "Waterfront" Signs to
COMMERCIAL & PEARL STS.

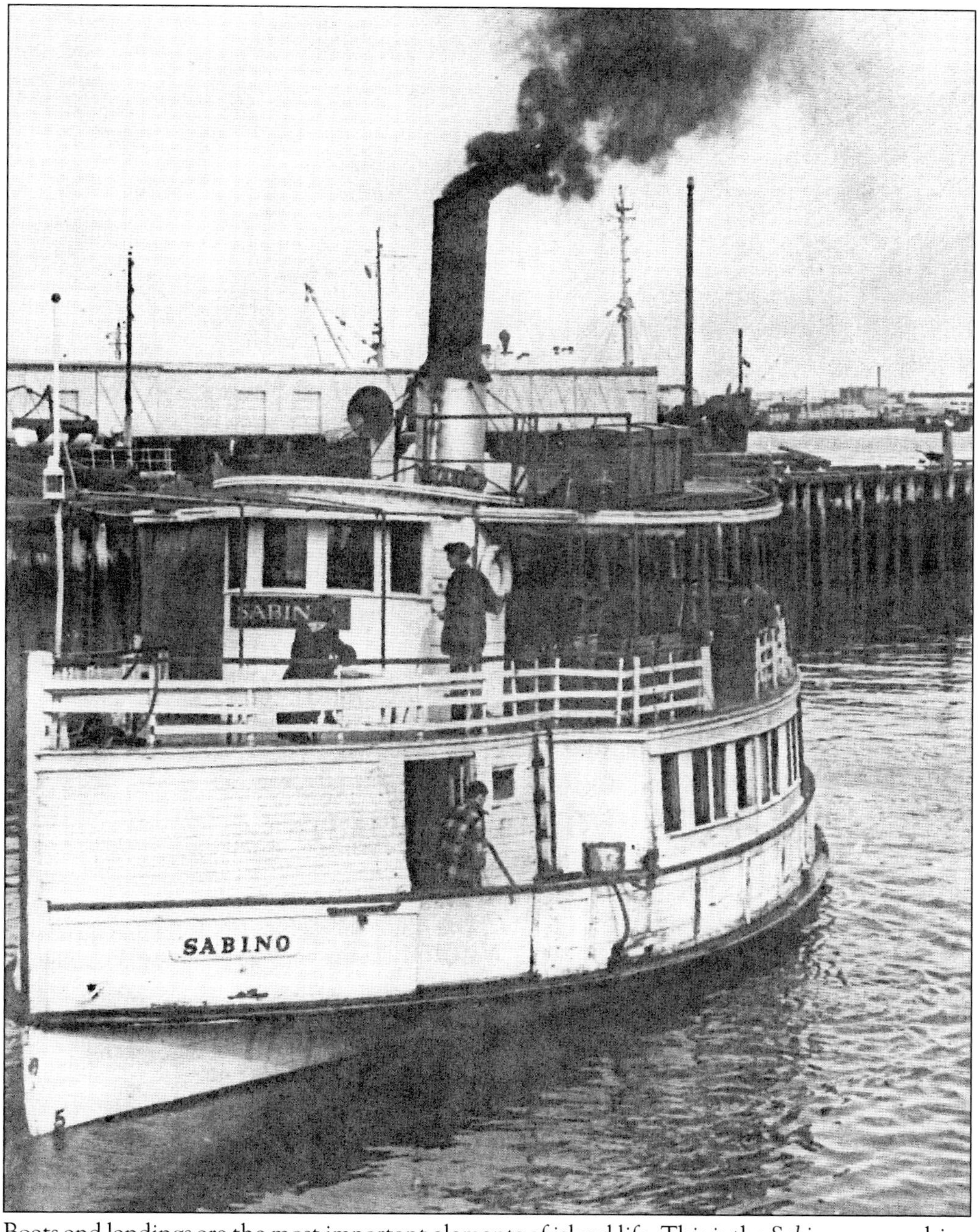

Boats and landings are the most important elements of island life. This is the *Sabino* approaching the dock in Portland.

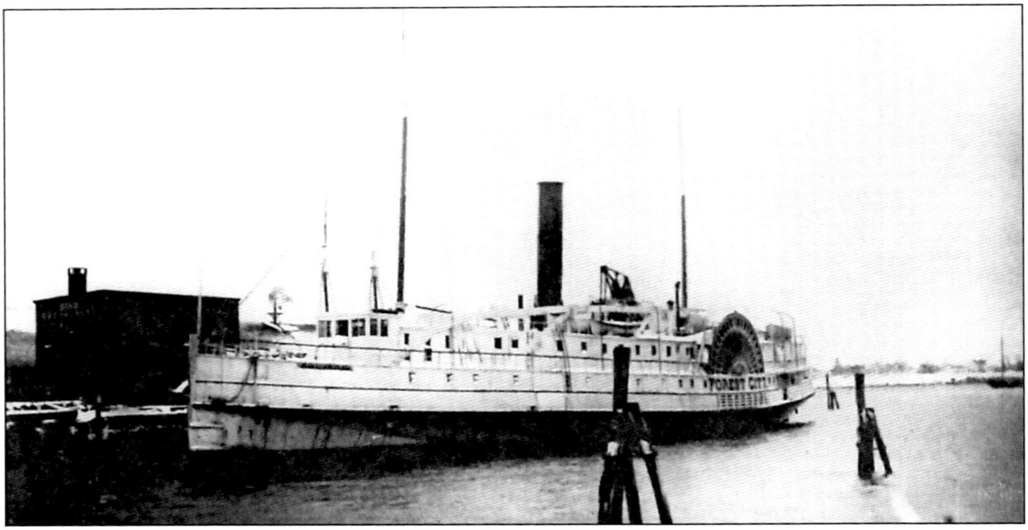

The *Forest City*, an early paddle steamer.

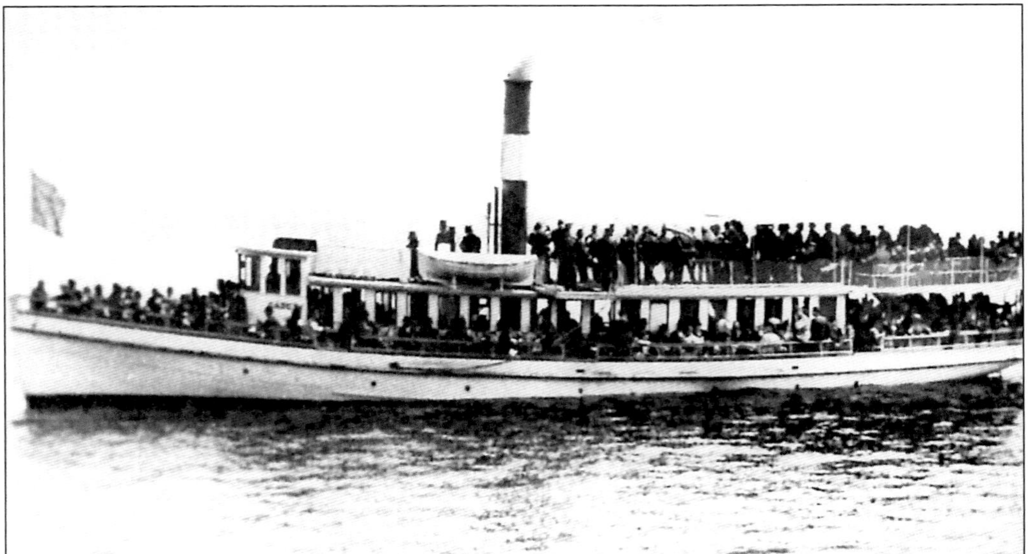

The *Cadet*, one of the largest ships to travel the bay, looks packed to the gills in this photograph.

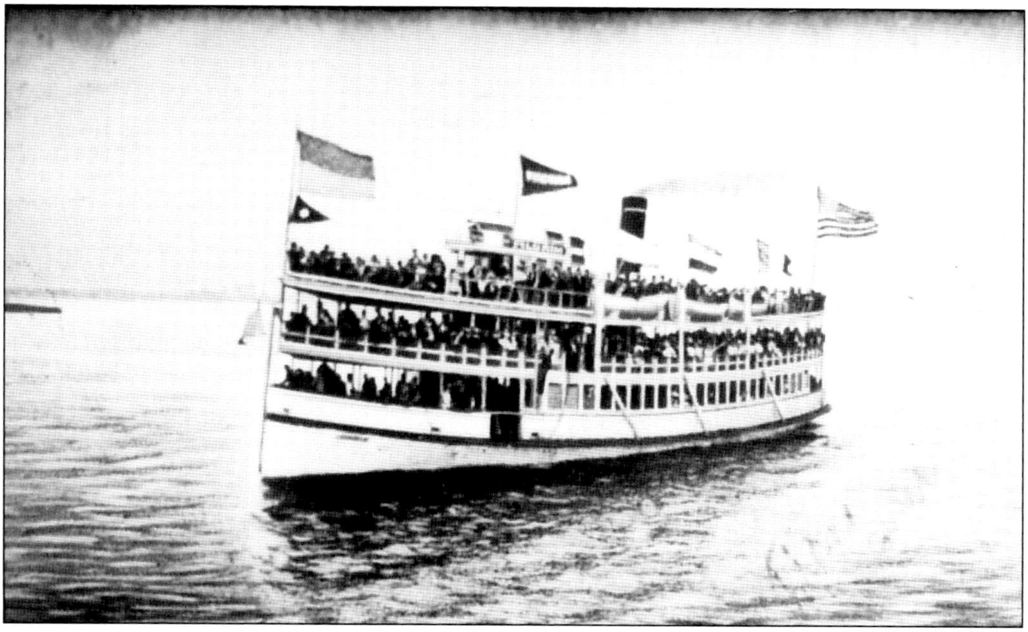

The island excursion steamer *Pilgrim* taking a group of excited tourists to the islands.

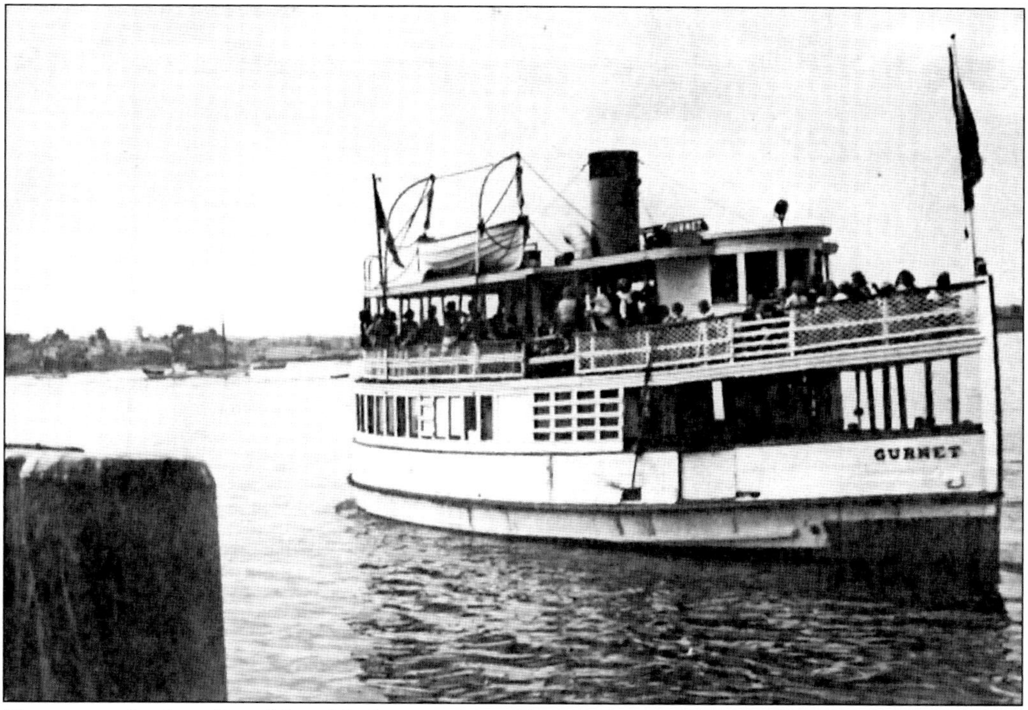

Gurnet was built at Boothbay Harbor in 1914. She was 58 feet long and had an 18-foot beam. First powered by steam, she was converted to diesel in 1926. She joined the fleet of island steamers in Casco Bay in 1916, and was the last of the old wooden steamers to leave the Casco Bay Lines fleet.

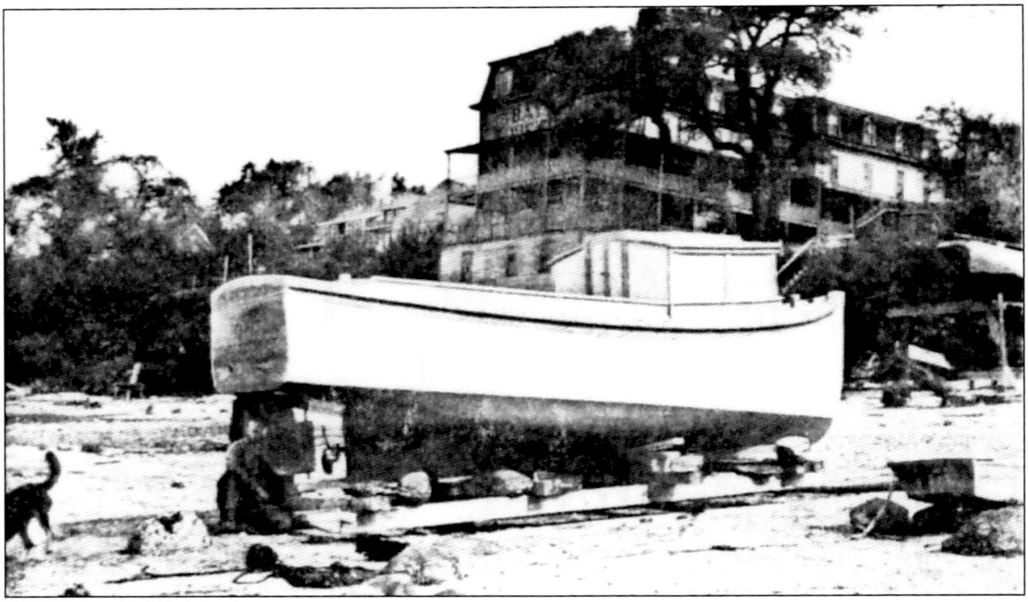

This boat was built by Don Crandall of Peaks Island in the 1930s. Many islanders had vessels which were used primarily for the purposes of work, but they also relied on these family vehicles for other purposes, such as ferrying family members to the mainland for important services or events.

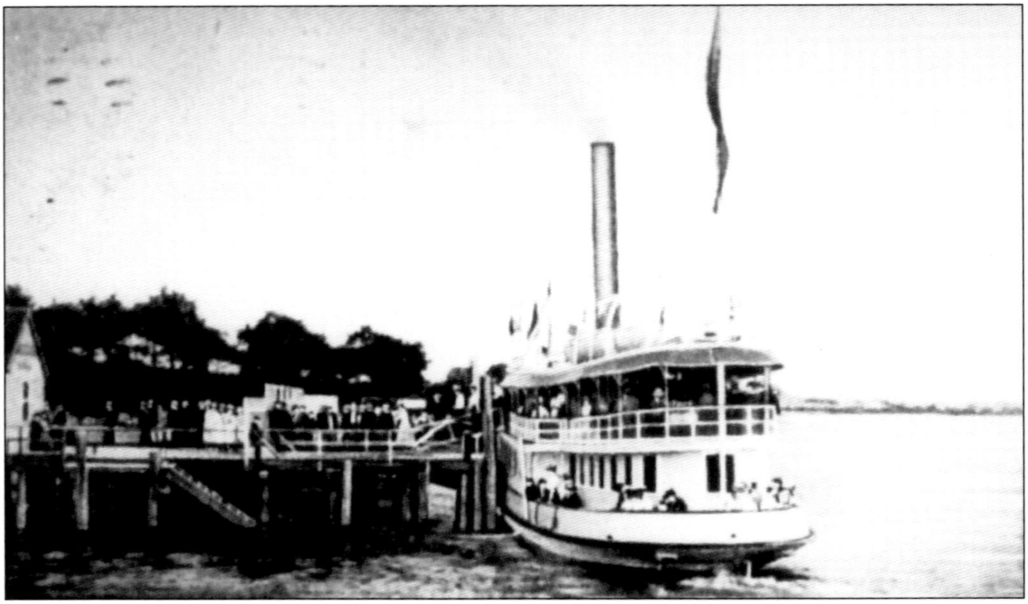

A busy steamboat landing at Peaks Island in the 1930s.

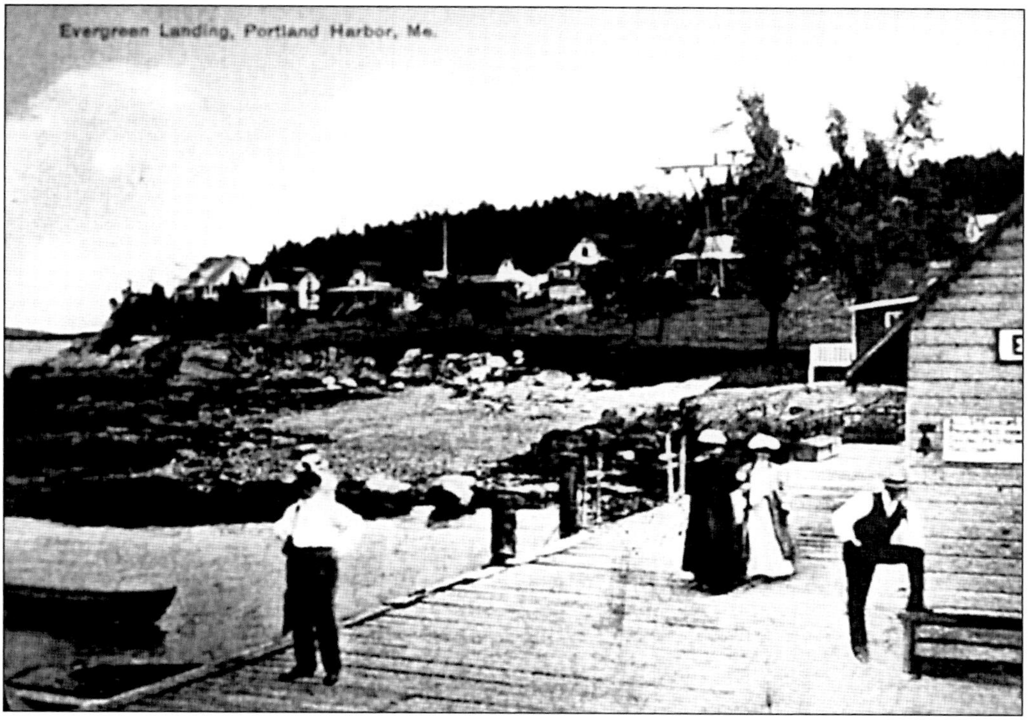

Evergreen Landing in Portland Harbor. It has a sandy beach and a great view of tiny Pumpkin Knob.

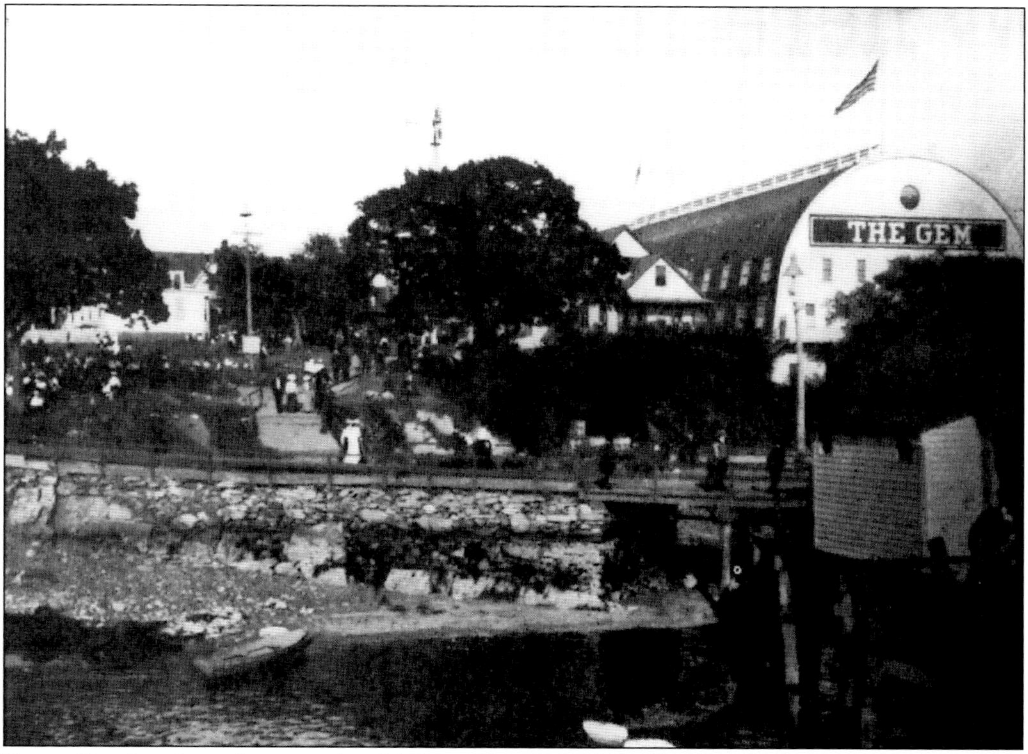

Forest City Landing, showing the old Gem Theatre and the bustling gardens.

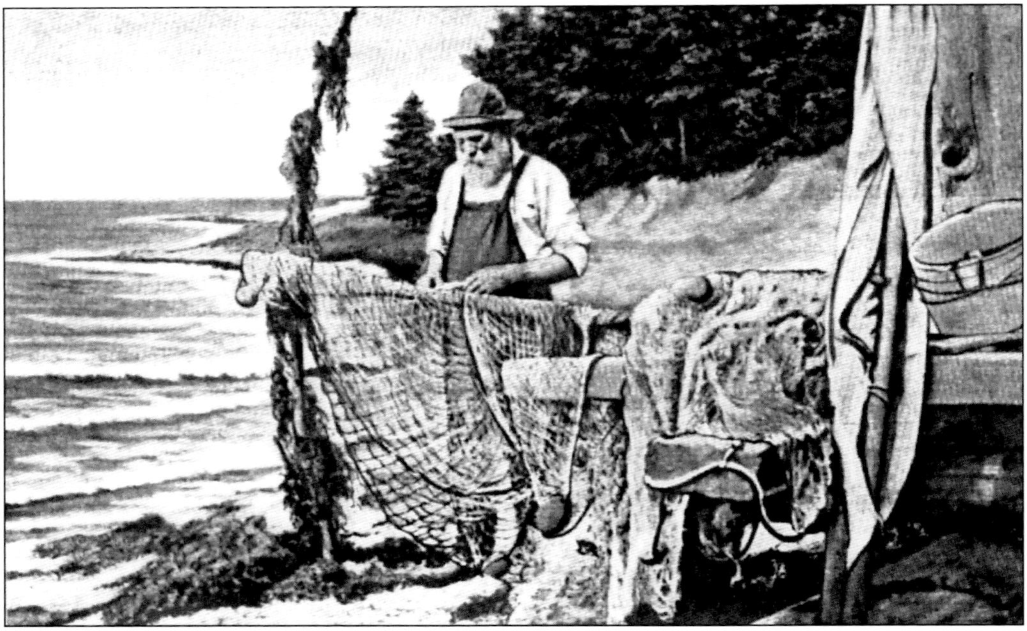

This old timer is carefully checking over his net.

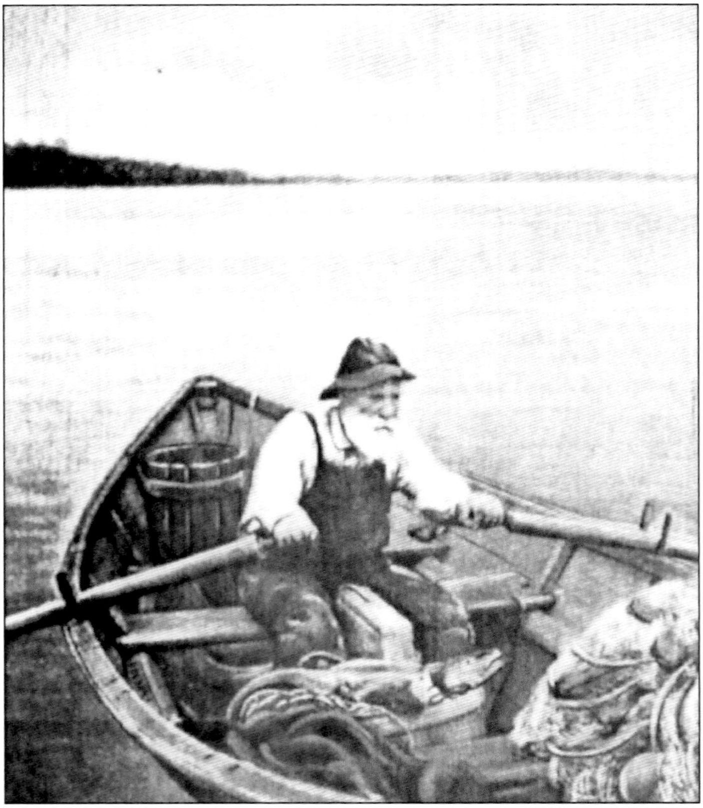

He then rows out to drop it over the side. The cork floaters will stay atop the water to mark the net's location.

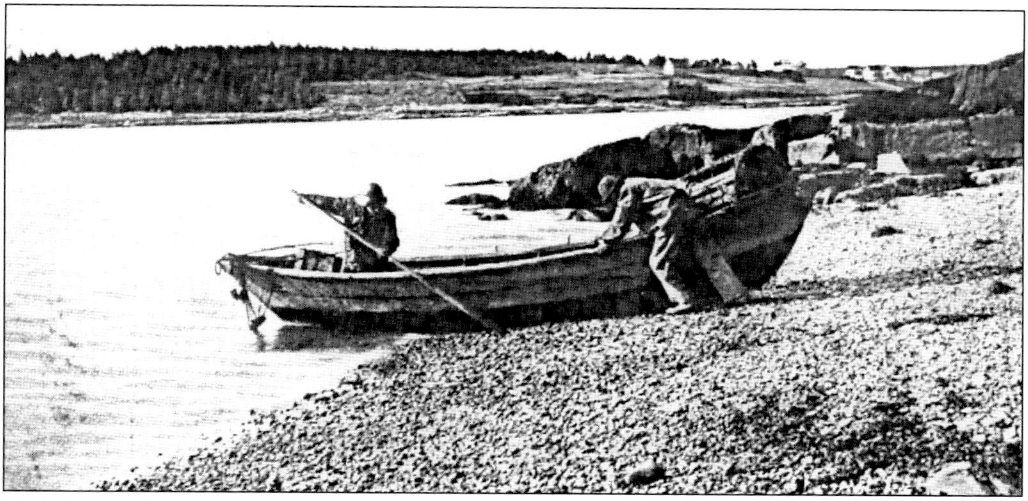

Tryin' to get her in!

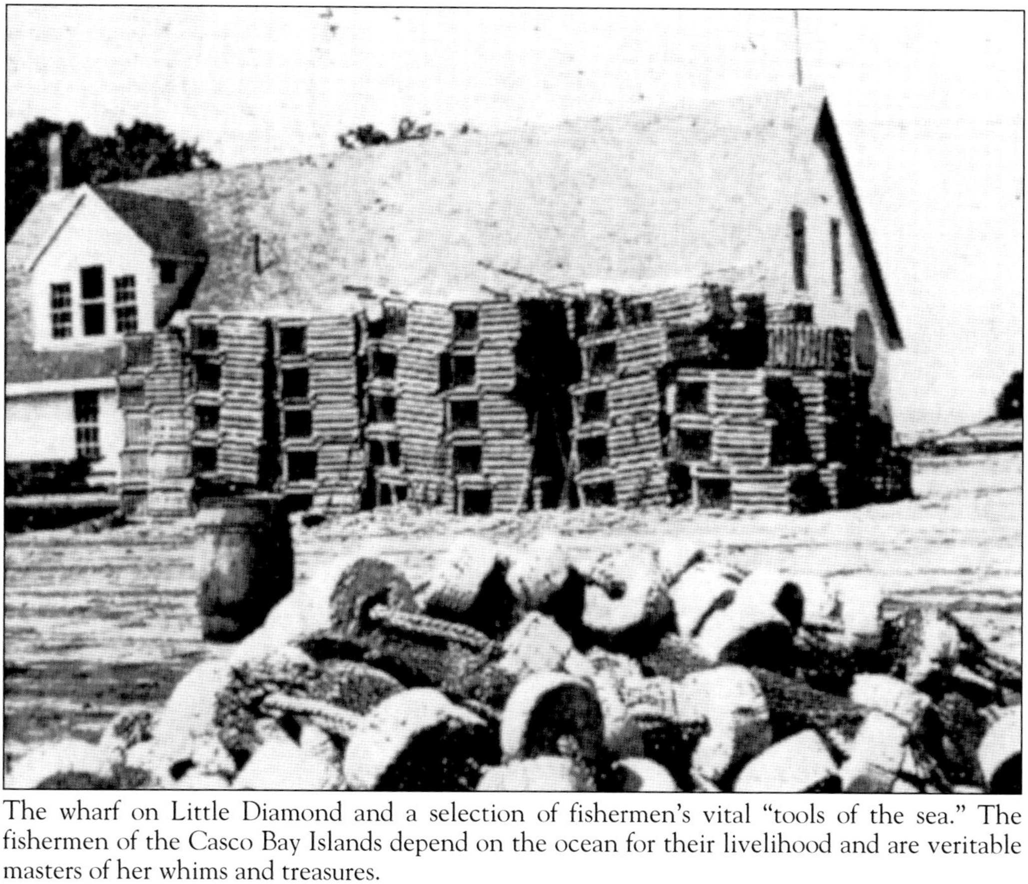

The wharf on Little Diamond and a selection of fishermen's vital "tools of the sea." The fishermen of the Casco Bay Islands depend on the ocean for their livelihood and are veritable masters of her whims and treasures.

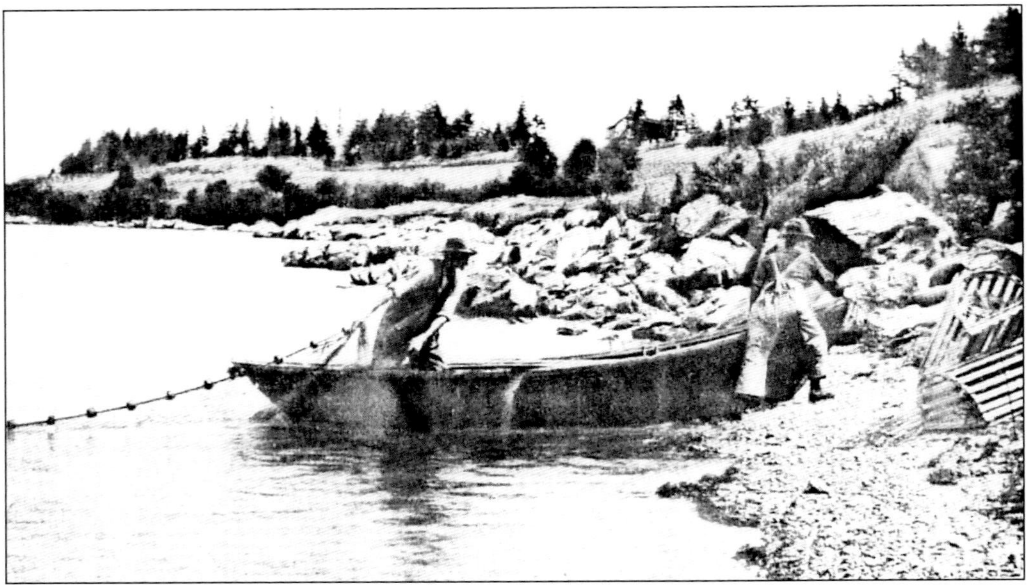

Tryin' to get her out!

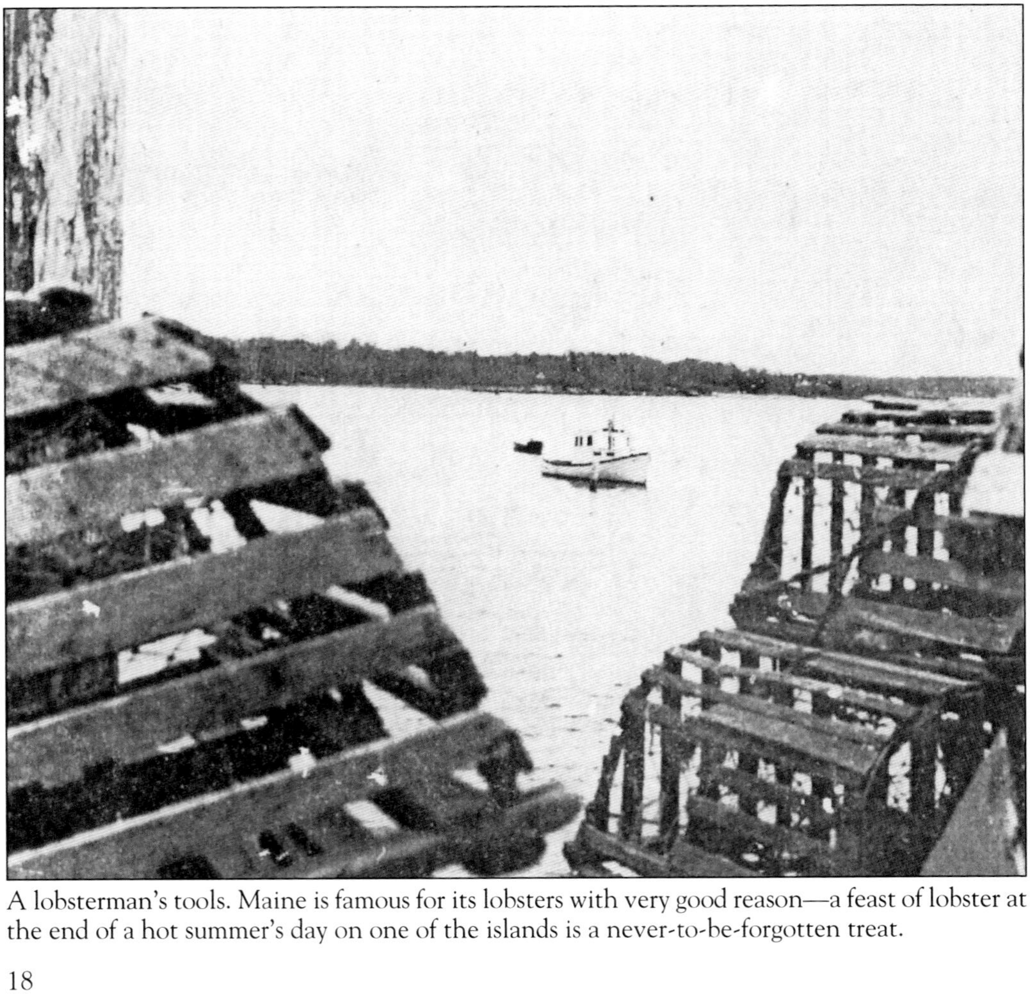

A lobsterman's tools. Maine is famous for its lobsters with very good reason—a feast of lobster at the end of a hot summer's day on one of the islands is a never-to-be-forgotten treat.

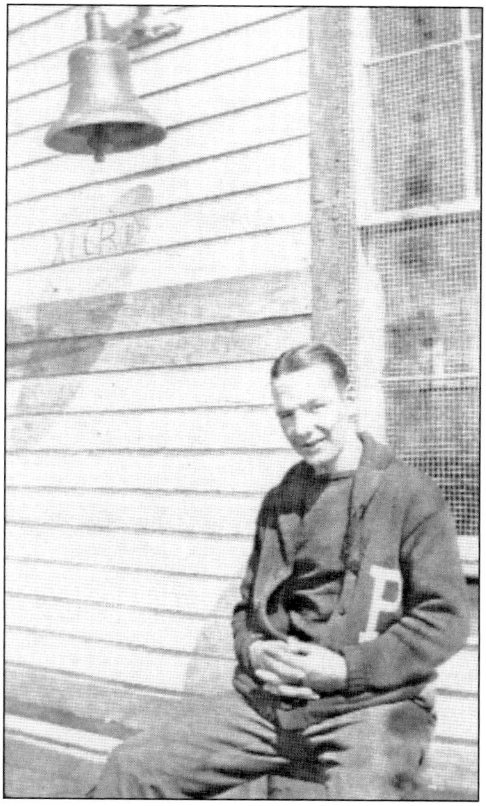

The bell shown in this photograph was rung by hand by waiting passengers to guide the boat to the wharf during "pea soup" fogs.

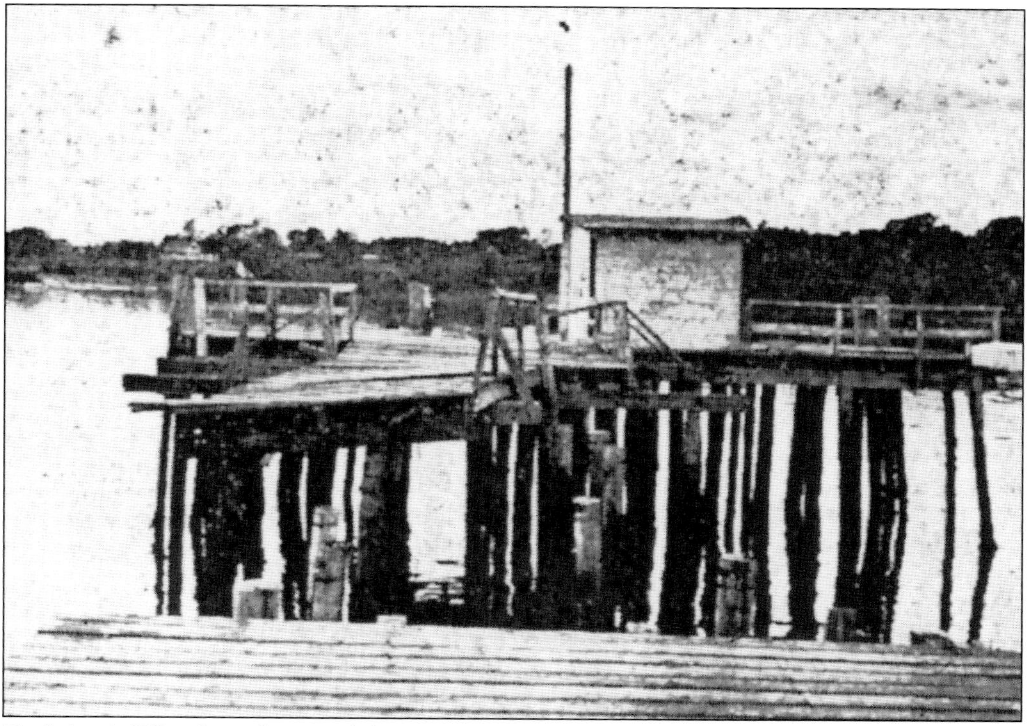

Trefethen's Wharf was destroyed during a hurricane and was never rebuilt.

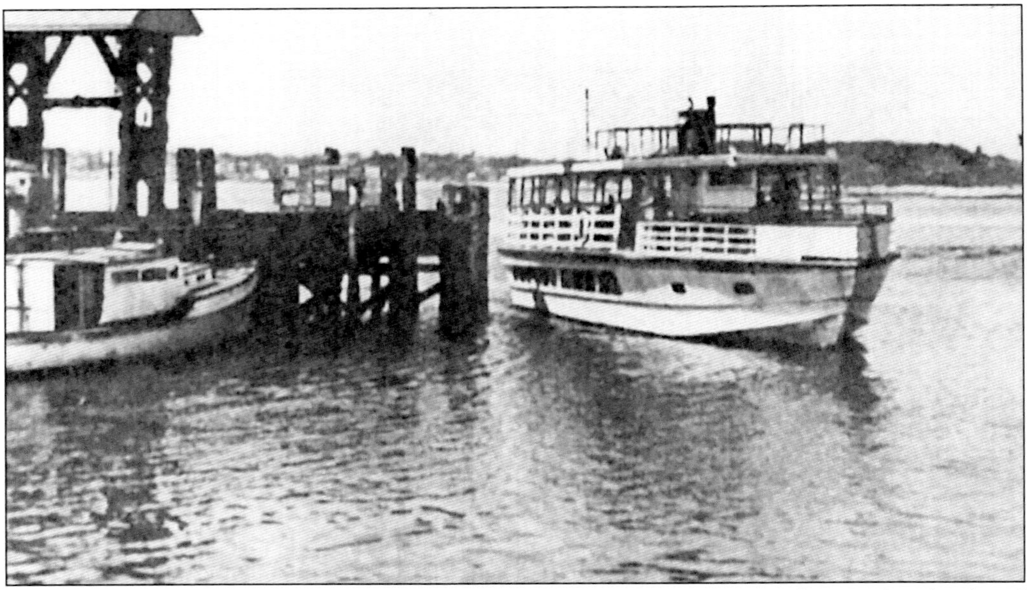

The *Sunshine* was used on the Casco Bay Lines' night runs from Portland to Peaks Island and through the "roads." In 1956 she ran aground in a fog off Great Diamond Island. The captain and passengers on this late-night run had no ship-to-shore communication, so they built a fire and waited until the first morning boat came by. All of the passengers climbed to safety, but despite several attempts to move the *Sunshine*, she could not be dislodged. She was finally salvaged and abandoned. Visitors usually see only the summertime delights of the islands, but locals are very well aware of the dangers of the sea.

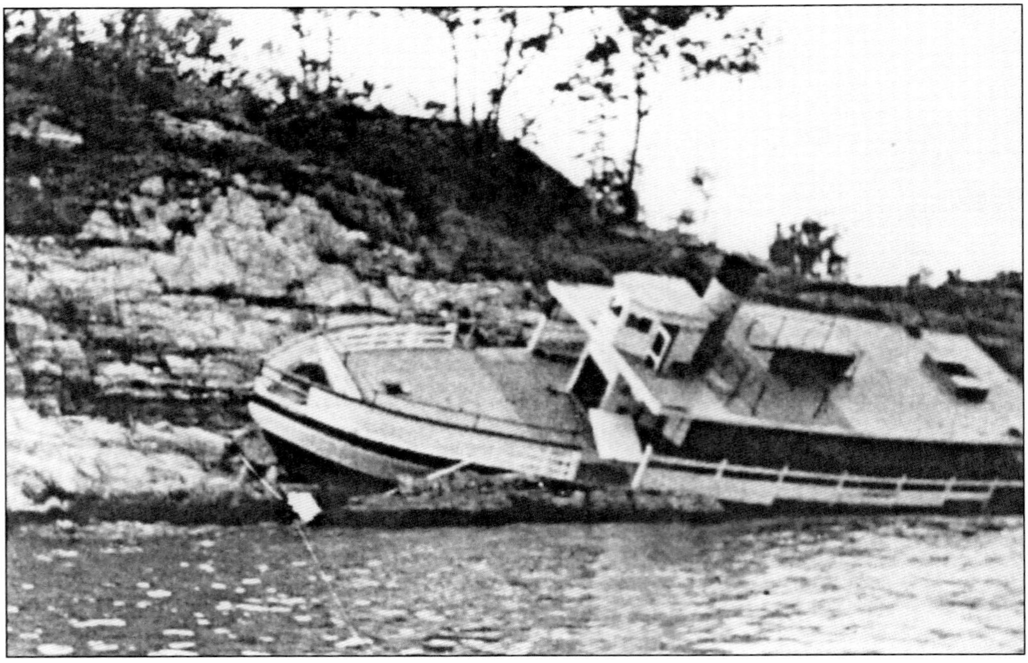

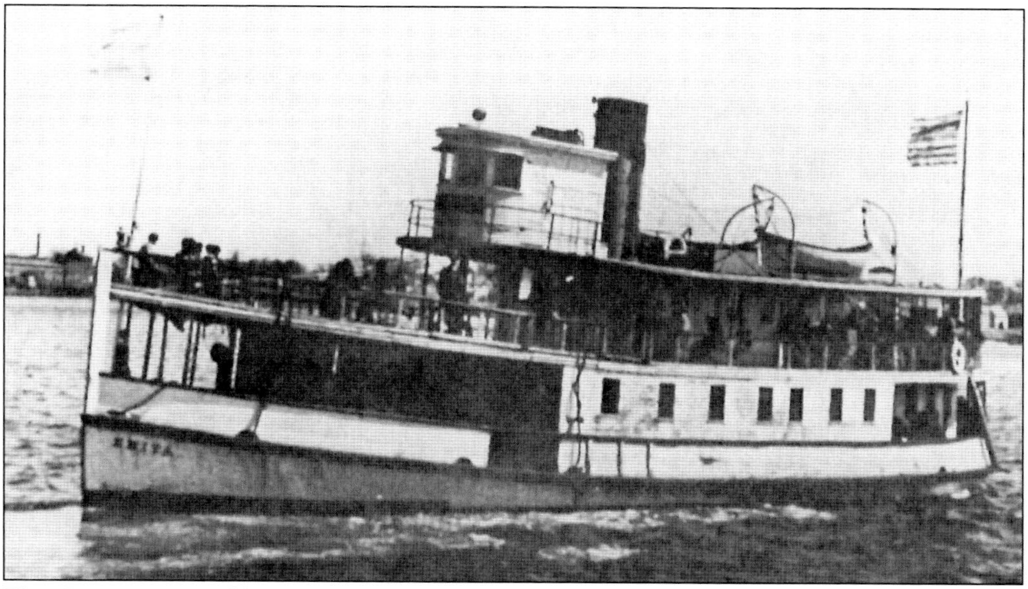

The *Emita* was an old favorite in Casco Bay. Built in 1880 at Athens, New York, she was originally destined for service on the Hudson River. First a steamer, and later converted to diesel, she remained in service summer and winter until 1952. Left to rot along a river, she was torched one Halloween by pranksters.

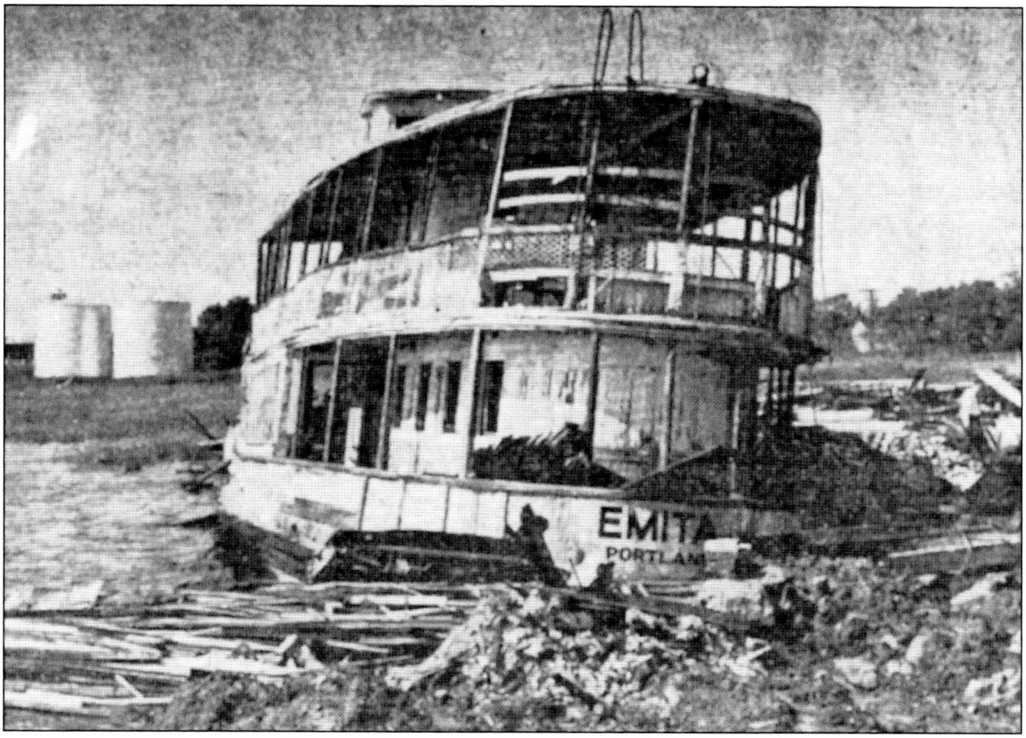

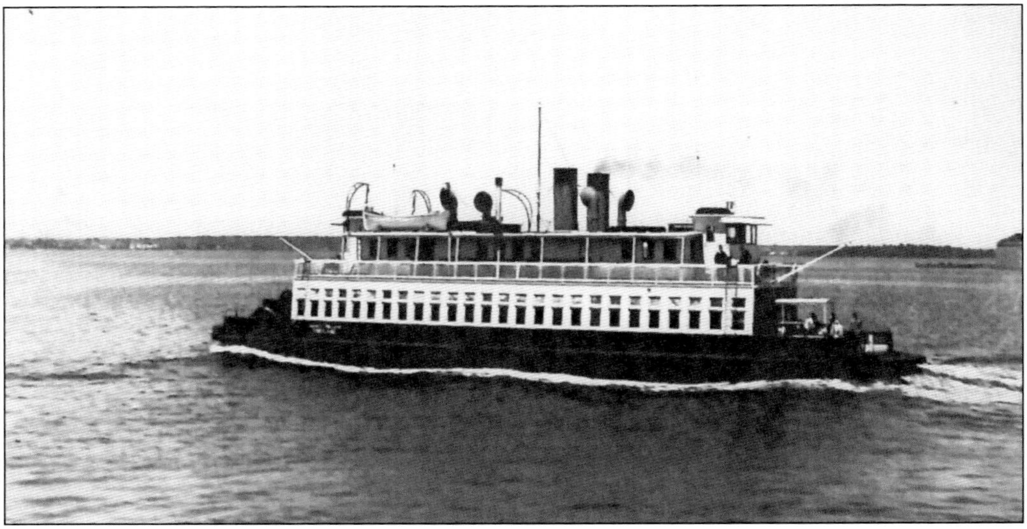

The *Nancy Helen*, one of the early car ferries. She was another victim of fire—a sad ending for such a fine ship.

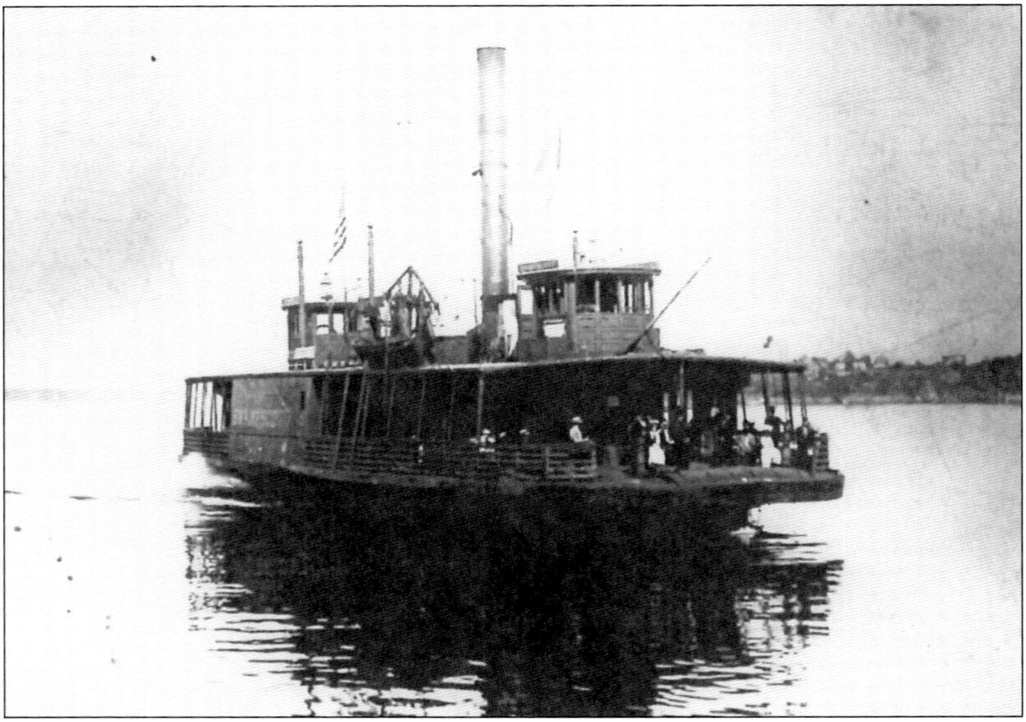

Yet another fire victim—the *Swampscot*.

Two

Peaks Island Homes

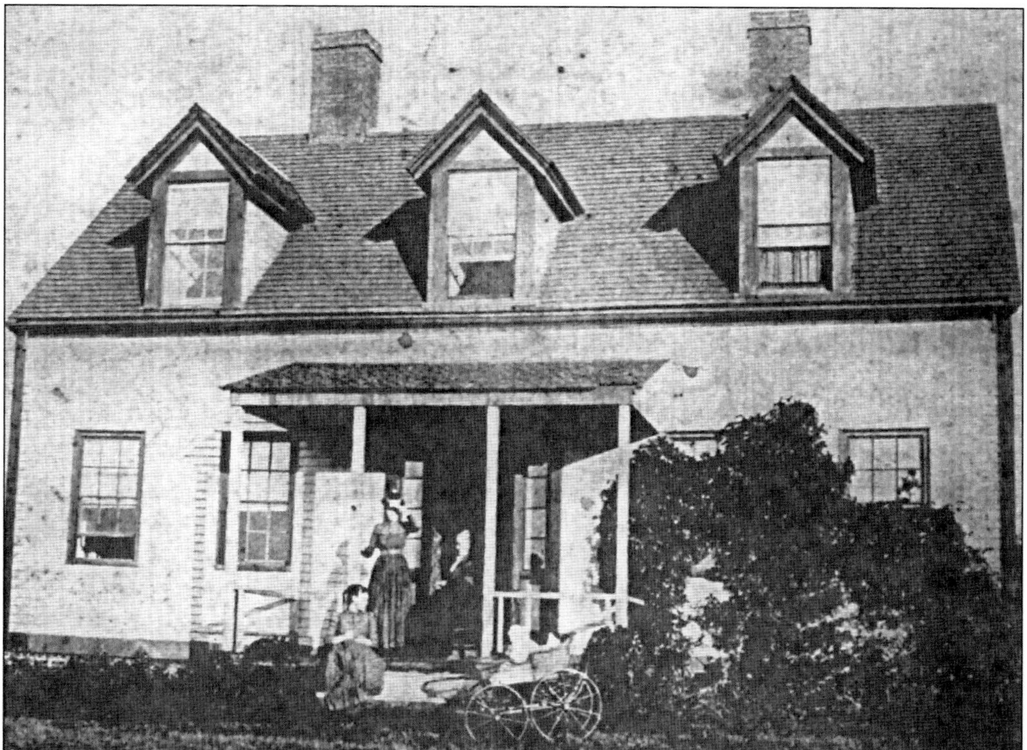

One of the earliest homes, the Trefethen homestead was built c. 1700.

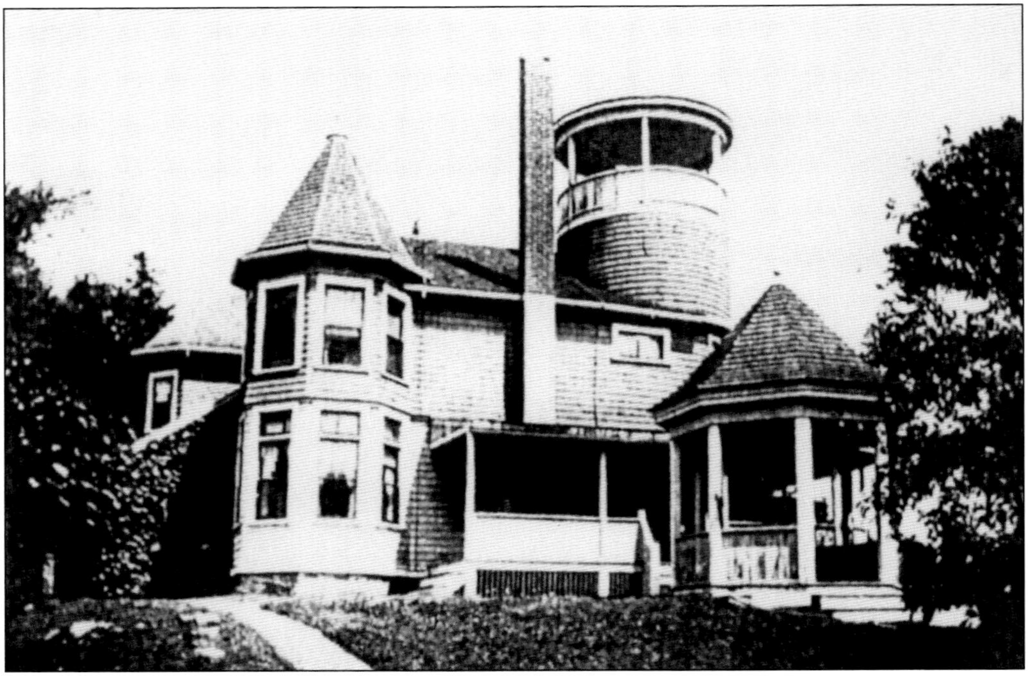

A very elaborate cottage—it even boasts a lookout tower for sea-scanning with a telescope.

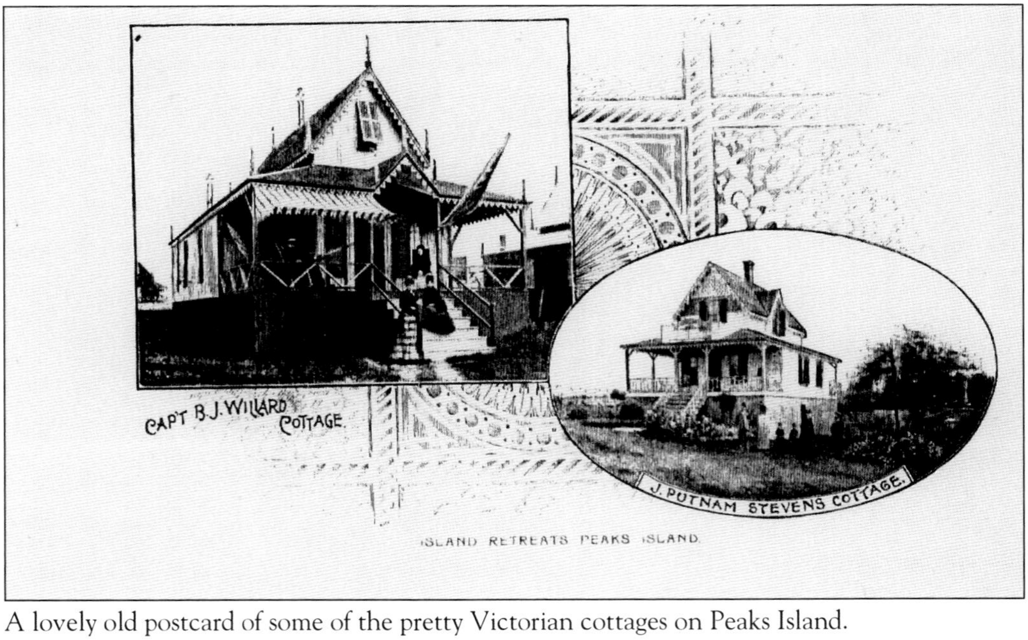

A lovely old postcard of some of the pretty Victorian cottages on Peaks Island.

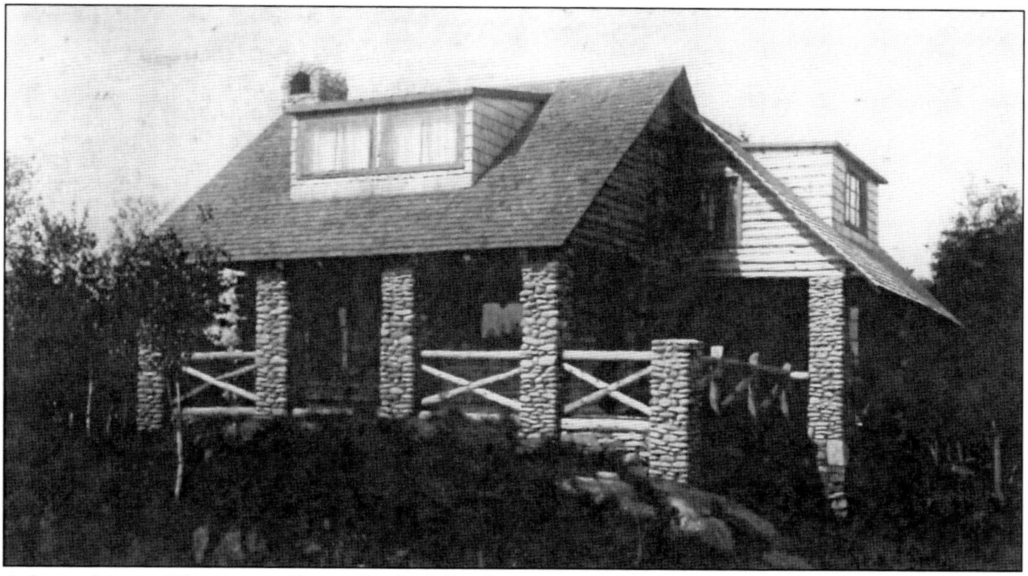

A log cabin on Utowanna Farm, Peaks Island.

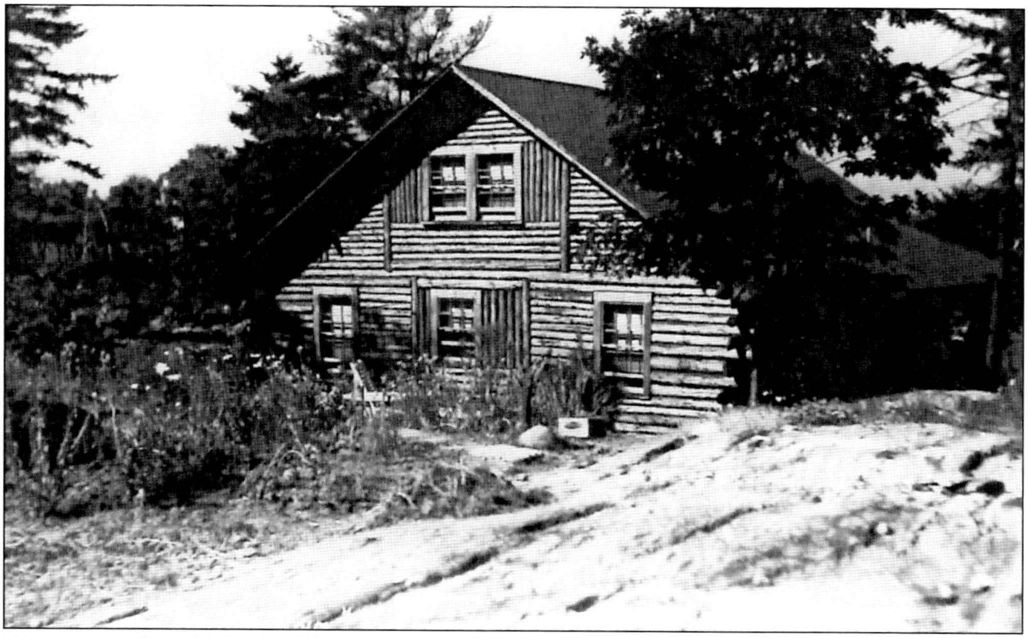

Trees were plentiful for building a variety of homes over the years.

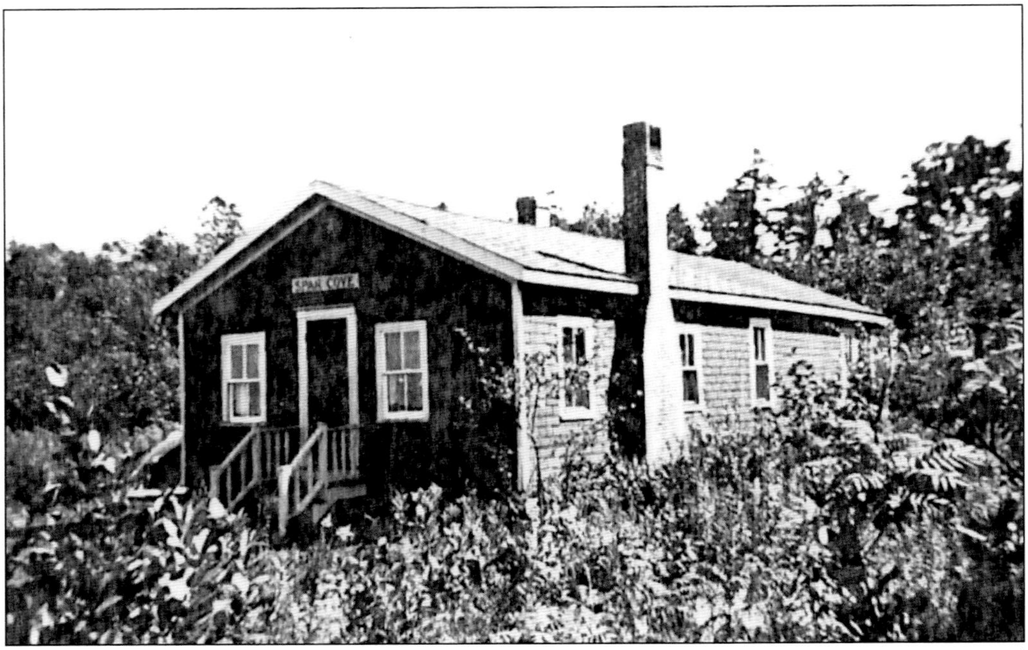

This World War II military building was made into a home after peace came. It was named "Spar Cove" because of its location.

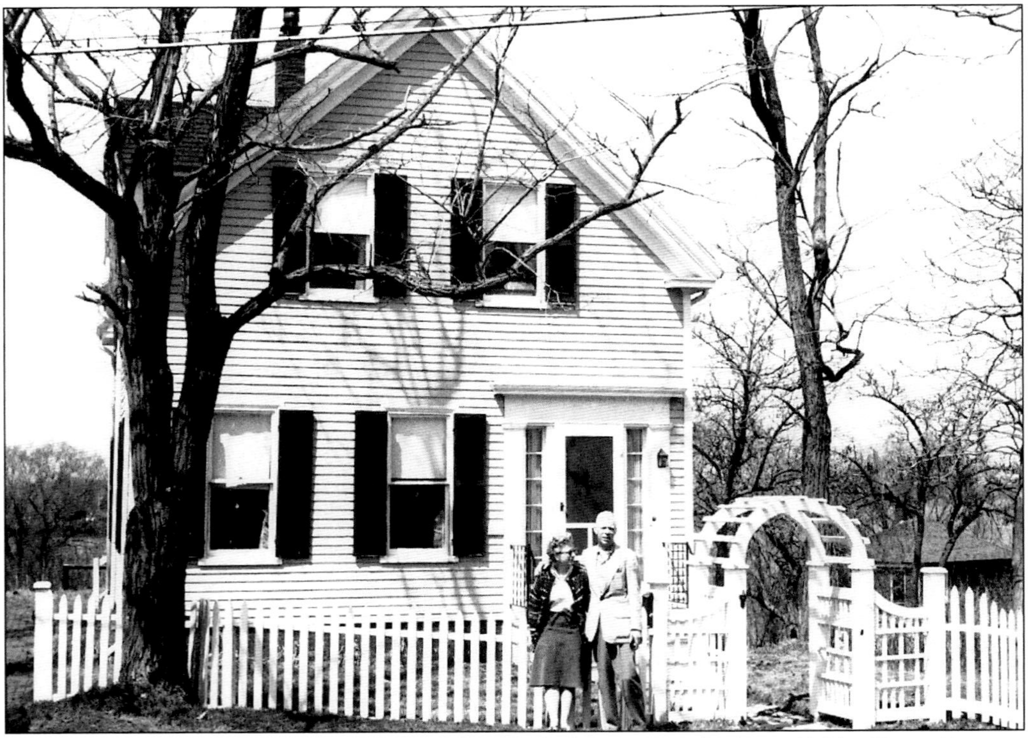

One of the three Parson houses on Peaks Island. The homes were built c. 1880 by Henry Parsons for his three daughters, Arlette, Trulette, and Charlette. This is Trulette's, a teacher at Peaks Island School.

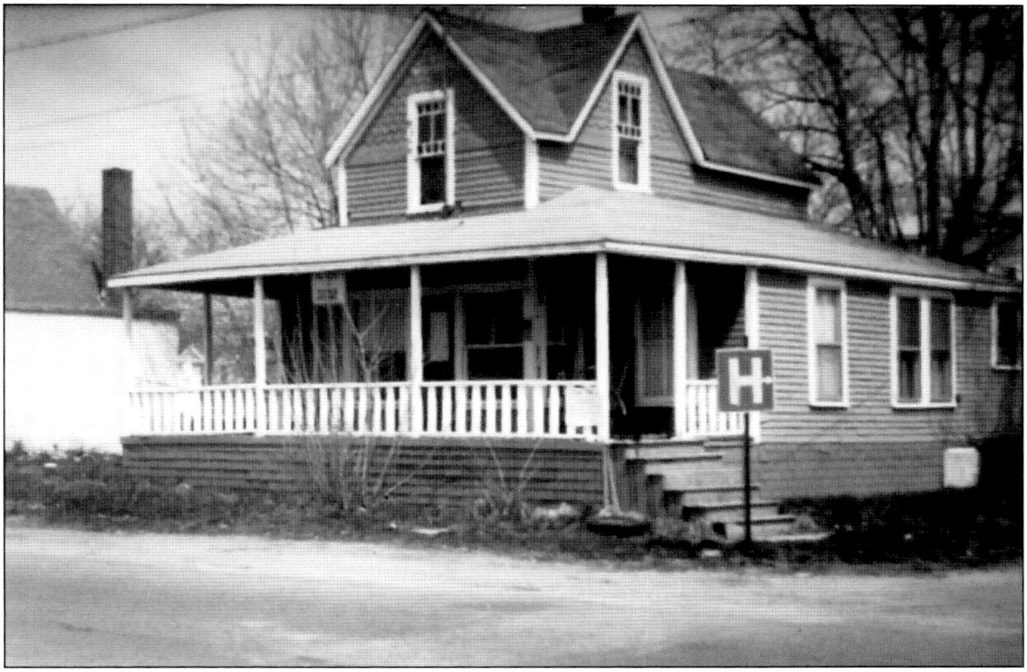

This house on Island Avenue was moved to a new location with a large crowd gathered to watch. The new fire station, the public library, and the community center are now located on this site.

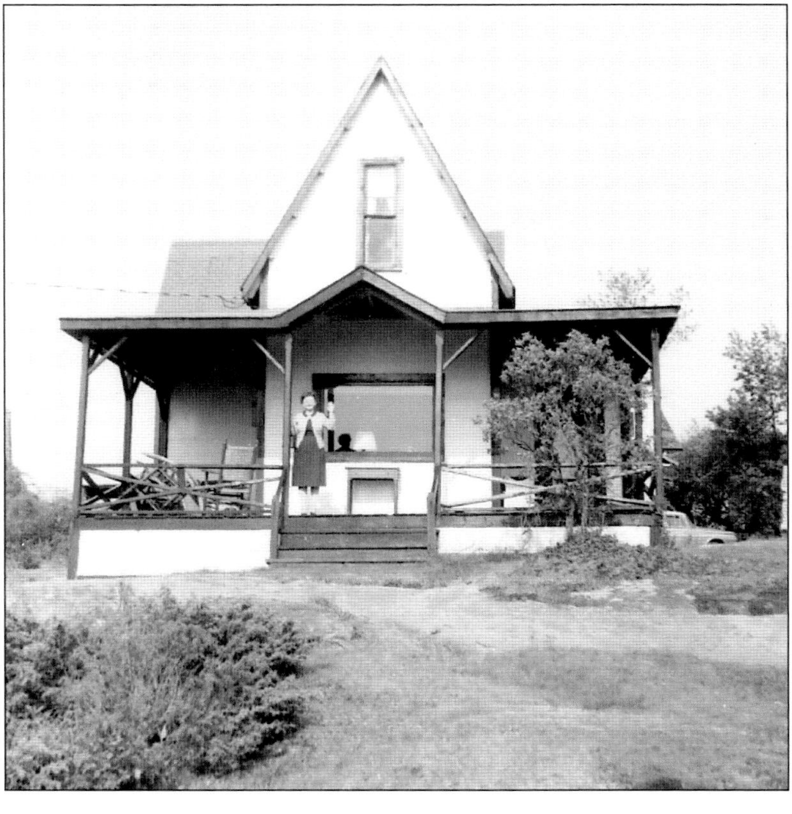

The Lowell Cottage on Willow Street.

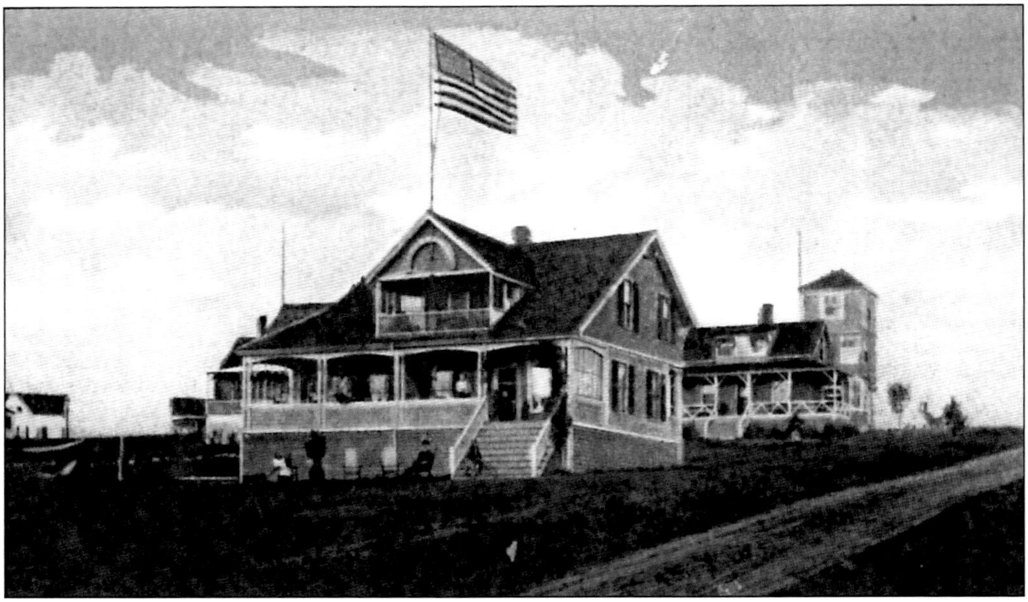

One of the largest summer boarding houses—always popular, always full.

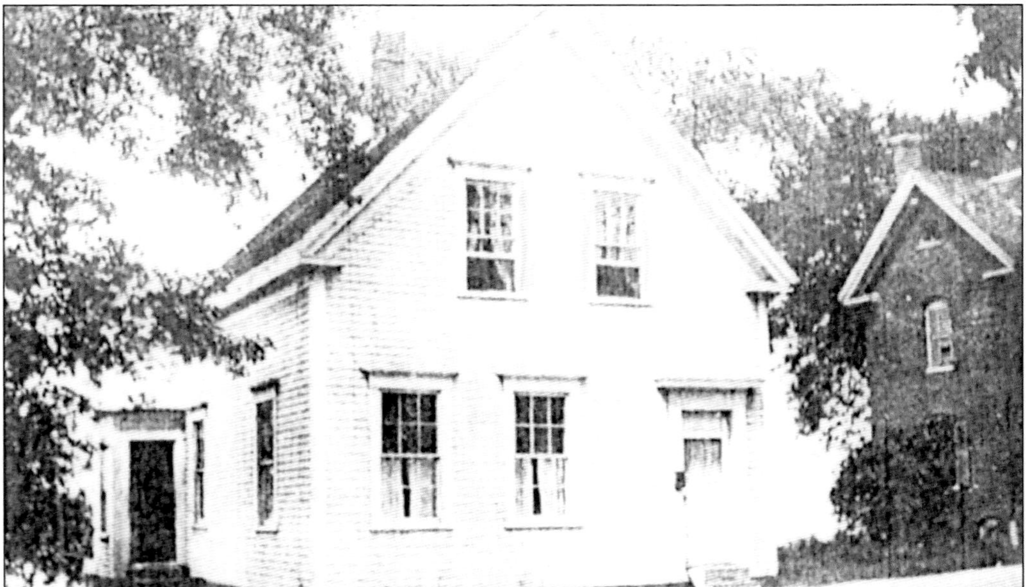

The Randall homestead. Cliff Randall captained the Casco Bay Lines for many years and was one of our best-loved islanders.

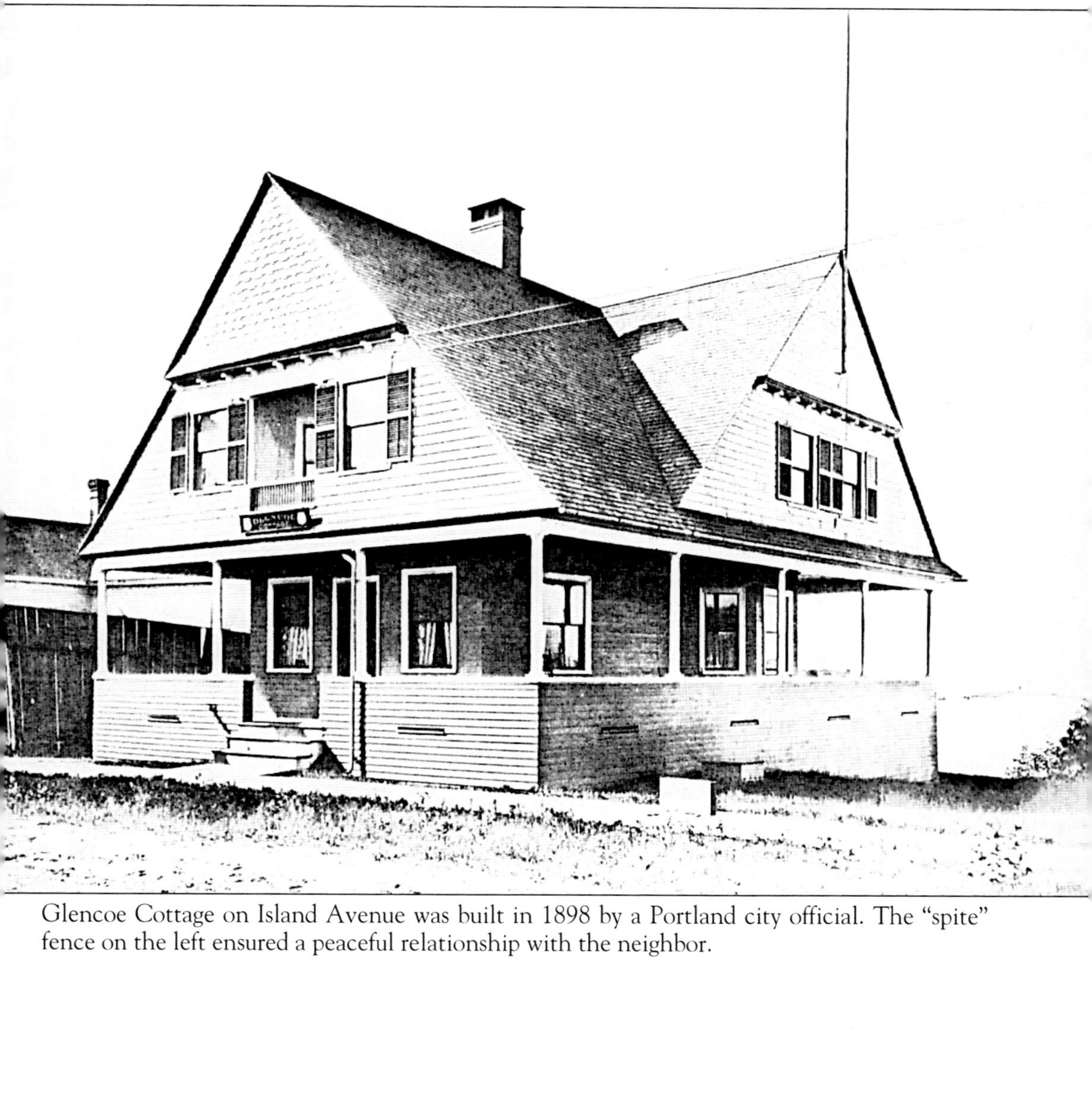

Glencoe Cottage on Island Avenue was built in 1898 by a Portland city official. The "spite" fence on the left ensured a peaceful relationship with the neighbor.

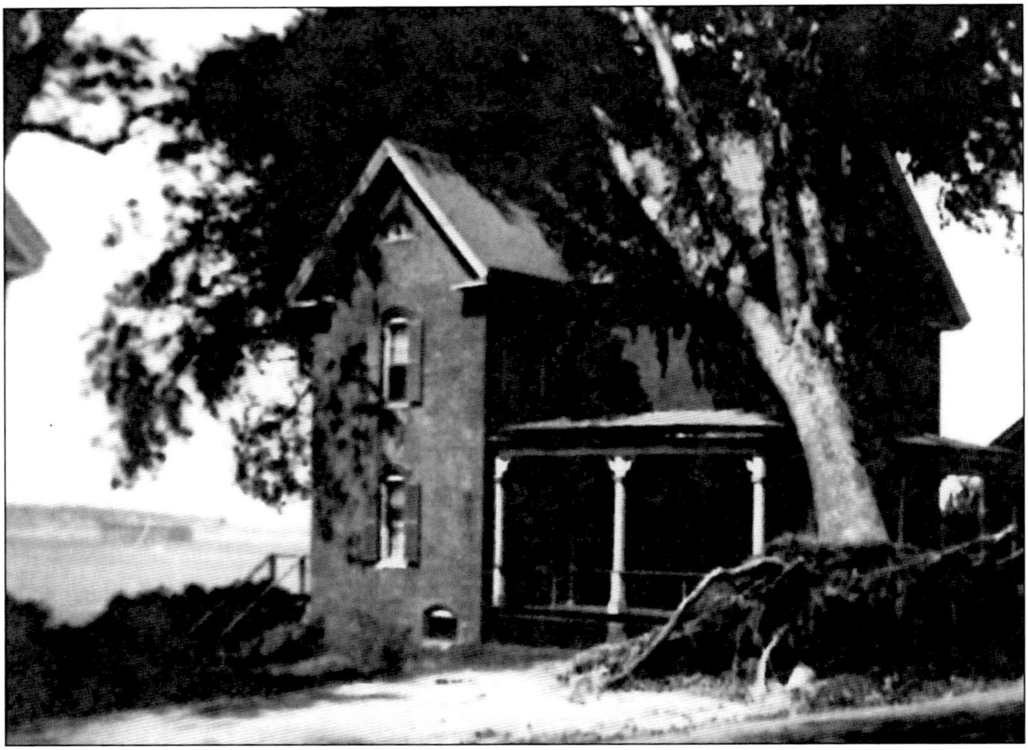

The first brick house. While wooden homes would often be heavily damaged during the forceful storms which drove off the ocean, this one only ever suffered damage to its porch. It actually managed to escape structural damage when a hurricane toppled this tree in 1954.

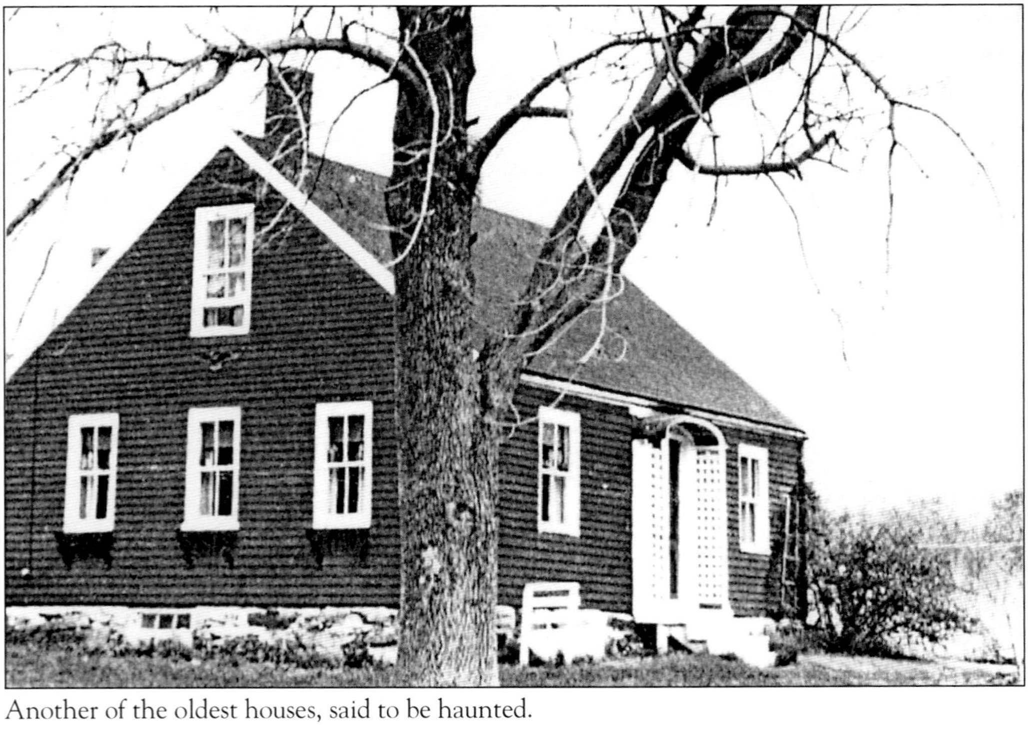

Another of the oldest houses, said to be haunted.

Three

Peaks Island
Schools, Churches, and Burial Grounds

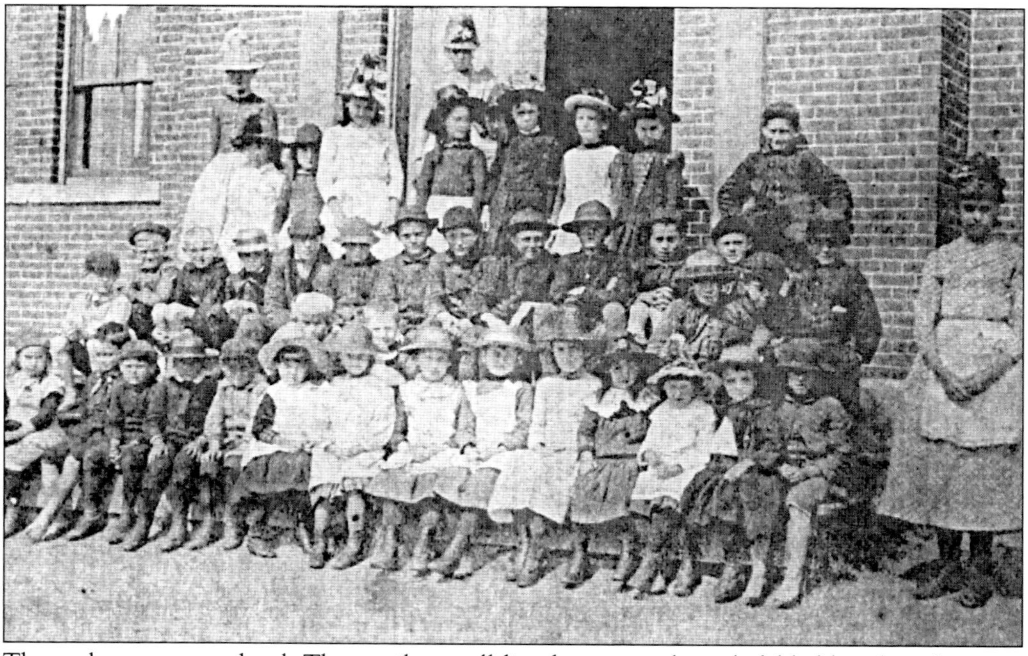

The early grammar school. The pupils are all lined up properly with folded hands and serious faces. You can almost hear the teacher saying, "People will always remember you this way, so look pleasant, please!"

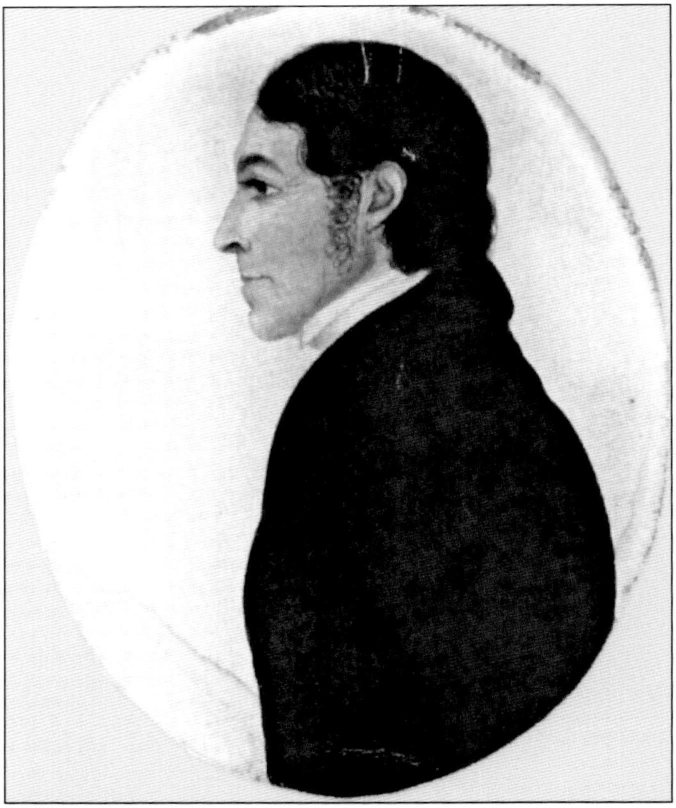

Joseph B. Reed, Peaks Island's first schoolmaster, in a drawing from 1810.

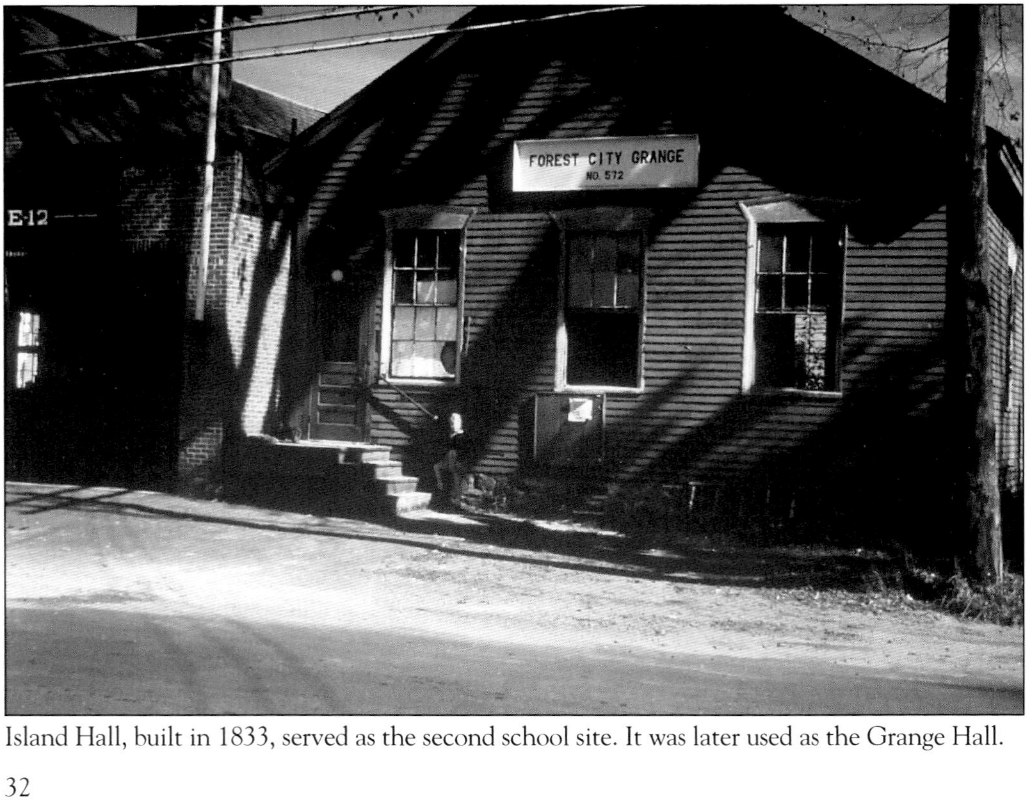

Island Hall, built in 1833, served as the second school site. It was later used as the Grange Hall.

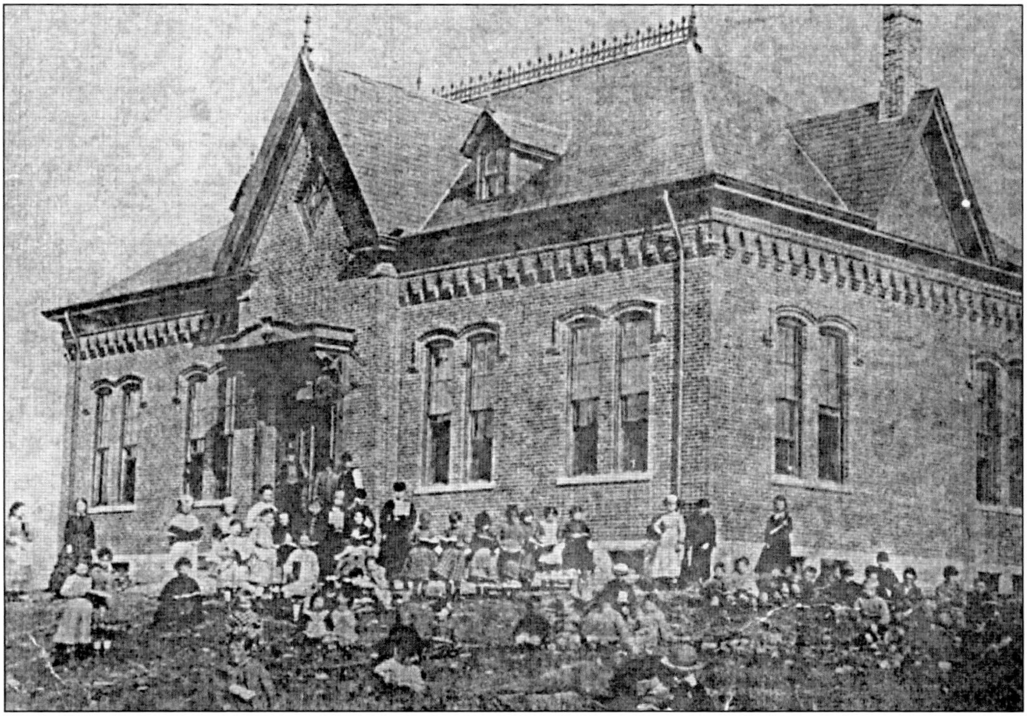

Peaks Island School in 1924 from a very well-loved and well-worn photograph.

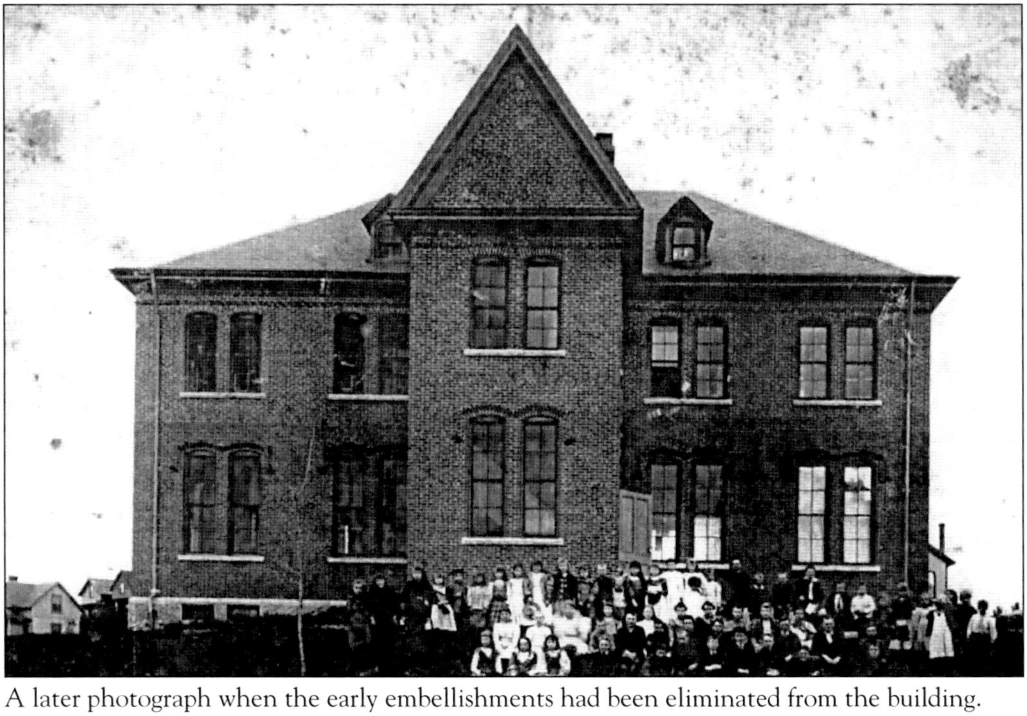

A later photograph when the early embellishments had been eliminated from the building.

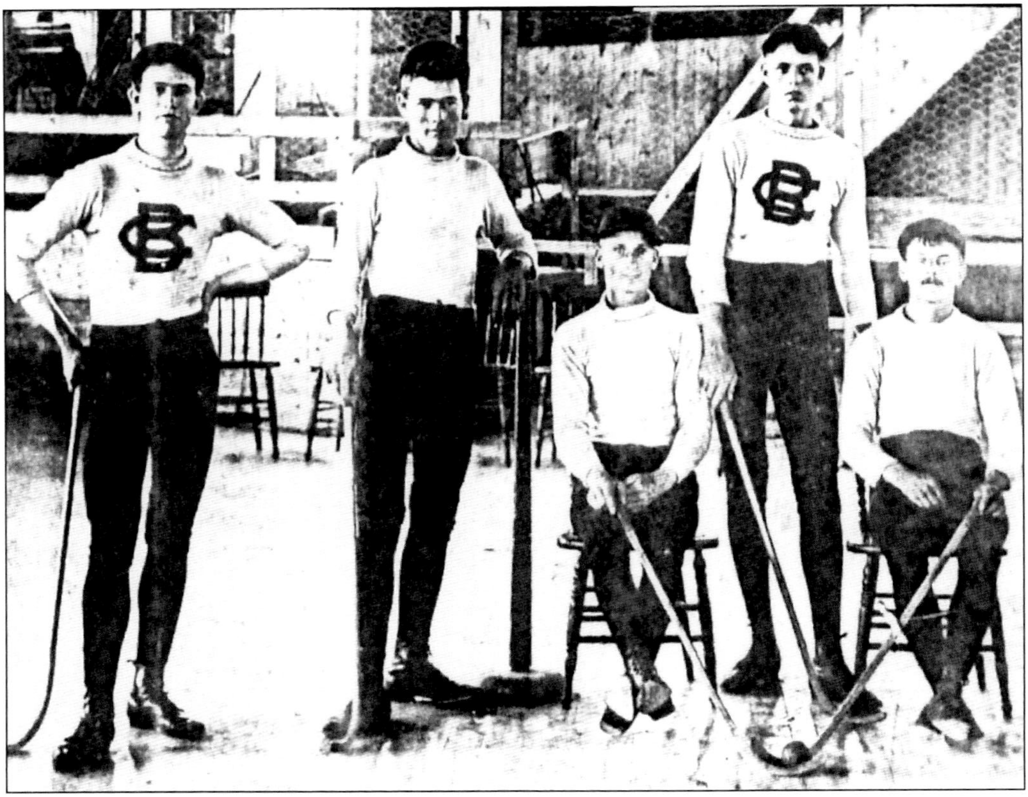

The hockey team in the late 1800s.

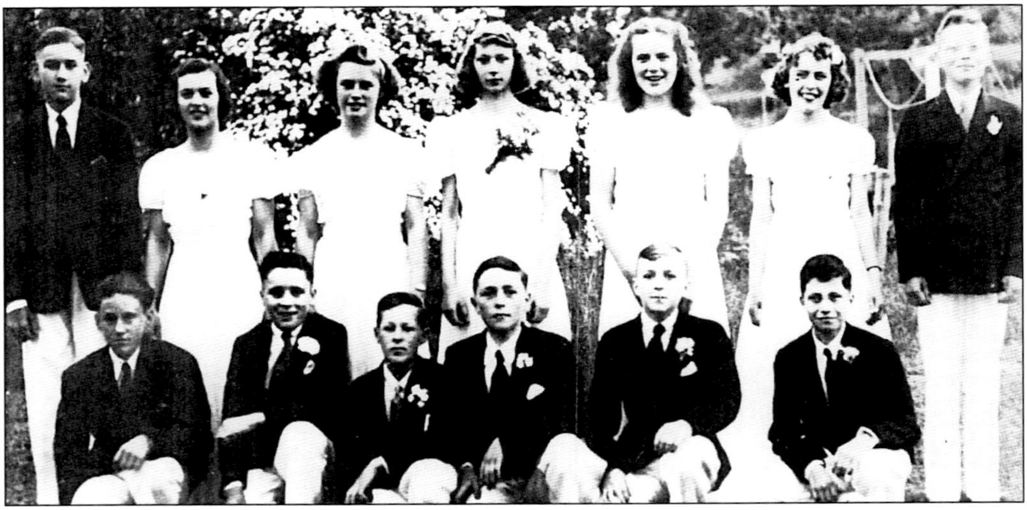

The Peaks Island School class of 1940. From left to right are: (front row) Dwight Brackett, Thomas Collins, Bruce MacVane, Bill Shute, Richard Hasson, and Bill Boulter; (back row) Roscoe Smith, Janette Skillings, Shirley Hill, Mary Ventres, Jane Carleton, Mary Latham, and Norman Allison. The relative isolation of the islands allows children to roam farther and with more safety than they can in towns and cities, giving them the freedom many modern children envy.

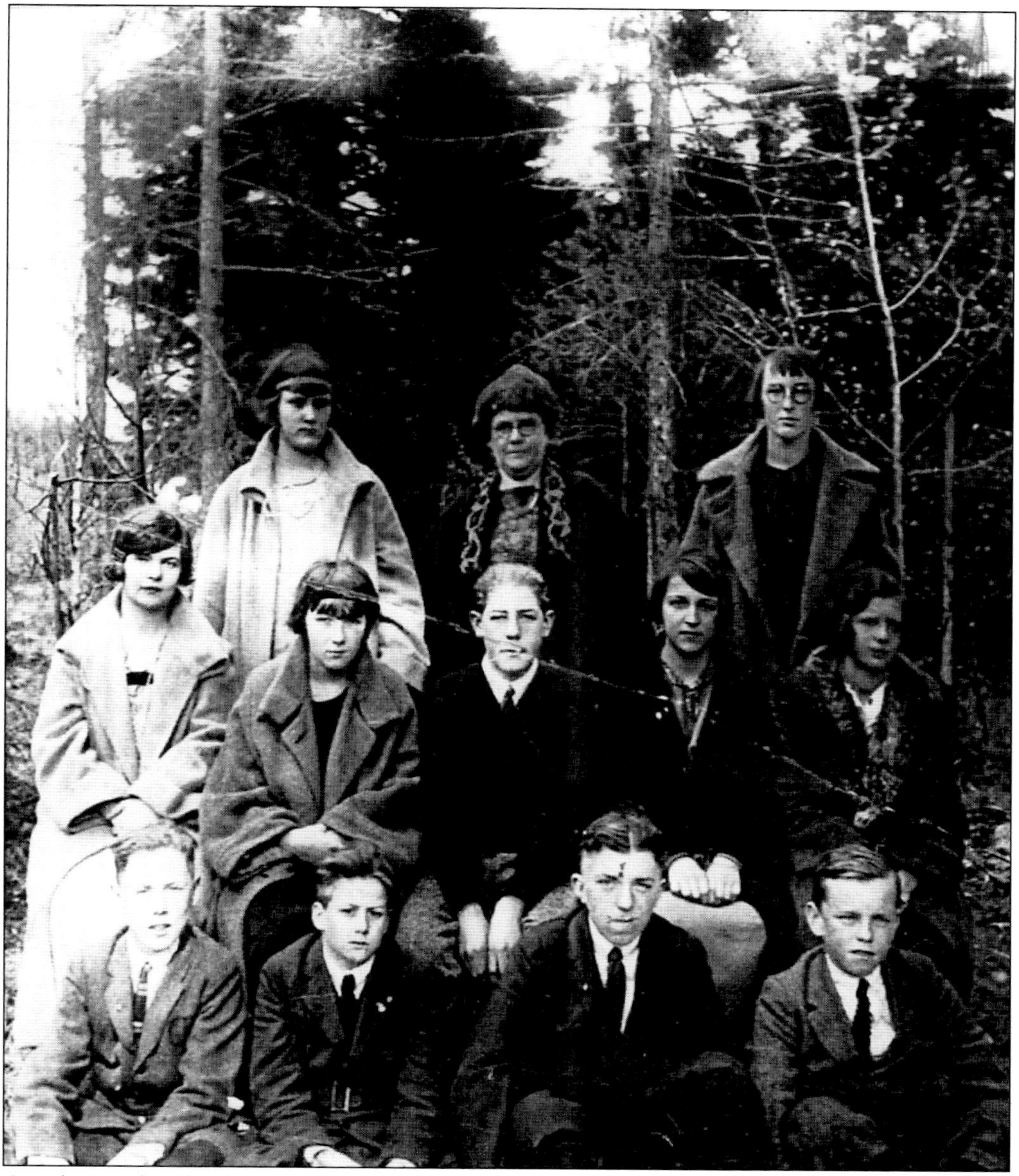

Another Peaks Island School class. From left to right are: (front row) Ernest Pettengill, Wilfred Kennedy, Donald Crandall, and John Henderson; (middle row) Virginia Cleaves, Dorothy Hamilton, Arthur True, and Louis Brackett; (back row) Lillian Wright, Ethel Frost, and Dorothy Powell.

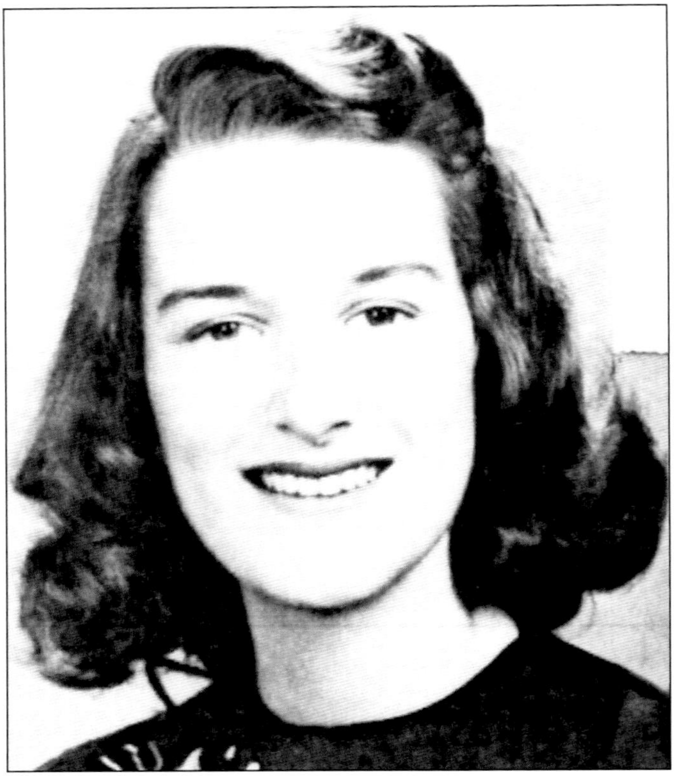

Our two Peaks Island students that became valedictorians at Portland High School, the first public high school in the nation. This is Joan (Jody) Smith, class of 1948.

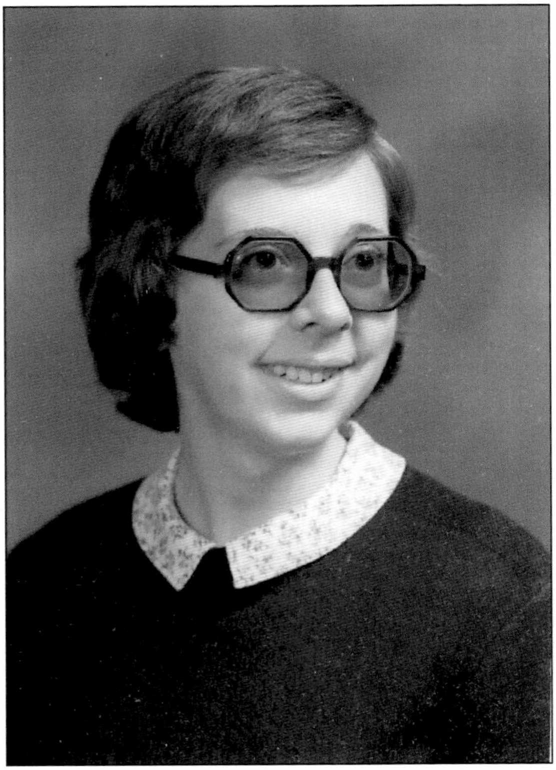

Kendra Mary Erico, class of 1975.

Life on the islands has always been quite self-contained. As well as schools, religious meeting places were built so that islanders could take care of the spiritual side of their lives without having to travel to the mainland. Brackett Memorial Church held its first service in 1860. The community on Peaks Island in the nineteenth century was very strictly graded, as can be seen from a glance at the church records from February 1870. The church contained forty-five numbered pews which were "bought" by families who would occupy that pew each Sunday. The more expensive pews were located at the front of the church, and seated the most well-to-do families on the island. The names which appear on the floor plan of pew assignments from February 1870 are: Brackett, Fisher, Frellick, Jones, Lane, Maxwell, McDonald, Parsons, Skillings, Smith, Sterling, Torrington, Trefethen, and Wheatley.

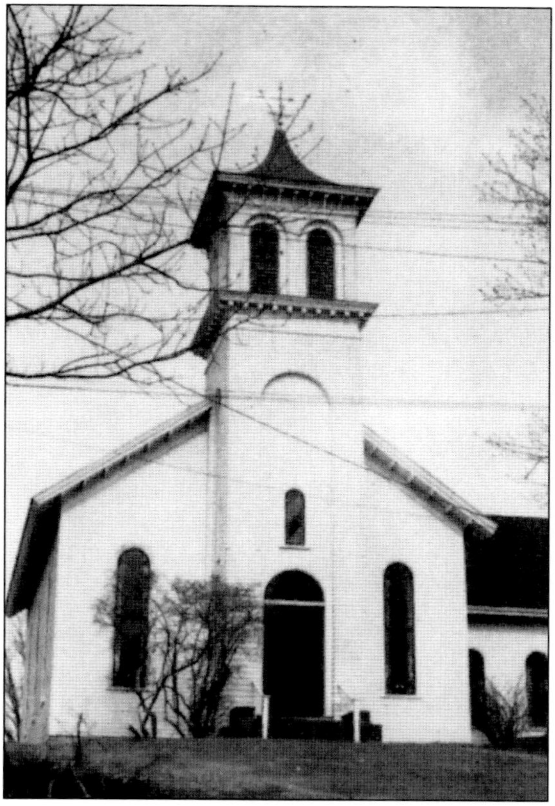

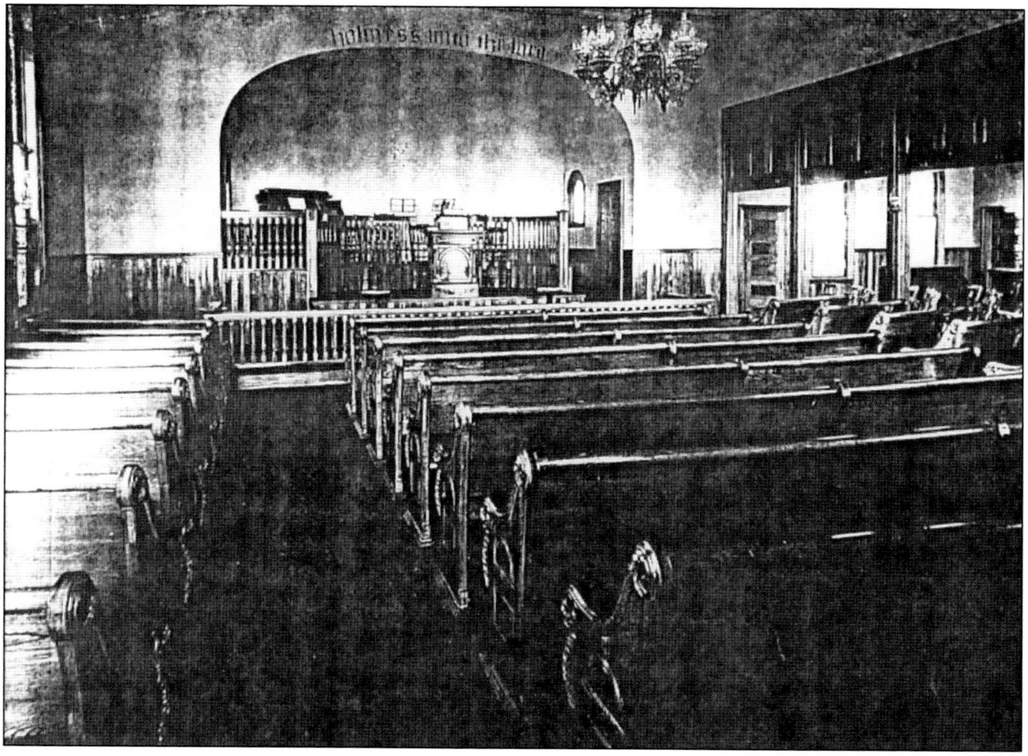

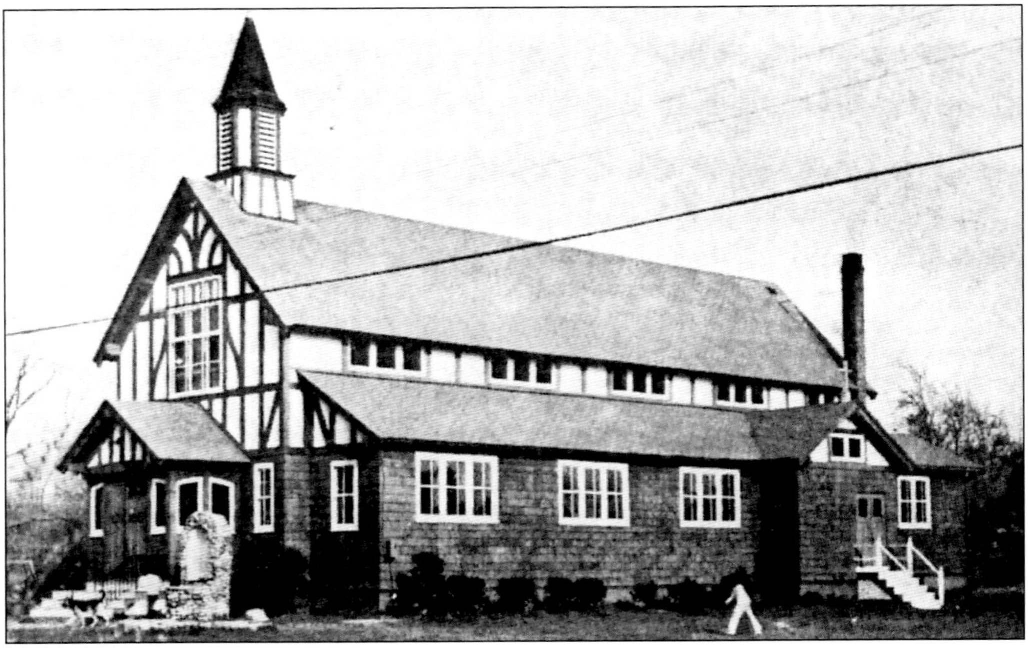

In 1924 a portion of Littlejohn's sheep pasture was purchased and St. Christopher's Catholic Church built thereon.

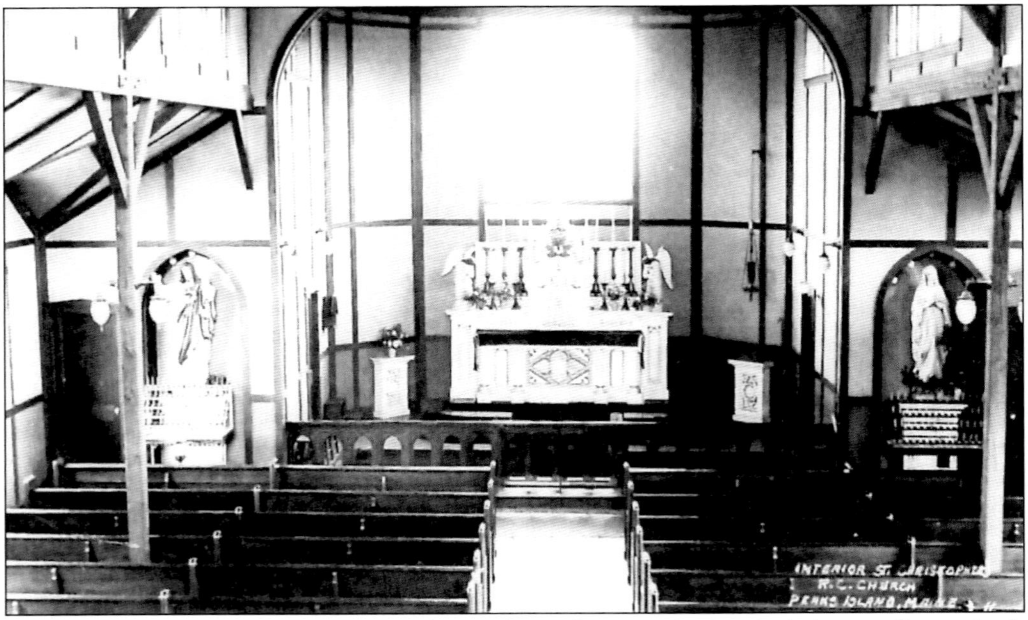

A photograph of the interior of St. Christopher's showing the lovely lighting effects which occur at certain times of day.

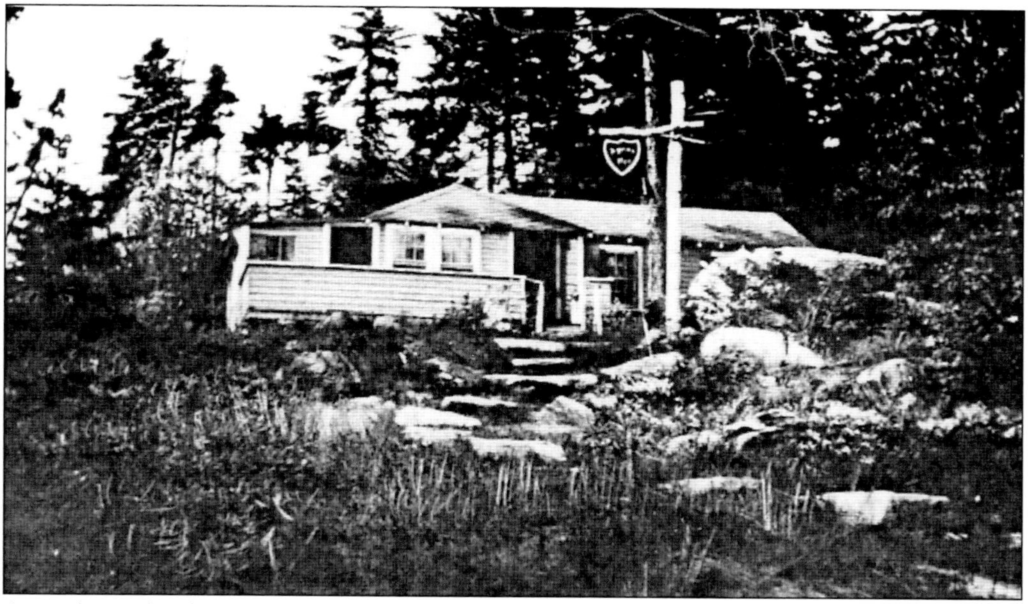

A residence for the chaplain of St. Christopher's, "St. Anthony's by the Sea," was built on a secluded road on the backshore.

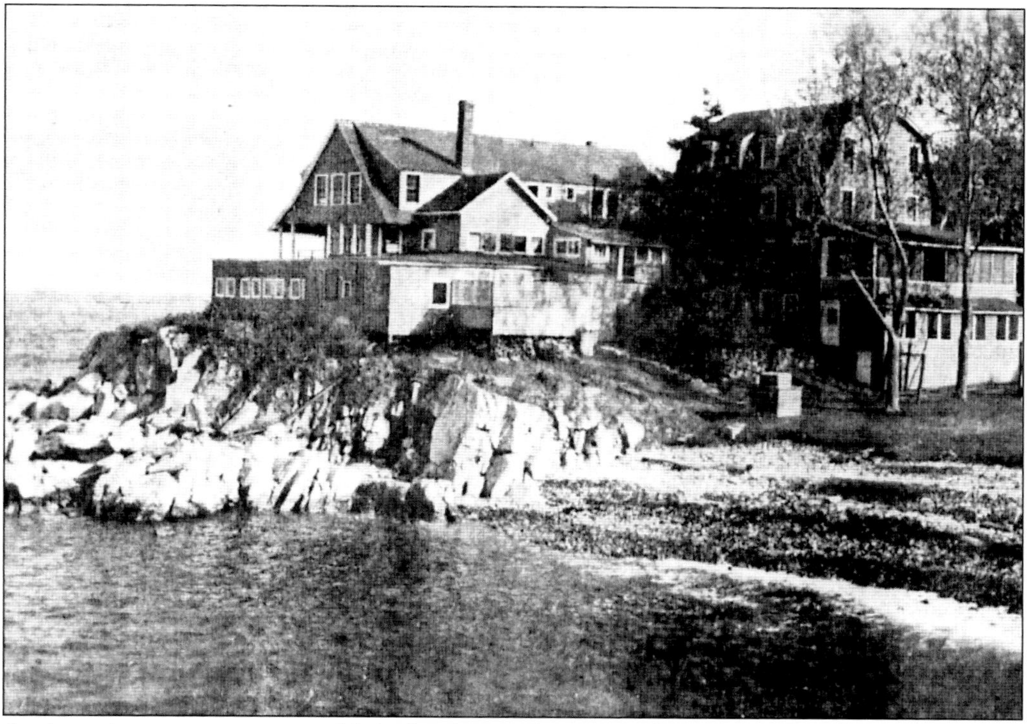

An imposing structure was established to house the sisters who came to St. Christopher's from Boston. The spectacular view was truly inspiring for them.

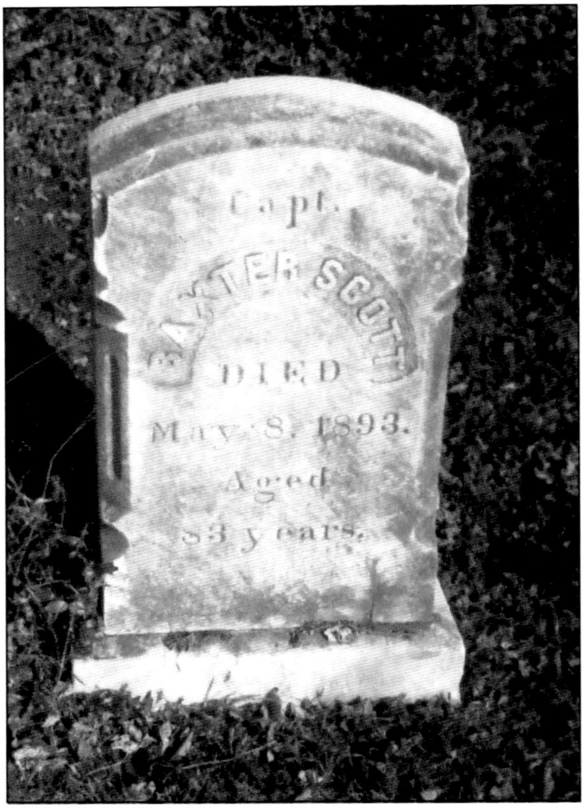

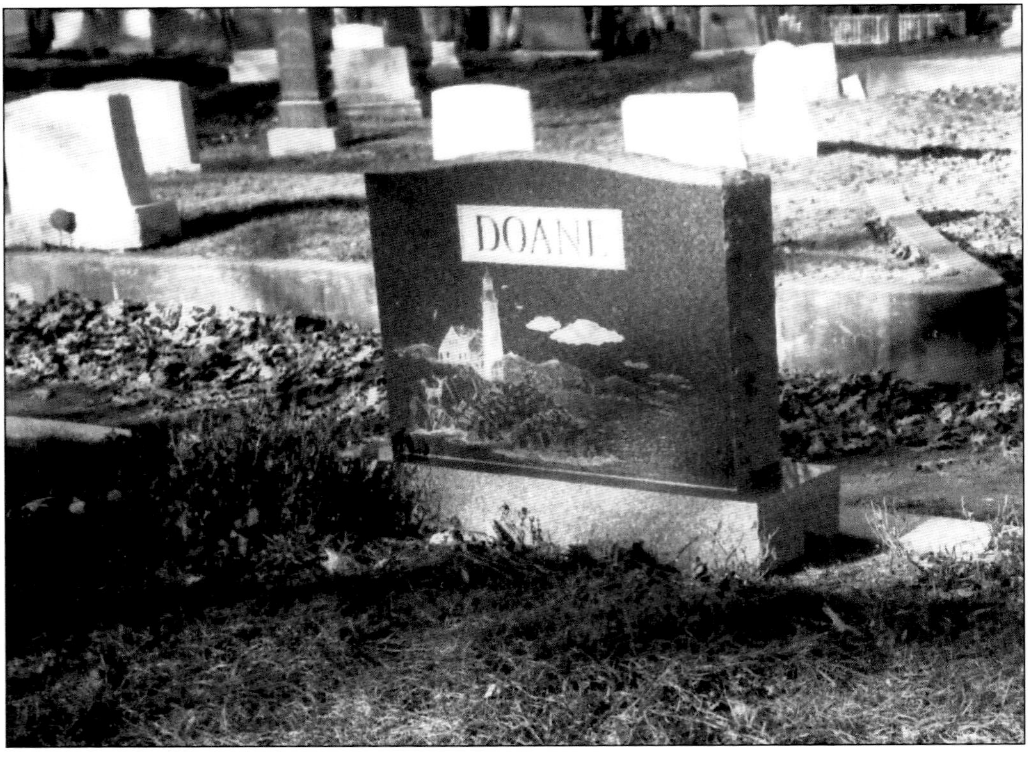

There are four cemeteries on Peaks Island—Brackett, Trefethen, Ye Olde Trott Burying Ground, and Pond Grove. The headstones date from the early 1800s to the late 1900s.

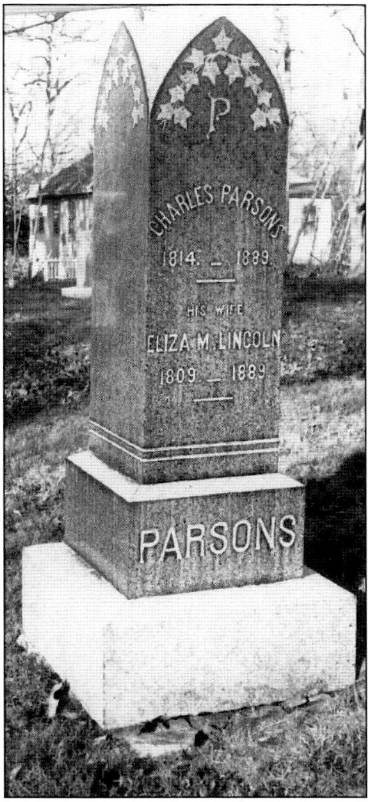

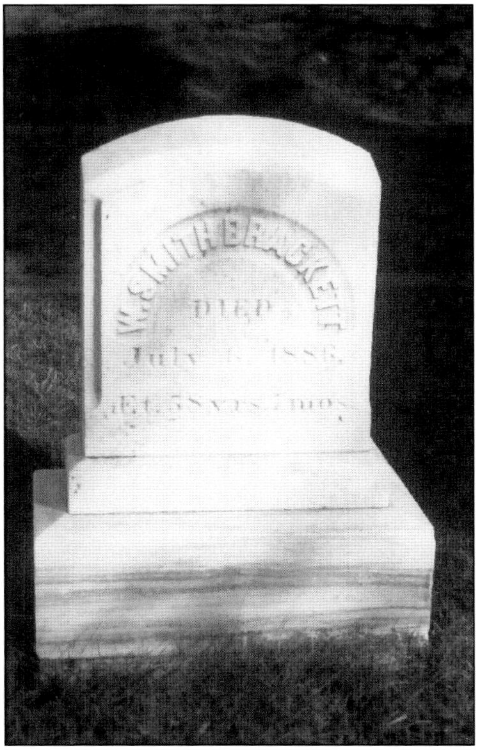

There is one mystery grave in Brackett cemetery, that of Captain John Shaw. Captain Shaw was appointed the first lighthouse keeper on Matinicus Rock in 1829 by President John Quincy Adams. He died in a Portland hospital in 1831, but no one is quite sure why he is buried on Peaks Island.

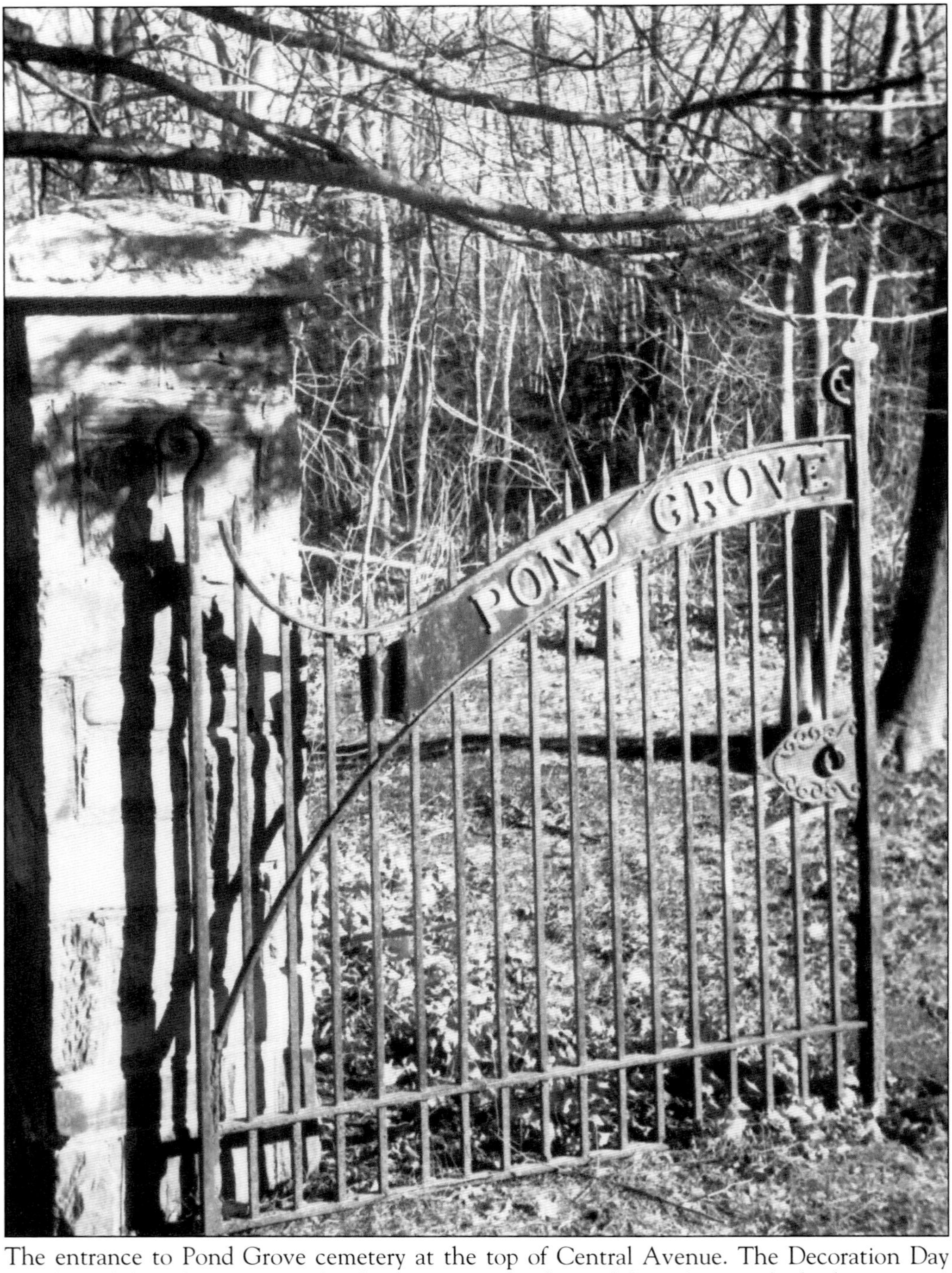

The entrance to Pond Grove cemetery at the top of Central Avenue. The Decoration Day Parade ends here for a service after flowers are strewn from a lobster boat in the harbor.

Four

Peaks Island Businesses

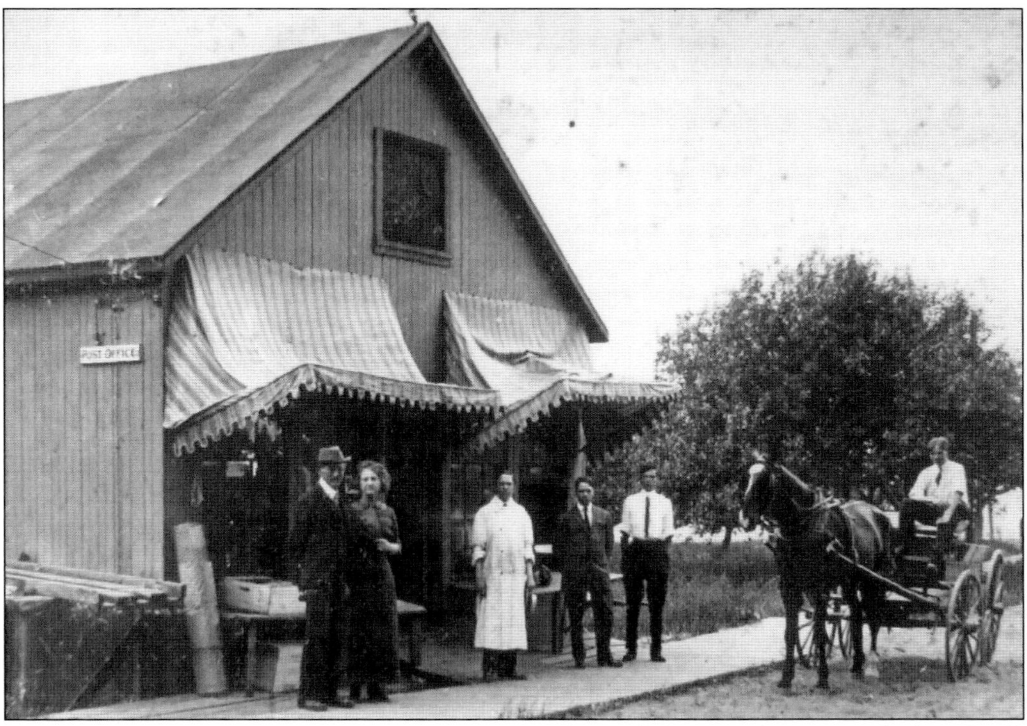

The first grocery store on Peaks Island, located near the Trefethen Landing. Note the boardwalk that ran all the way to the Forest City Landing.

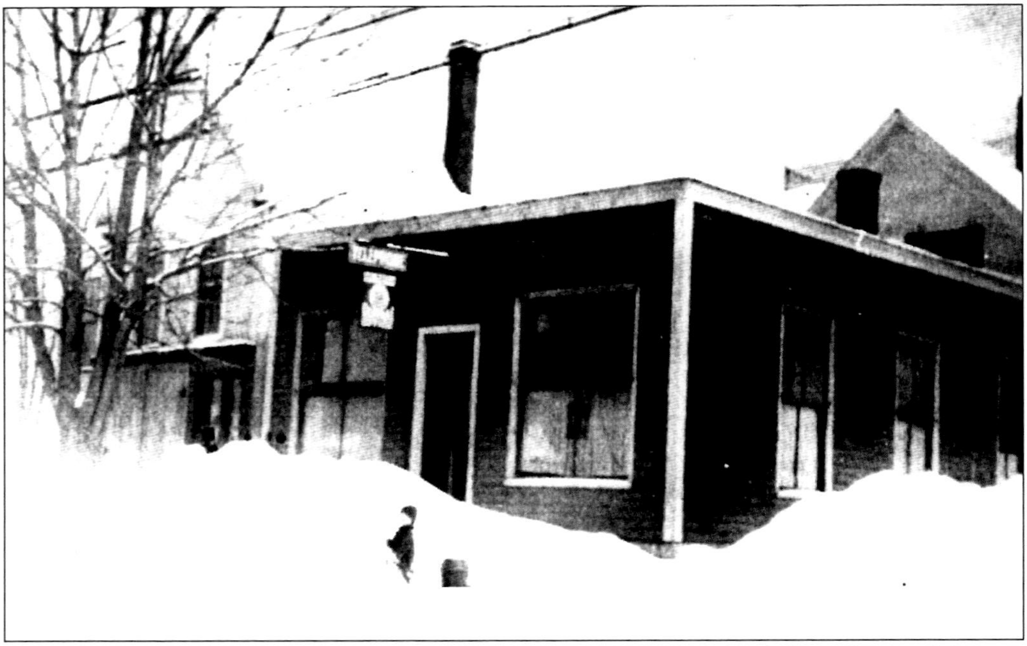

The twentieth century may have been slow in coming to Peaks Island, but when it did come it made life a little more secure. The operators of the first telephone switchboard closed the switchboard at 10 p.m., but one of them would sleep in the anteroom in case an emergency call came in. During the 1930s fire they remained at their stations all day until the flames on the roof threatened to destroy it.

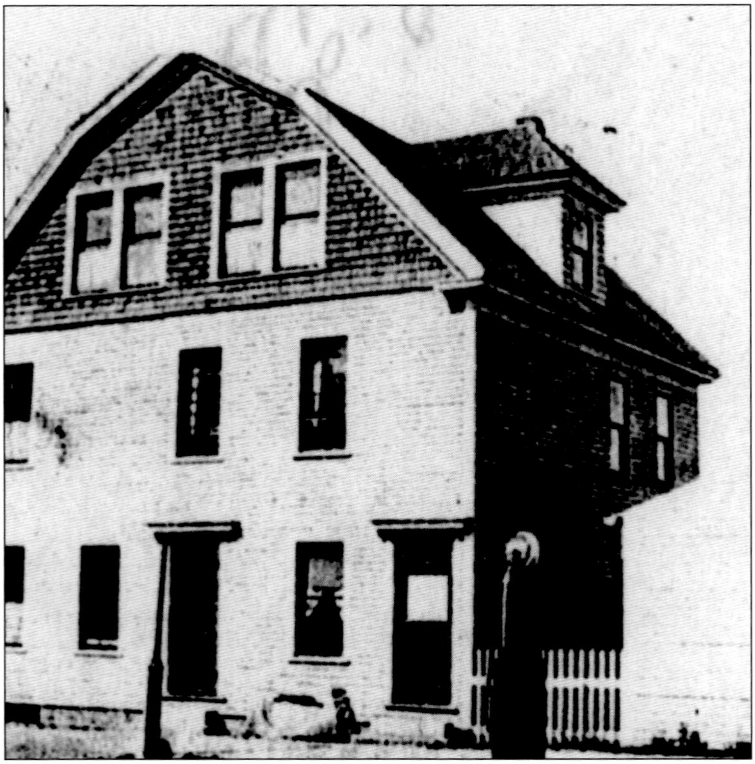

The post office was on the lower floor of this building. A summer substation also operated in the Trefethen area.

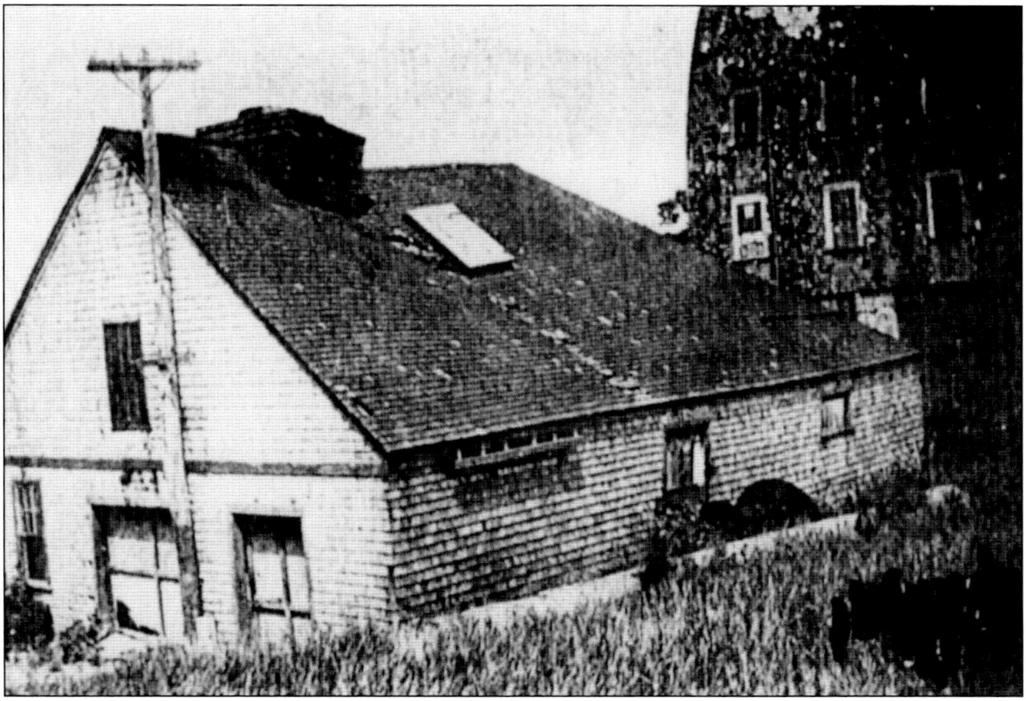

Carbide was made for business purposes at this site.

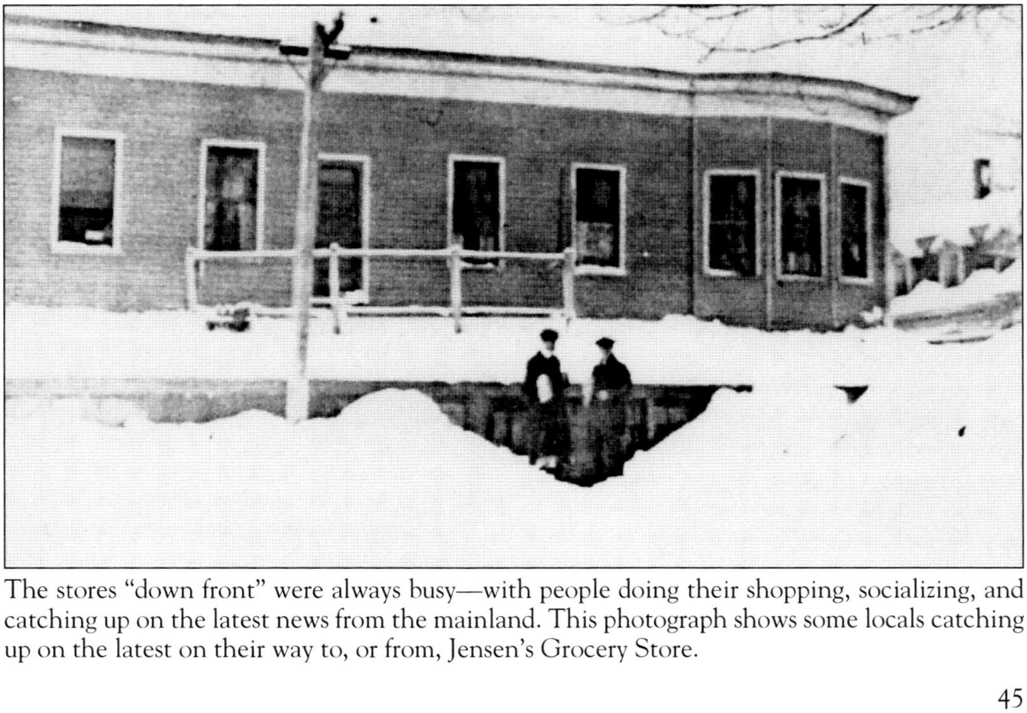

The stores "down front" were always busy—with people doing their shopping, socializing, and catching up on the latest news from the mainland. This photograph shows some locals catching up on the latest on their way to, or from, Jensen's Grocery Store.

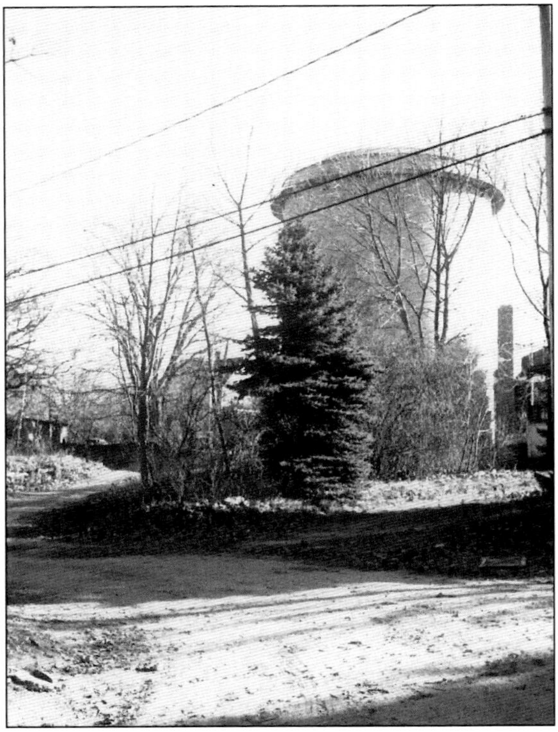

This tank held 400,000 gallons of water piped over from Sebago Lake on the mainland. Set atop Brackett Hill to provide flow, visitors always found its water delightfully cool and refreshing. The house located alongside the tank was provided for the superintendent.

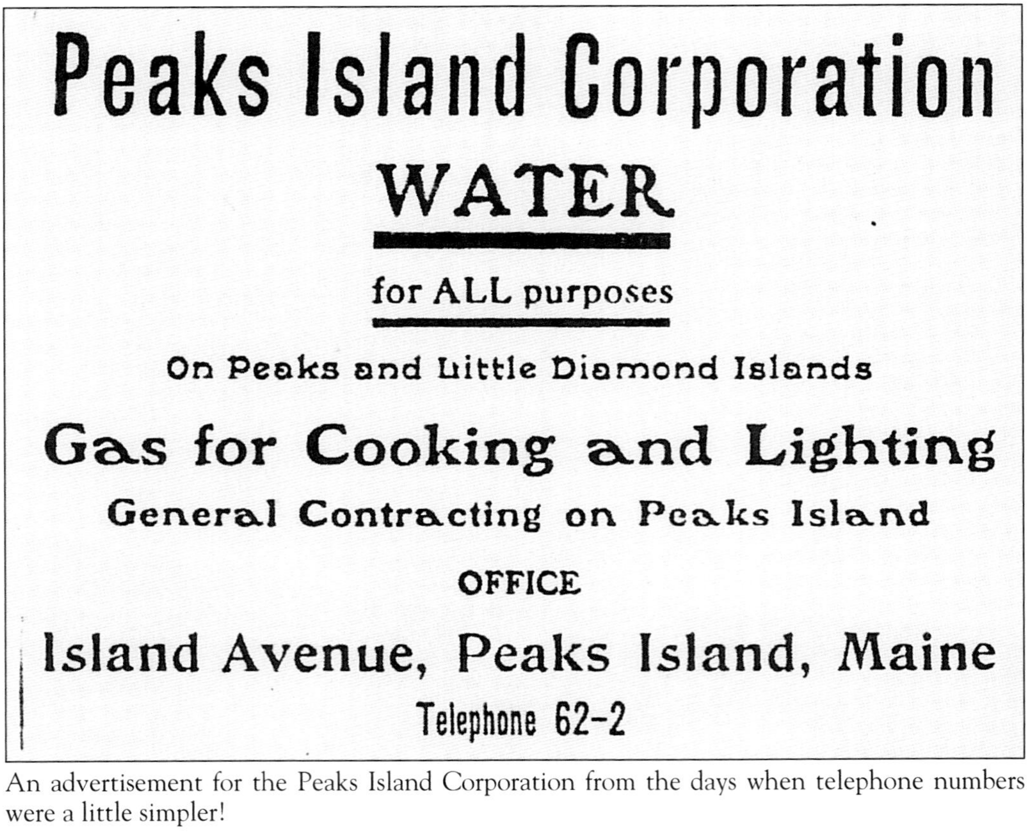

An advertisement for the Peaks Island Corporation from the days when telephone numbers were a little simpler!

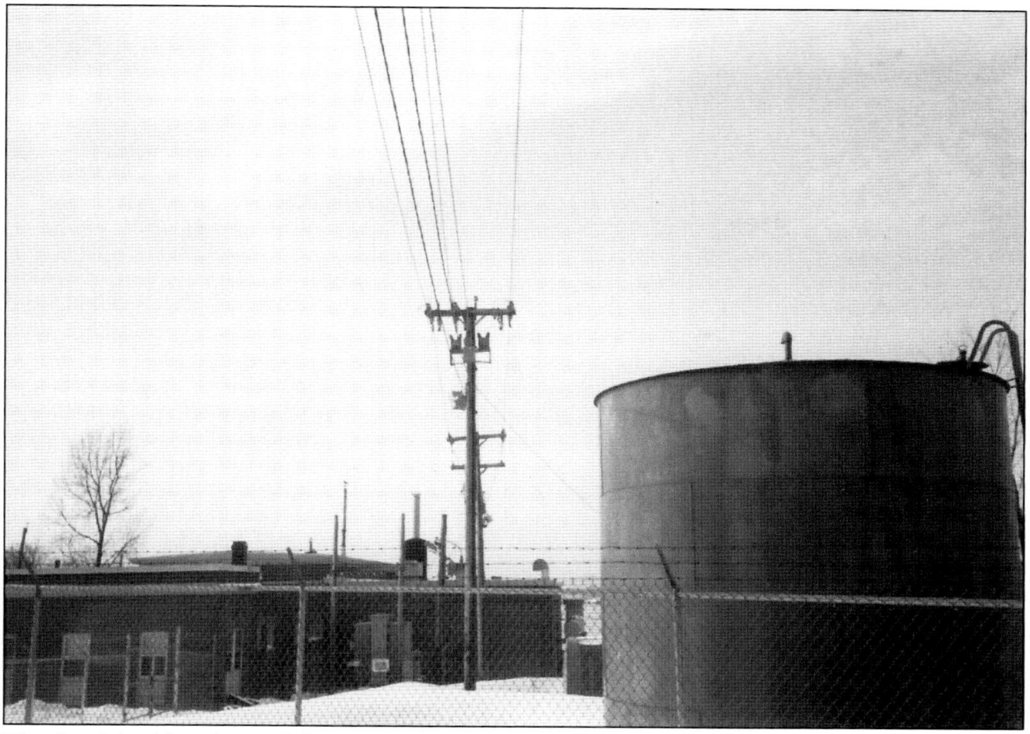

This brick building housed the power plant for the island. The tanks of oil were kept completely filled in the fall and winter in case the cove became icelocked and the supply boats could not enter. The population of Peaks Island drops significantly in the winter, but those who stay need to keep warm!

Casco Bay
Light and Power Co.

Supplying Electricity to the Following Islands

Peaks Island

Little and Great Diamond Islands

Long Island   Cushings Island

Great Chebeague Island   Cliff Island

In the early days of electricity service and supply were maintained locally.

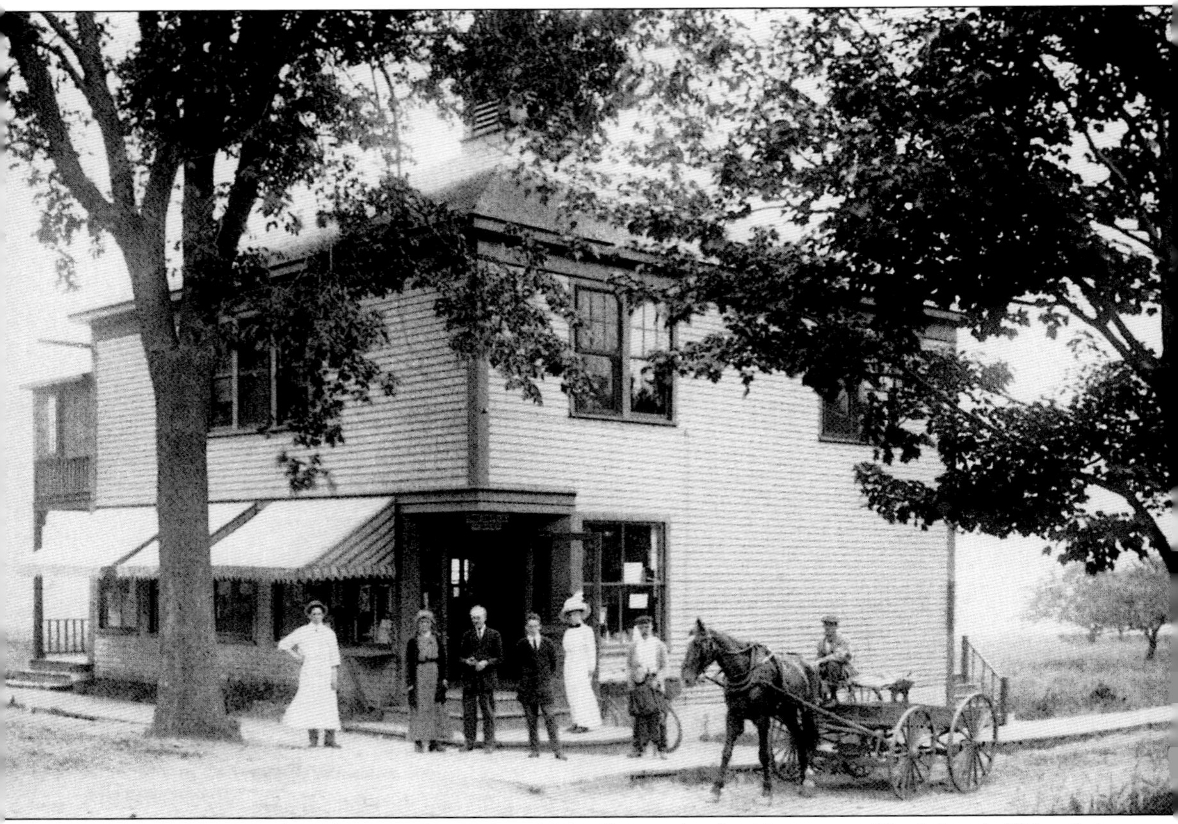

This photograph, taken in the early 1900s, shows the building near Trefethen's Wharf that housed the Peaks Island Post Office substation. People walked over every day to pick up their mail. In those days, having one's photograph taken was quite an event, and it looks as if all of the employees have gathered to have their picture taken.

The post office became Webber's store in the 1930s, and was known as a very special place that catered to the summer visitors who lived nearby and at Evergreen Landing. No tobacco or alcohol was sold there.

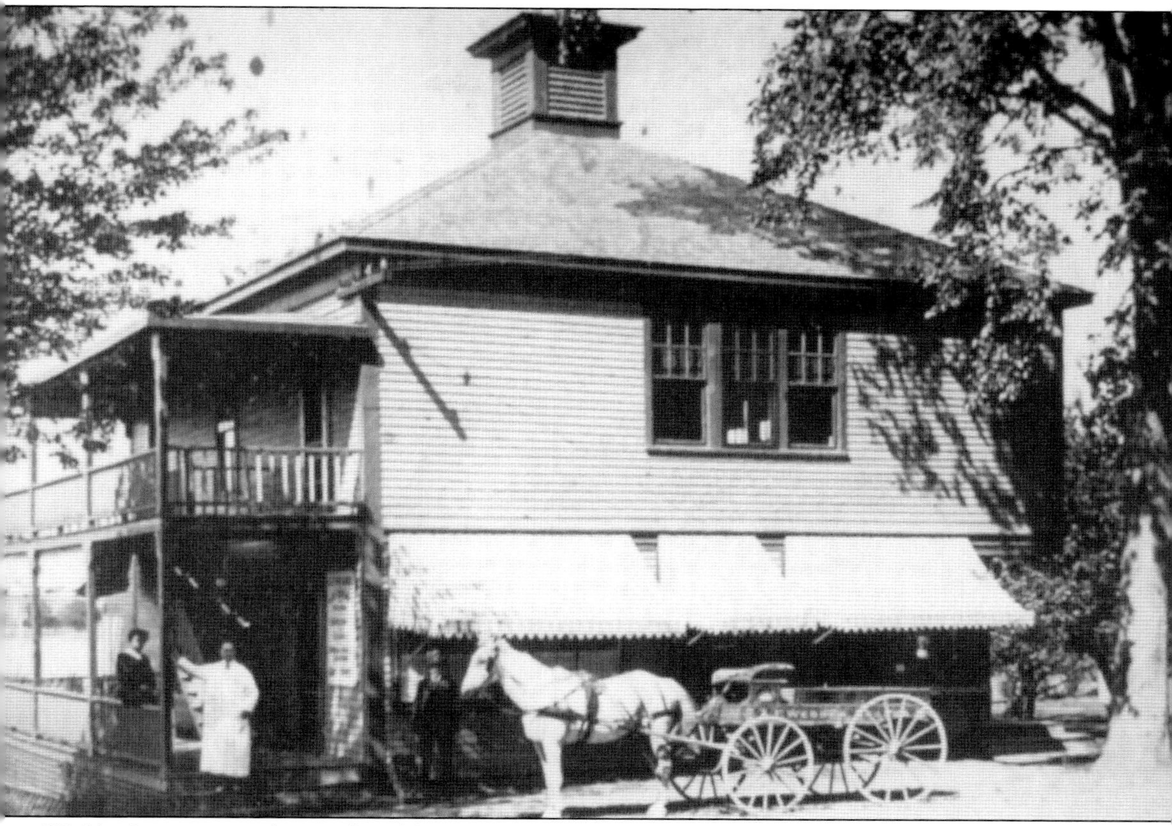

Webber's store complete with a delivery wagon.

DR. BLACK'S HOSPITAL

Peaks Island, Maine

Special Attention to Obstetrical, Gynecological and Female Surgical Cases.

Operating and Delivery Room Separate. Trained Nurses.

Private Rooms. Most Pleasant and Congenial Surroundings.

RICHARD P. BLACK, M. D.

Island Avenue Tel. 111 Peaks Island, Maine

There has usually been at least one local doctor to deal with emergencies on site. Nowadays all medical attention is received on the mainland.

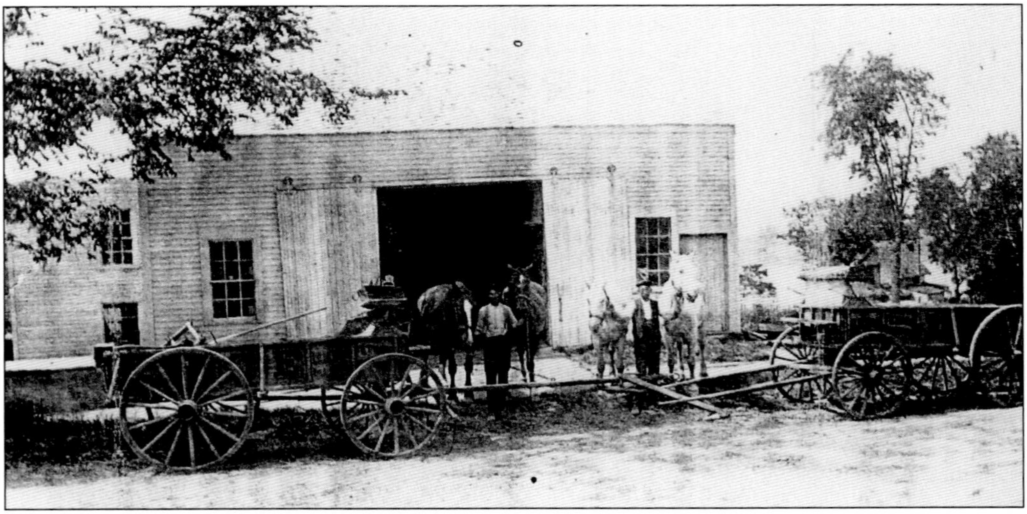

Howard Crosby Littlejohn ran an express delivery business in the early 1900s.

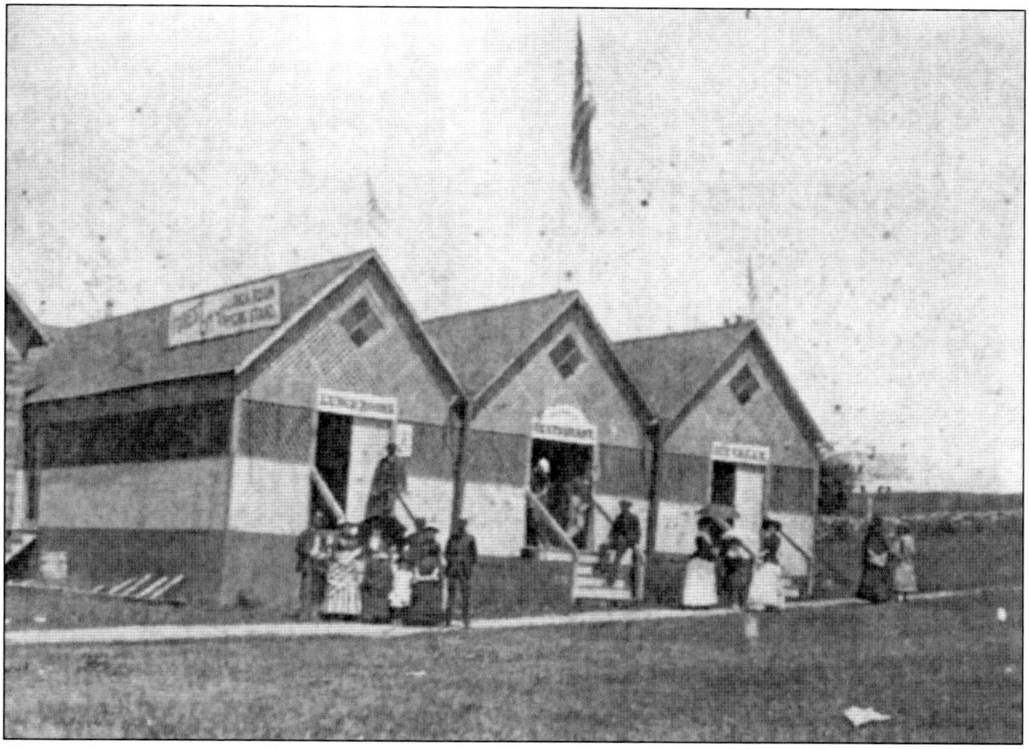

A popular restaurant and ice cream stand at Forest City. The name came from the fact that nearby Portland was popularly known as "Forest City."

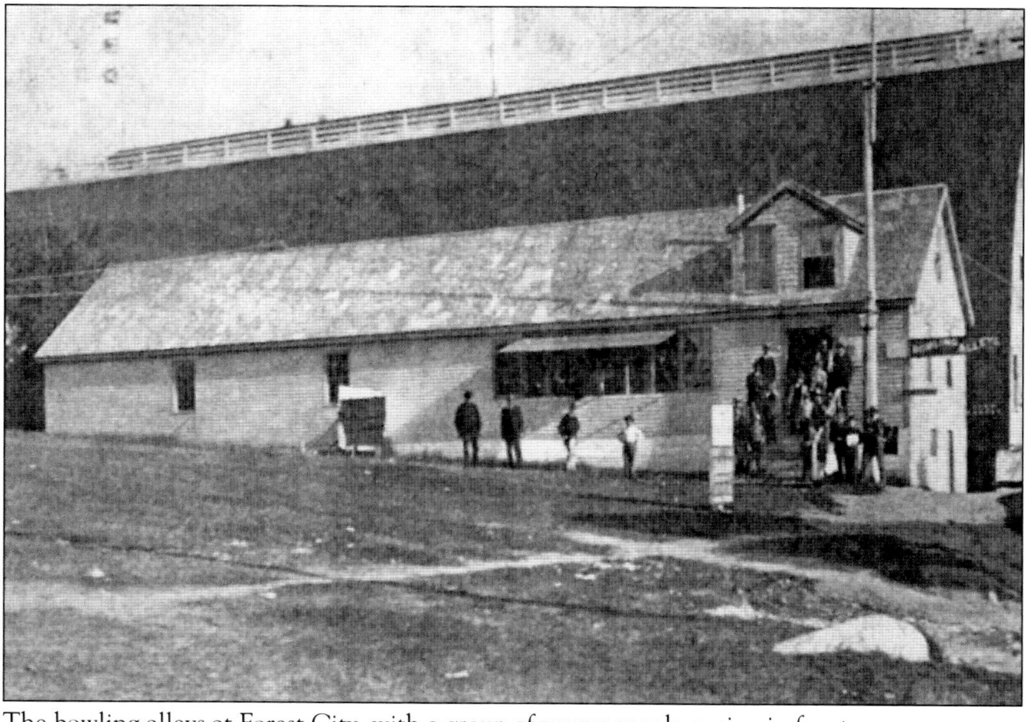

The bowling alleys at Forest City, with a group of young people posing in front.

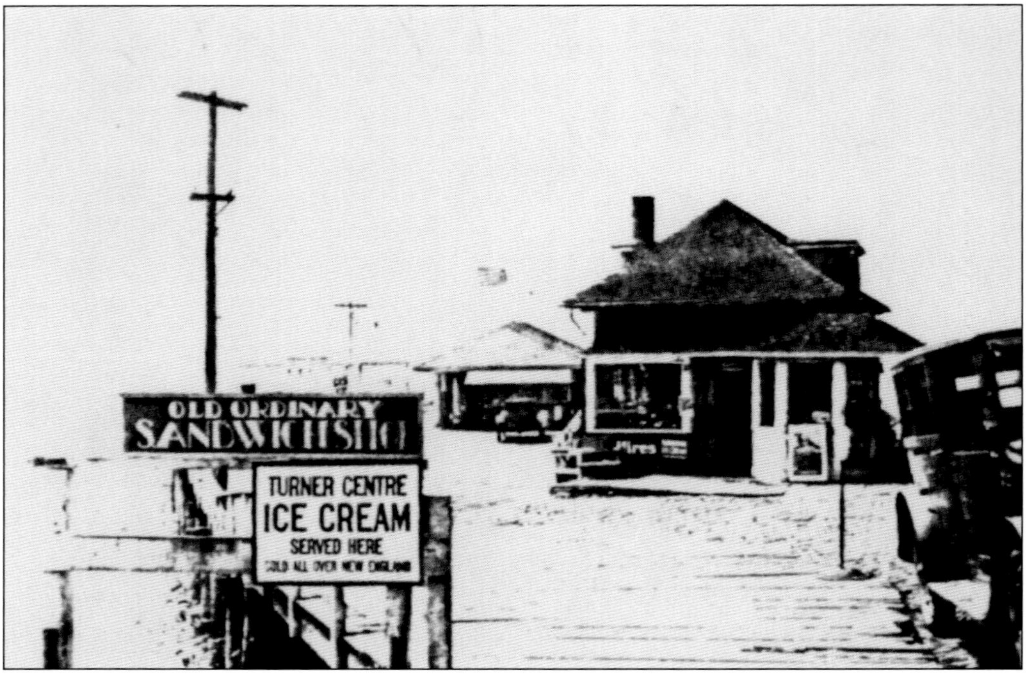

The volume of visitors to Peaks Island prompted residents to begin cottage industries and stores to cater to the tourists' needs. The building in the foreground of this 1930s photograph contained a small restaurant for visitors. The building in the background was the waiting room for passengers going to Portland.

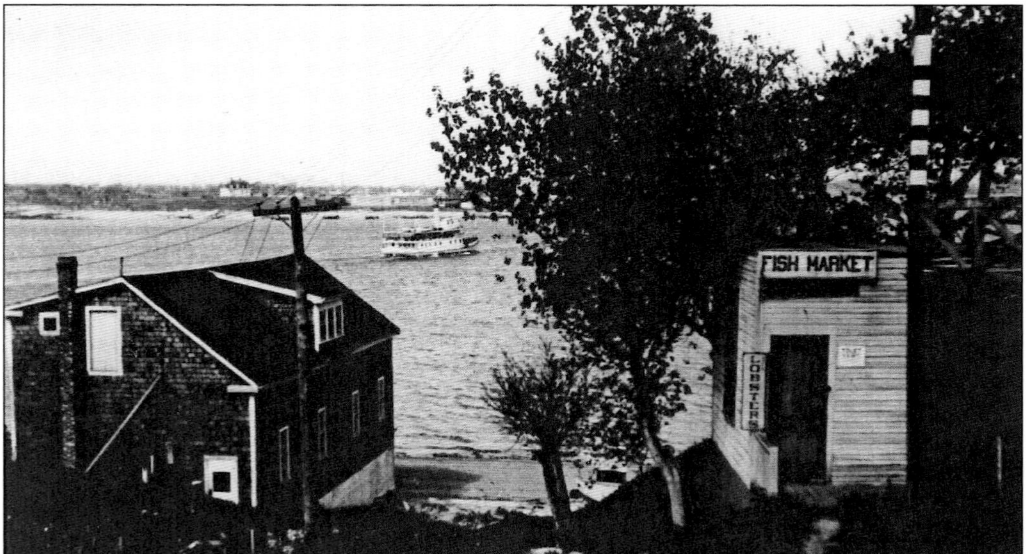

On the left of this photograph is a boat house for repairs and storage. The building on the right is a fish market where you could buy the day's fresh catch.

Five

Peaks Island Hotels

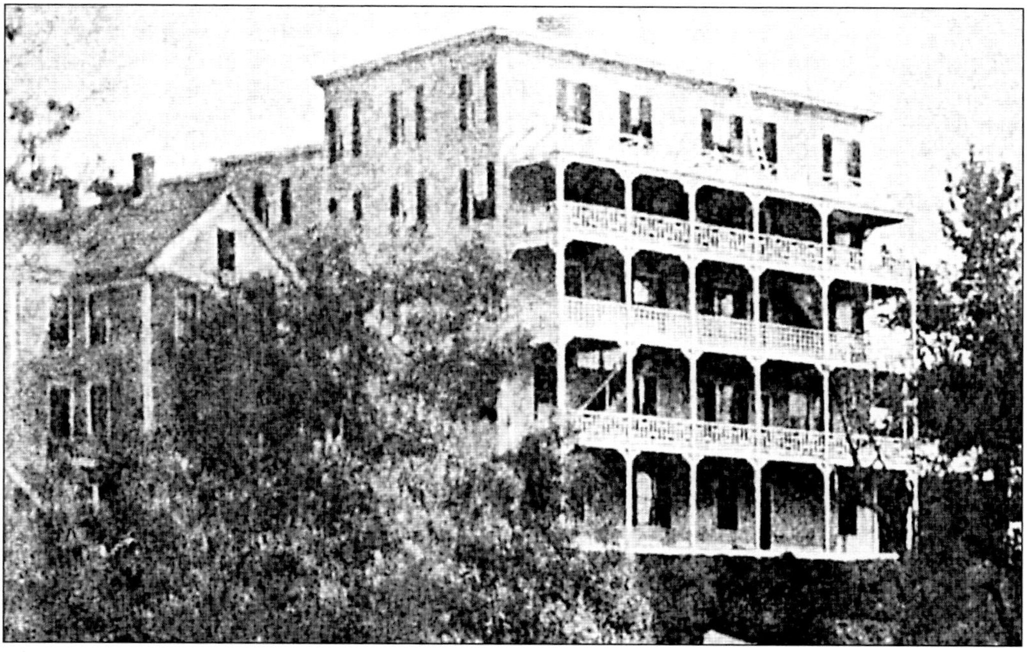

The Bay View House in 1865. This was one of the very early, and very opulent, hotels on Peaks Island. John T. Sterling was the proprietor at this time. Many visitors from the city would continue their sophisticated lifestyles while on vacation, and they expected all of the proper amenities and luxuries to do so.

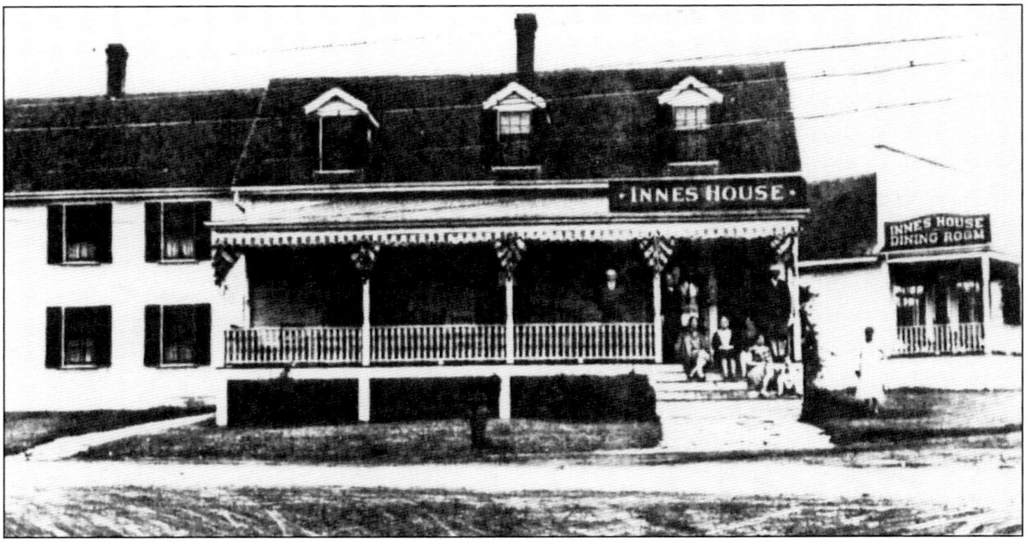

The Innes House, originally situated at the top of the hill on Welch Street, was moved down twice and finally located permanently on Island Avenue.

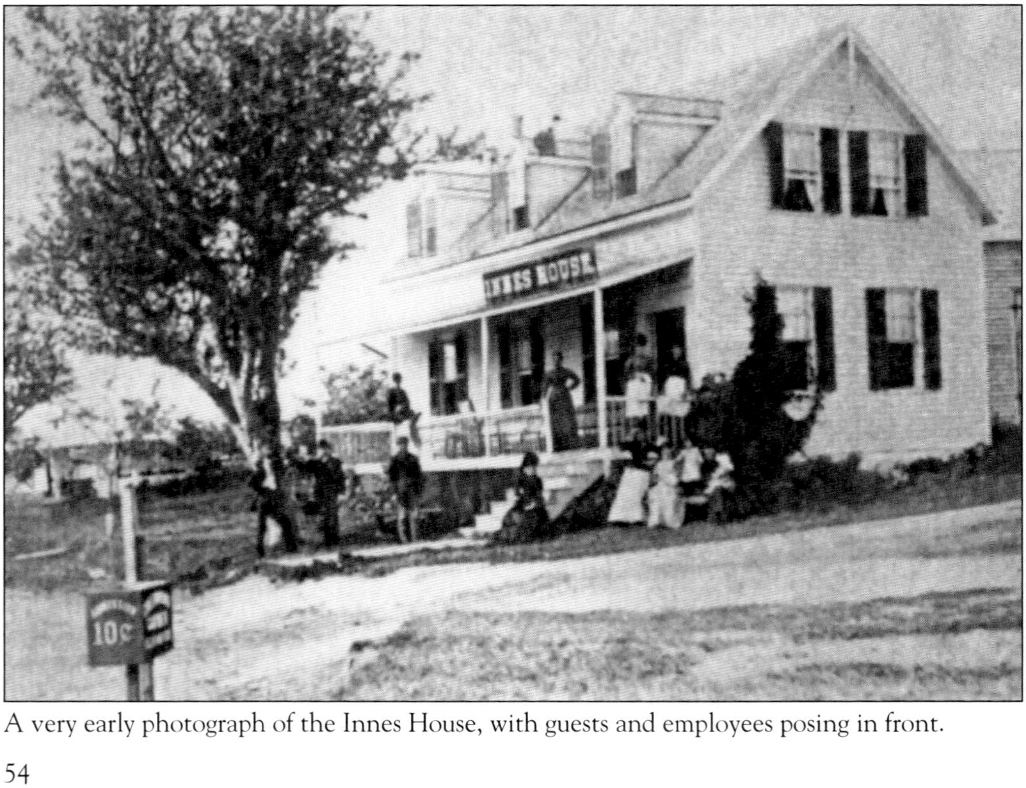

A very early photograph of the Innes House, with guests and employees posing in front.

LEADING HOTELS AND BOARDING HOUSES

ALONG THE ROUTE OF THE

CASCO BAY AND HARPSWELL LINES

	Accommodations	Rates: Per Day	Rates: Per Week
PEAK'S ISLAND			
FOREST CITY LANDING			
New Peak's Isl. House & Annexes—R. E. Rowe	600	$2.00 to $3.50	$12.00 to $20.00
Inness House—Mrs. Sarah Inness	60	2.00	8.00 to 10.00
Avenue House—M. C. Sterling	60	2.00	9.00 to 10.00
Harbor View House—E. P. Treworgy	40	. . . .	8.00 to 12.00
Bay View House—C. W. Howard	60	. . . .	9.00 to 12.00
Mineral Spring House—A. T. Sterling	25	1.00	7.00
Samoset Cottage—Mrs. J. B. Higgins	20	2.00	8.00 to 10.00
Hillside Cottage—W. J. Gardiner-Rooms only	12	. . . .	3.00 to 4.50
The Machigonne—J. A. Wiley " "	30	. . . .	3.00 to 5.00
Brackett House—J. F. Brackett " "	20	. . . .	3.00 to 5.00
Summer Retreat—Mrs. H A. Fisher " "	15	. . . .	2.00 to 4.00
Cliff Cottage—R. E. Sterling " "	20	. . . .	2.00 to 4.00
Toronto Cottage—A. V. Ackley " "	12	. . . .	2.00 to 3.00
Central Cottage—N. E. Skillings " "	20	. . . .	3.00 to 4.00
TREFETHEN'S LANDING			
Oceanic House—Mrs. R. T. Sterling	50	2.50	12.00
Ye Headland Inn—W. H. Simon	75	2.00 to 3.00	12.50 to 18.00
Valley View House—S. F. Heath	50	2.00	9.00 to 15.00
Hillside House—Mrs. J. C. Pedersen	25	. . . .	8.00 to 10.00
The Colonial—Mrs. W. H. Trefethen	20	. . . .	7.00 to 9.00
EVERGREEN LANDING			
Knickerbocker Hotel—Mrs. J. H. Anderson	75	2.00 to 3.00	10.00 to 15.00
CUSHING'S ISLAND			
Ottawa House—Boyce & Hatfield	250	3.00 to 4.00	15.00 to 30.00
		Spl. rates for season patrons	
LONG ISLAND			
Casco Bay House—C. E. Cushing	100	2.00	10.00 to 12.00
Dirigo House—Mrs. J. Perry	110	2.50	10.00 to 12.00
Granite Spring Hotel—E. Ponce	200	2.00 to 3.00	10.00 to 14.00
Beach Avenue House—W. A. Merrill	35	. . . .	8.00 to 10.00
GREAT CHEBEAGUE ISLAND			
WESTERN LANDING			
Sunnyside House—Mrs. J. E. Jenks	40	. . . .	10.00 to 12.00

This advertisement gives us an idea of the great number and variety of hotels and boarding houses on the Casco Bay Islands in their heyday. The islands' tourist trade stimulated business for the Casco Bay and other boat lines.

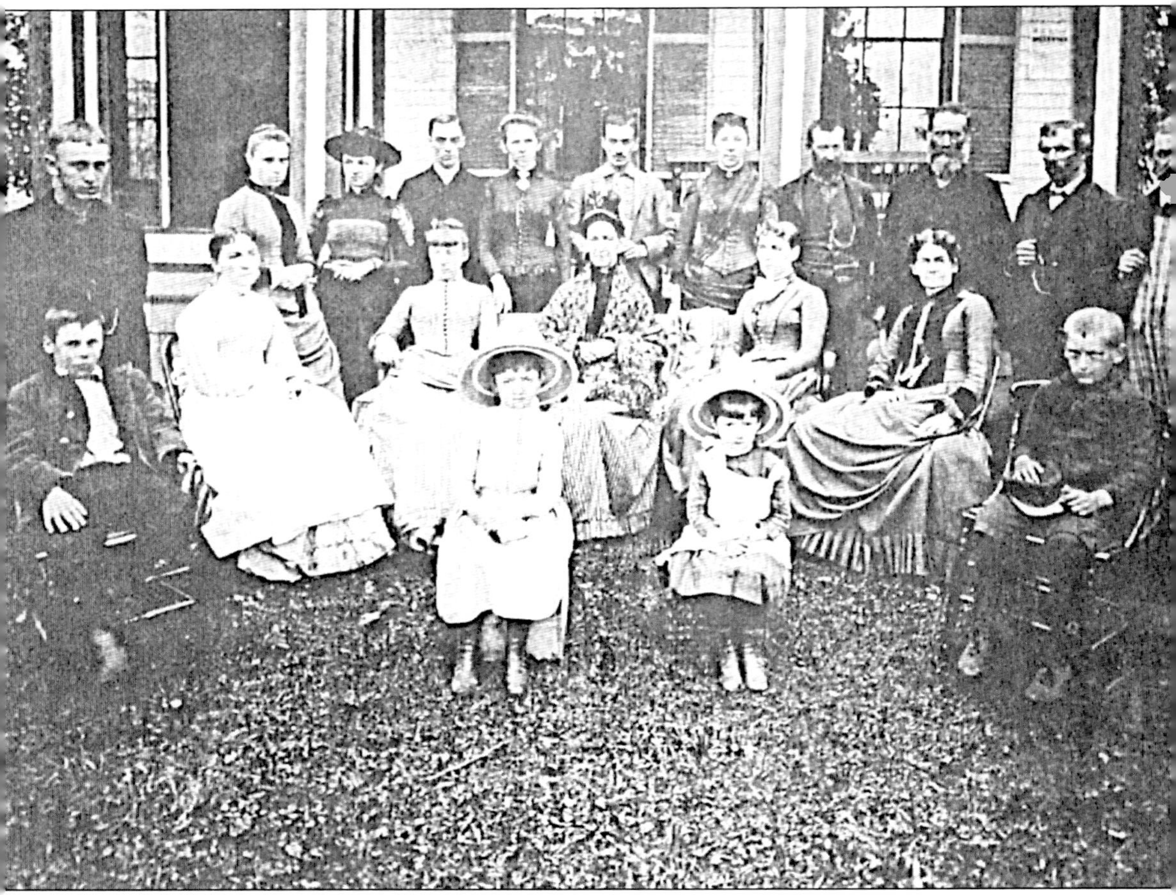

A Peaks Island family and friends gathered together for a photograph in 1886.

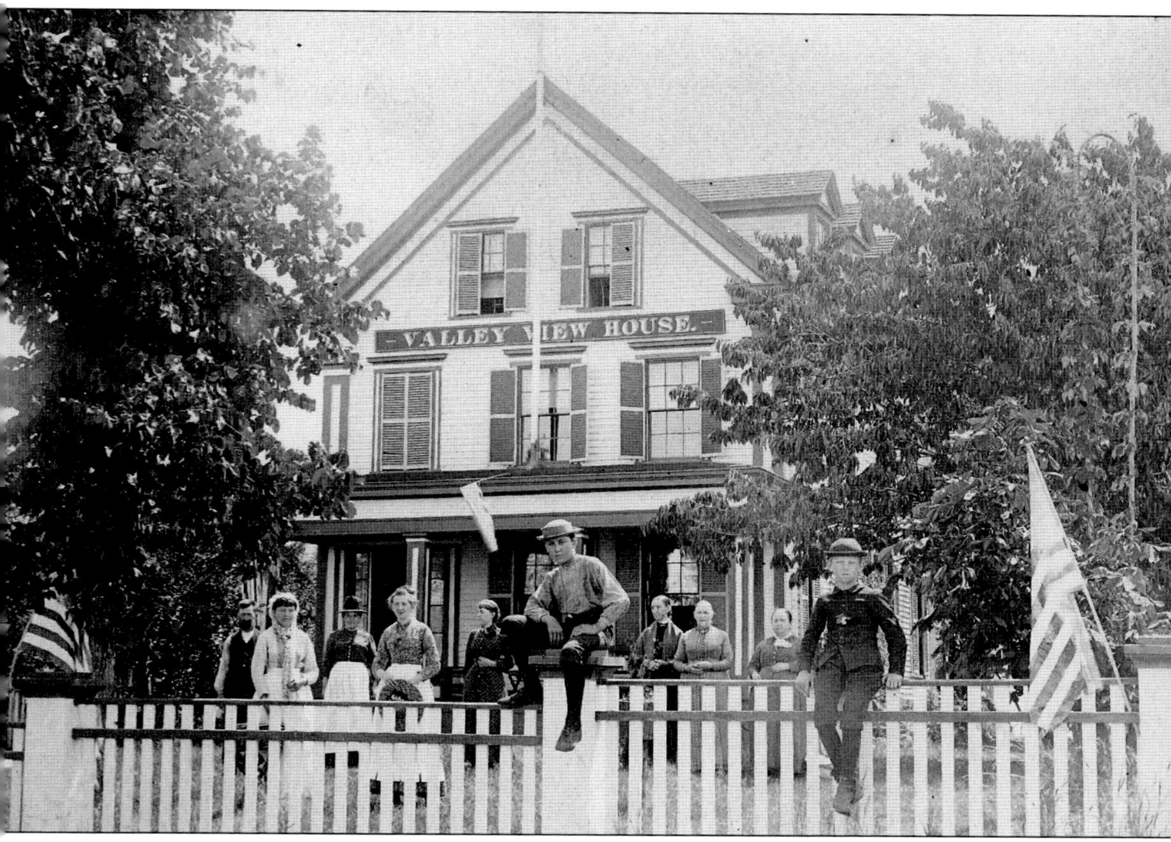

A delightful photograph of guests and staff posing outside Valley View House. It must have been a holiday—perhaps the Fourth of July—judging from the number of flags being flown.

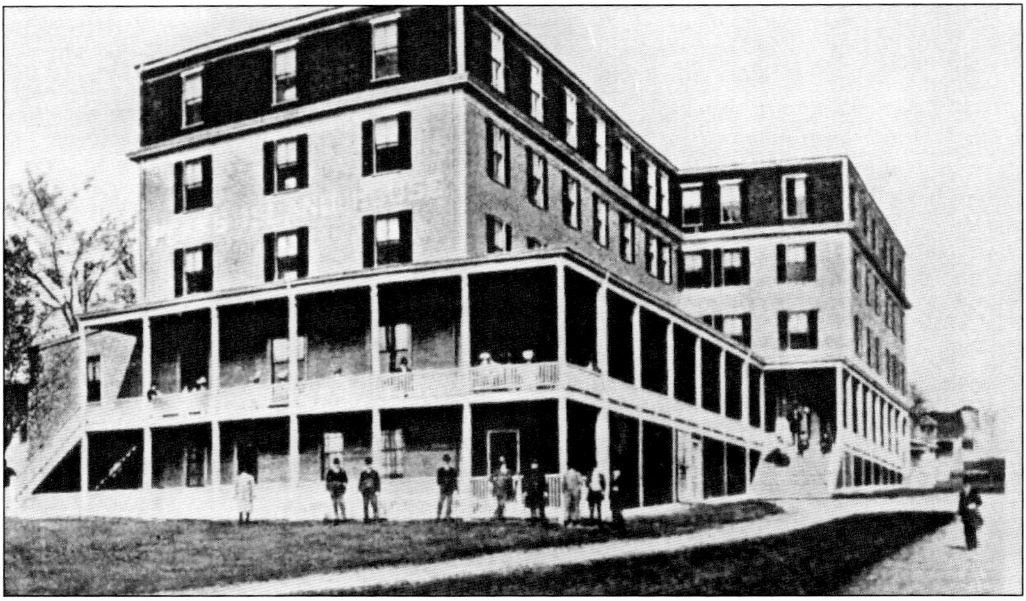

Peaks Island House was one of the most popular hotels on the island. The annex was built in response to the ever-growing number of visitors during the peak years of Peaks Island as a vacation resort.

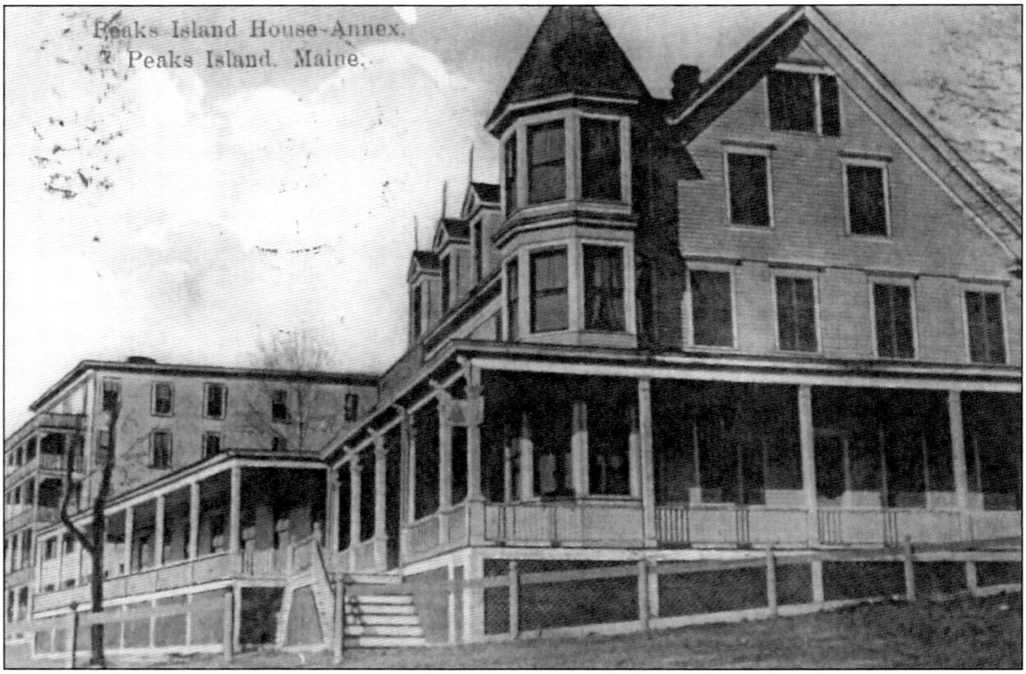

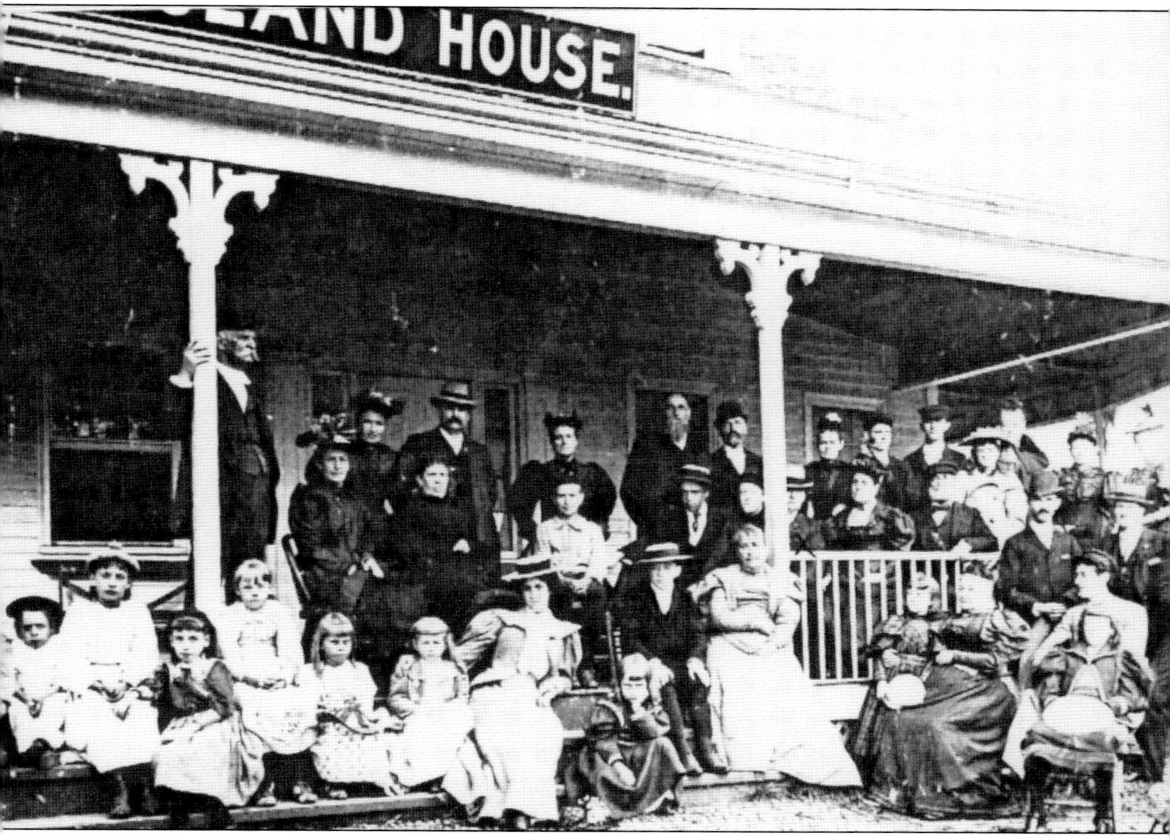

A group of well-dressed guests gathered on the porch of the Peaks Island House for a photograph in 1895.

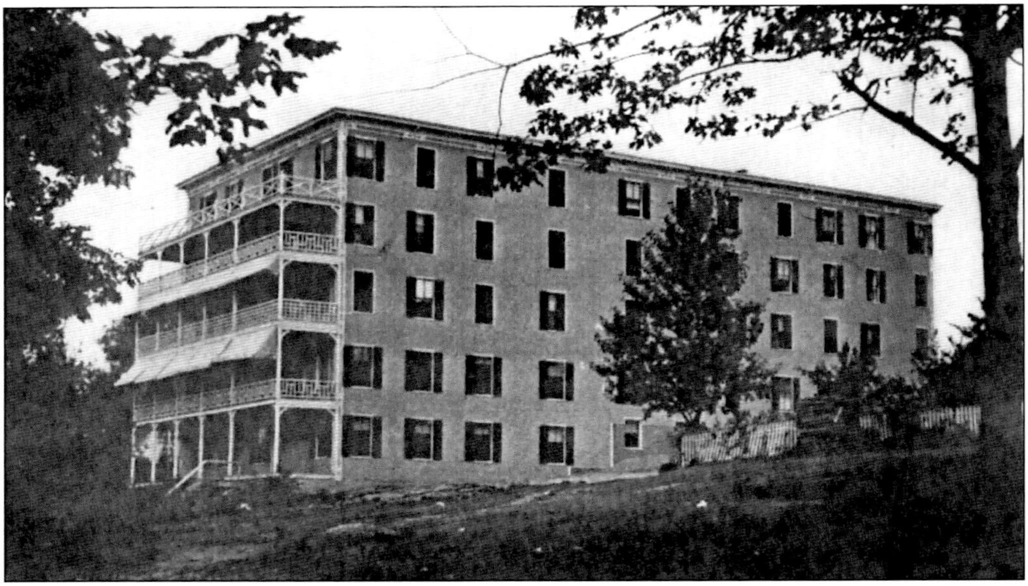

This size of this hotel, the Hotel Corona, gives us an idea of just how popular Peaks Island became in the summers of its busiest years.

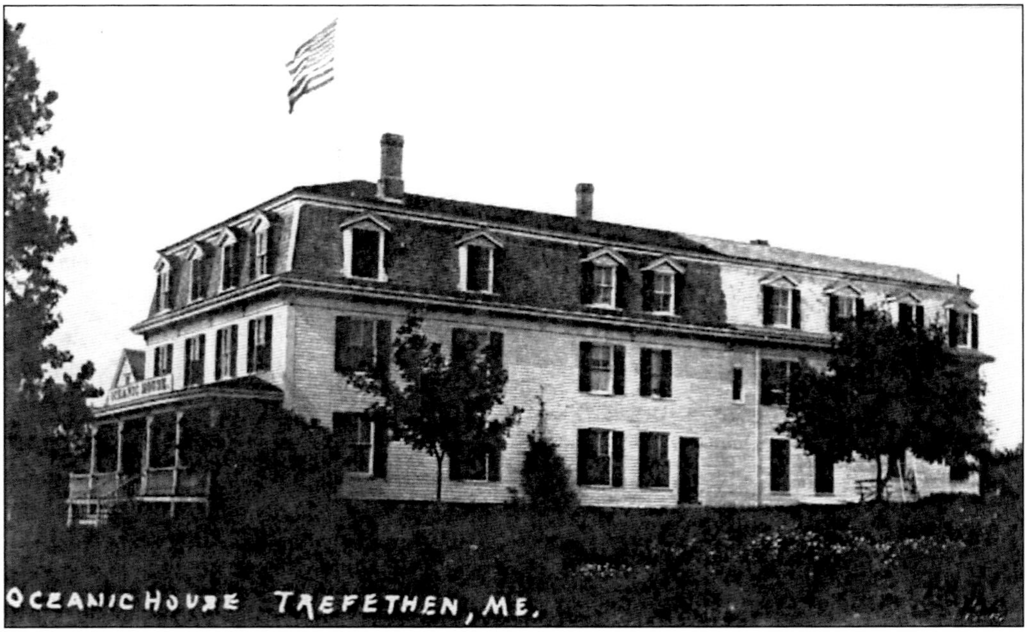

The Oceanic House in the Trefethen area of Peaks Island.

Six

Peaks Island People

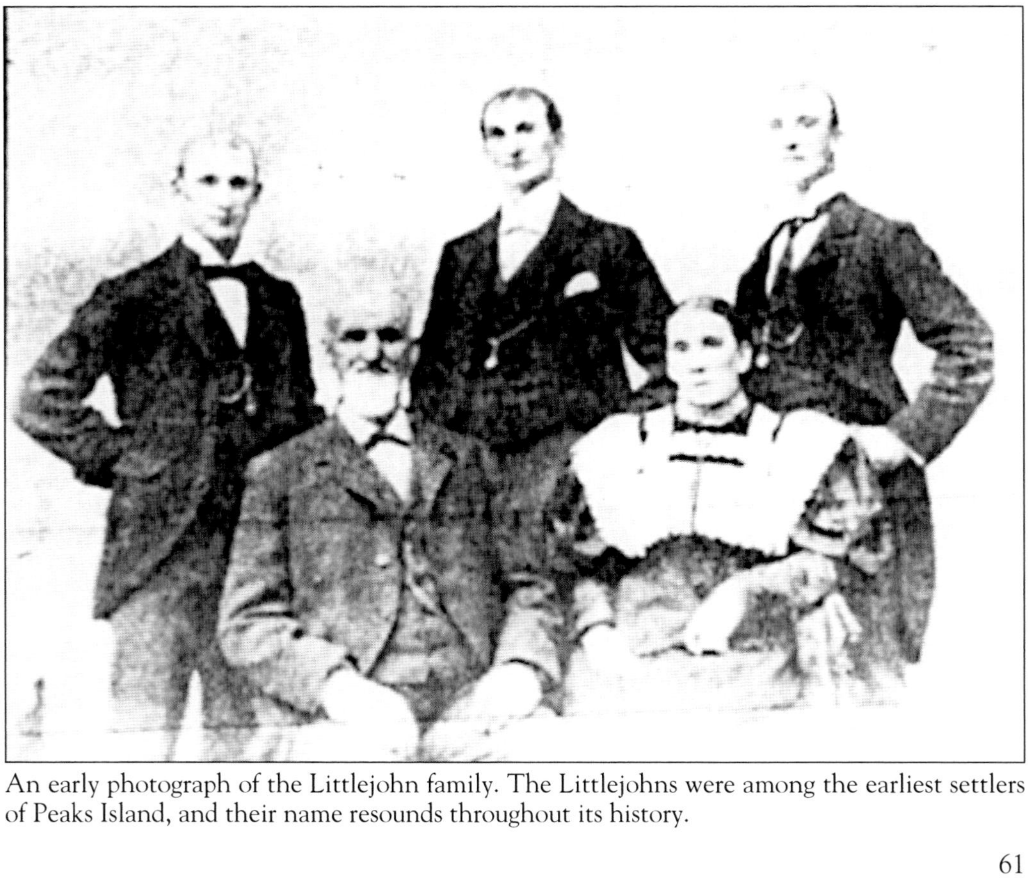

An early photograph of the Littlejohn family. The Littlejohns were among the earliest settlers of Peaks Island, and their name resounds throughout its history.

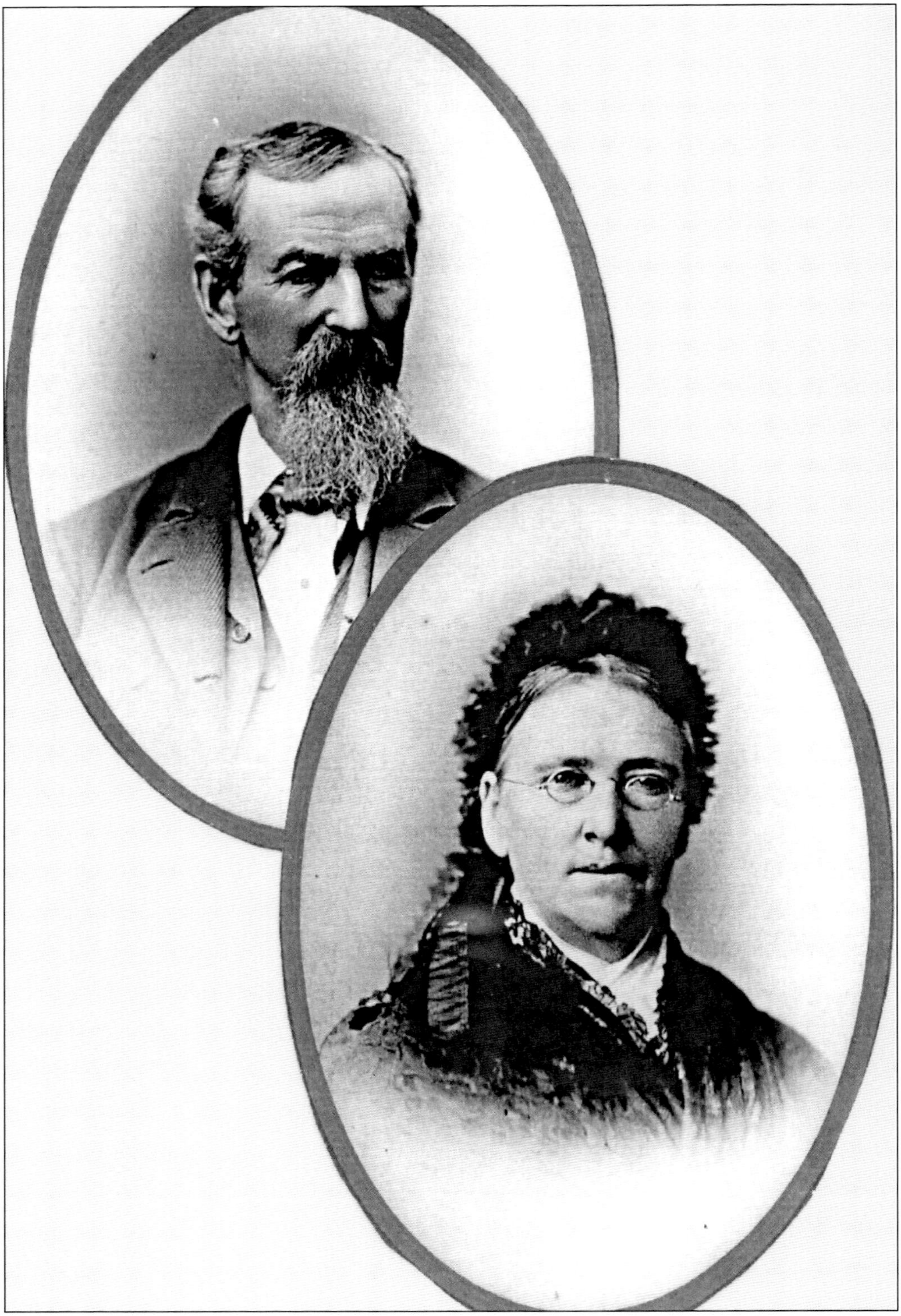

William Studley Trefethen and Emily Reed Trefethen, *c.* 1875. The Trefethens were also among the first settlers of Peaks Island.

Artist Roy Randall grew up on Peaks Island. The landscape of the Casco Bay Islands has inspired artists and writers for centuries, and the serenity and beauty of these hideaway places continue to attract those seeking a quieter, more relaxed lifestyle away from the cities.

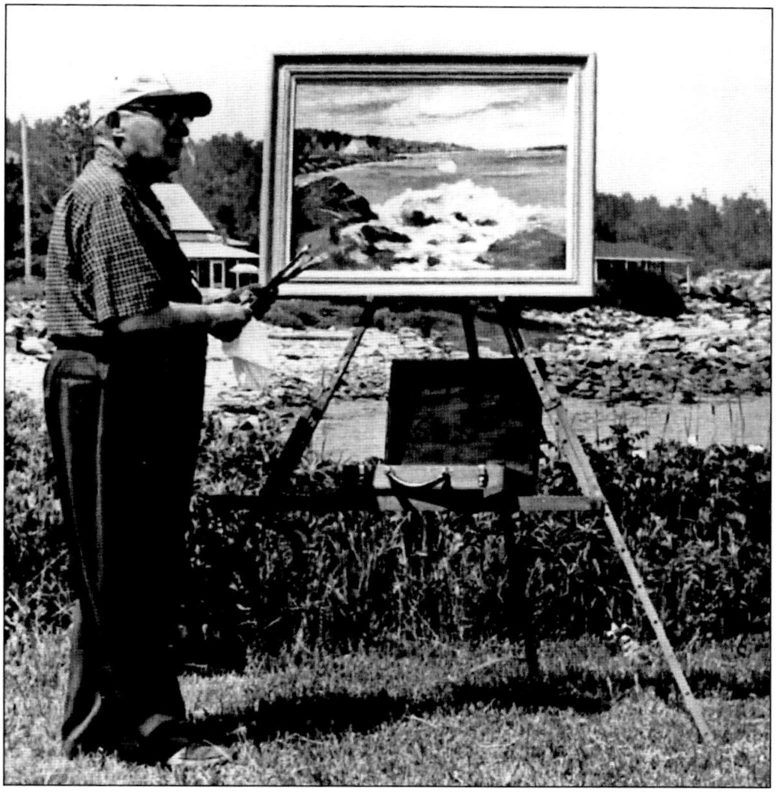

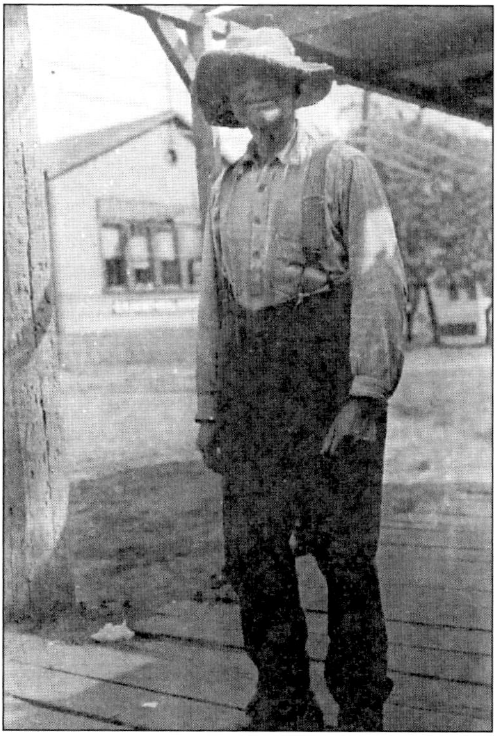

Captain Randall—a well-loved resident.

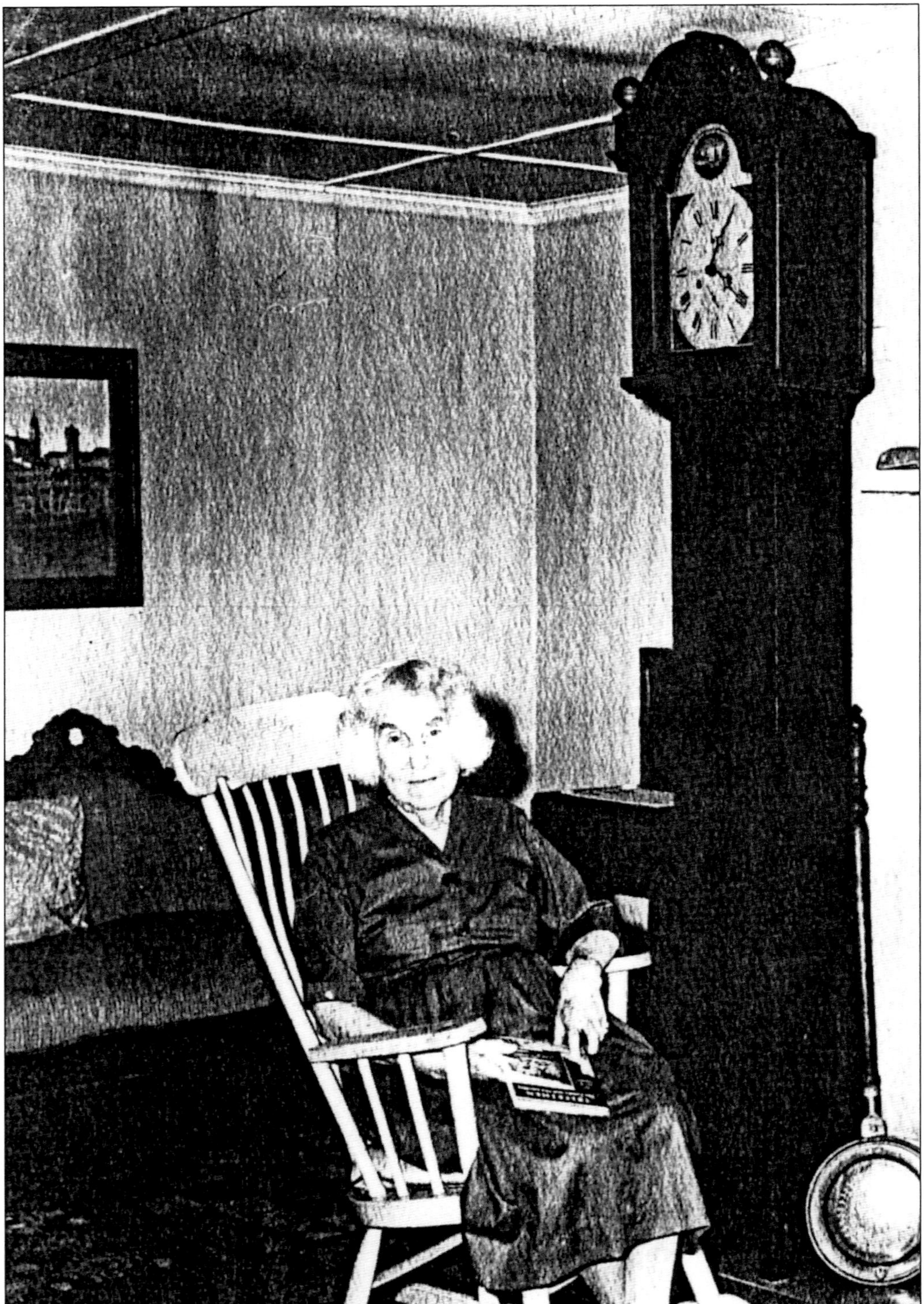

Jessie Bryan Trefethen, a retired professor of art at Oberlin College, Ohio, holds a copy of the book she wrote detailing the history of one of the earliest families on Monhegan and Peaks Islands—the Trefethens.

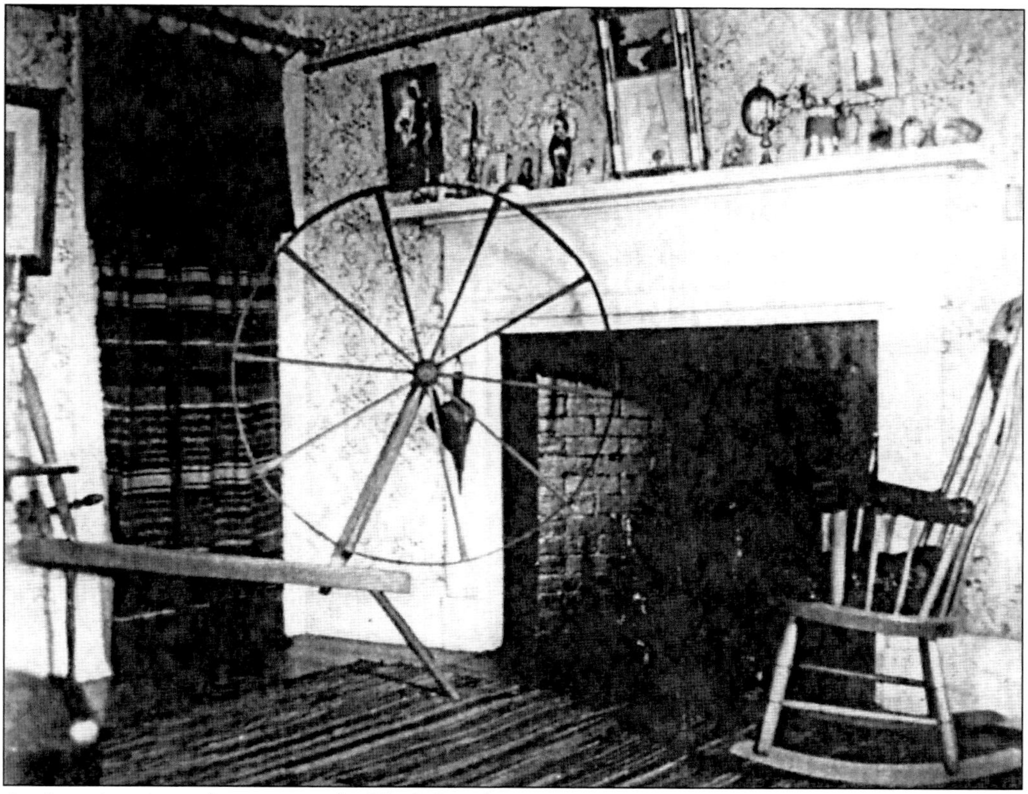

An interior view of a room in the Trefethen home.

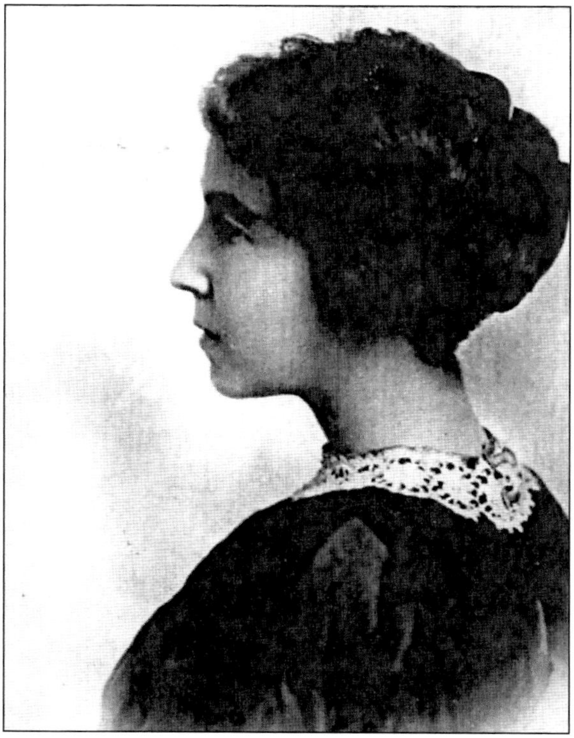

Jessie Bryan Trefethen at the age of about twenty.

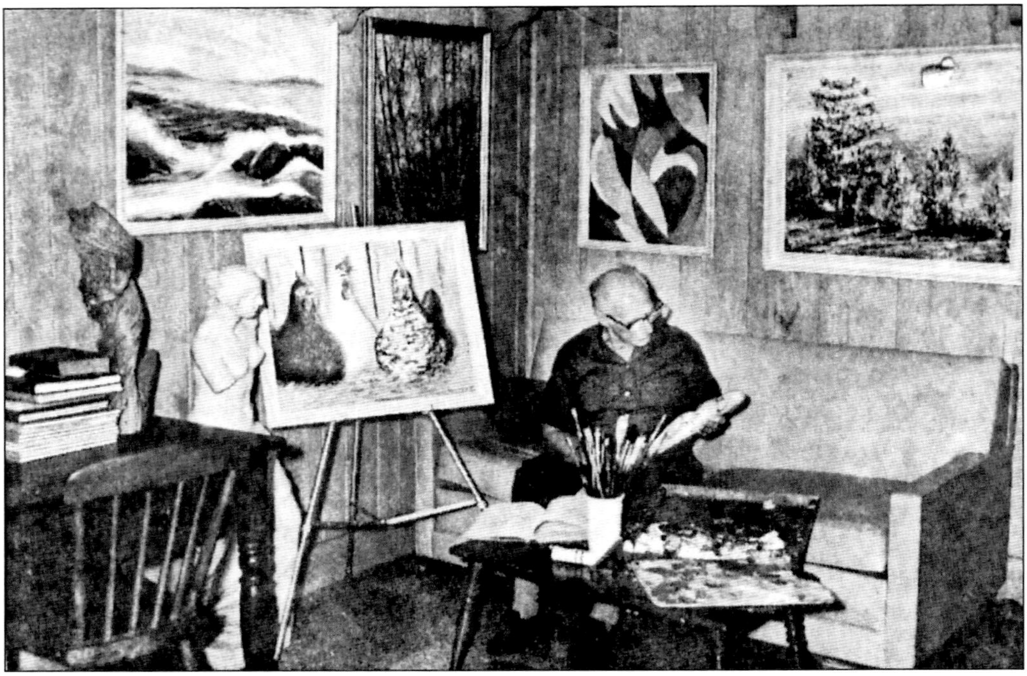

Ansel Sterling grew up on Peaks Island and later became an art teacher in the Westbrook schools. He and his wife Gladys, also a teacher, remodeled the Sterling homestead after their retirement. Sterling's paintings can be found in many area homes.

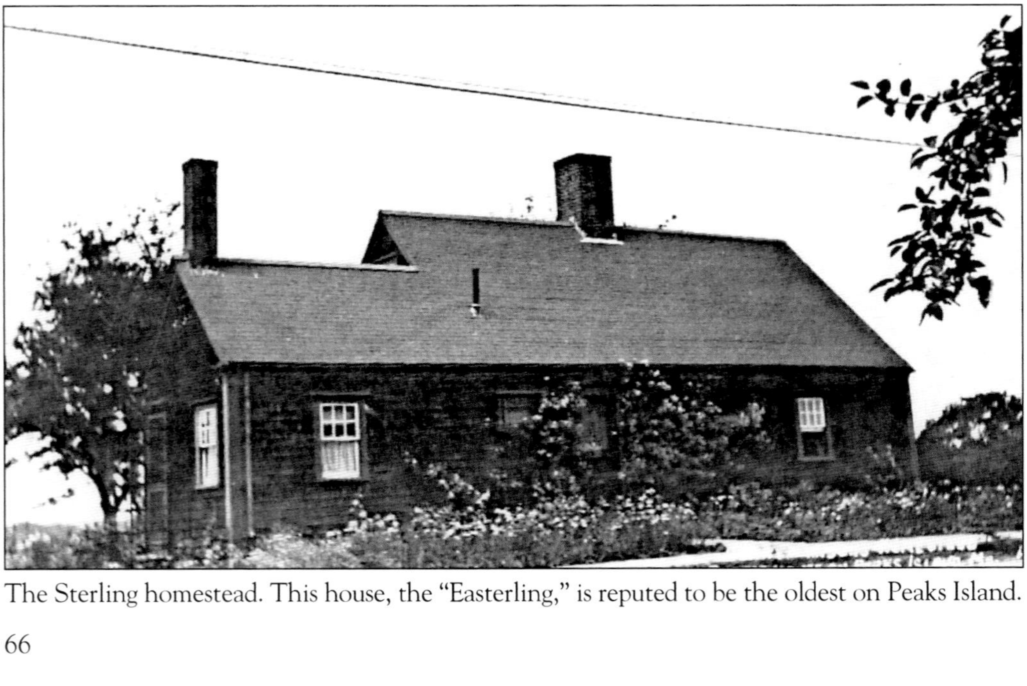

The Sterling homestead. This house, the "Easterling," is reputed to be the oldest on Peaks Island.

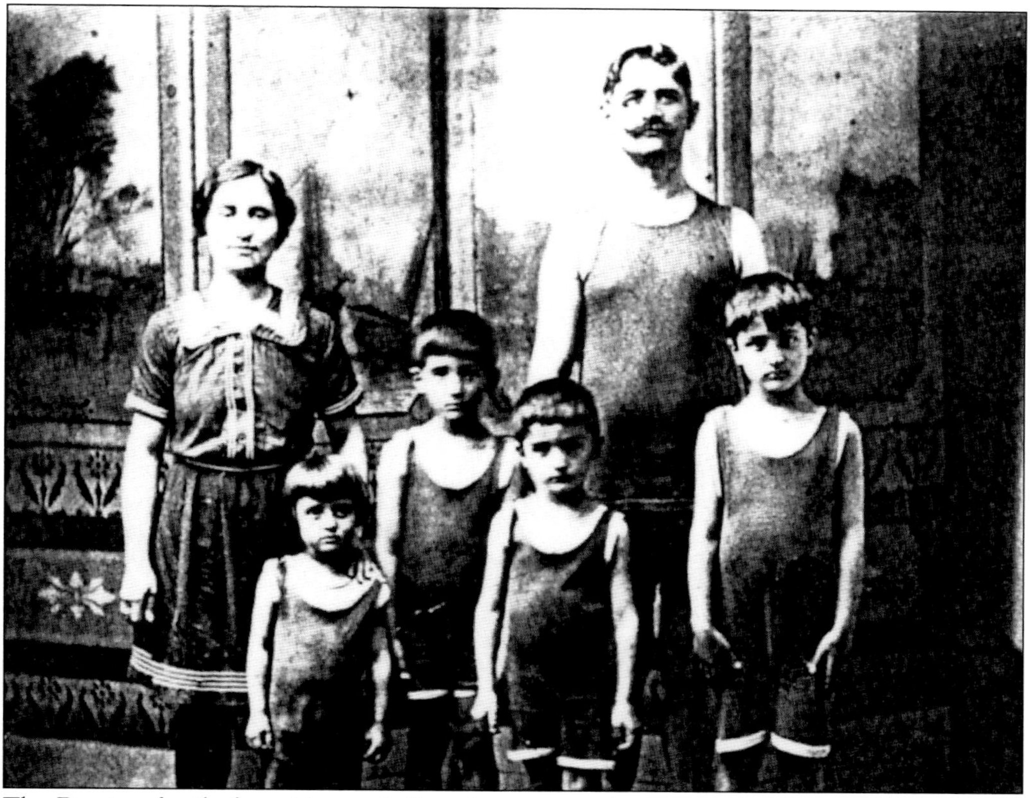

The Demitre family from Montreal, Canada, were regular summer residents on Peaks Island. They and their relatives had adjacent cottages, and spent the long summer months enjoying the island together.

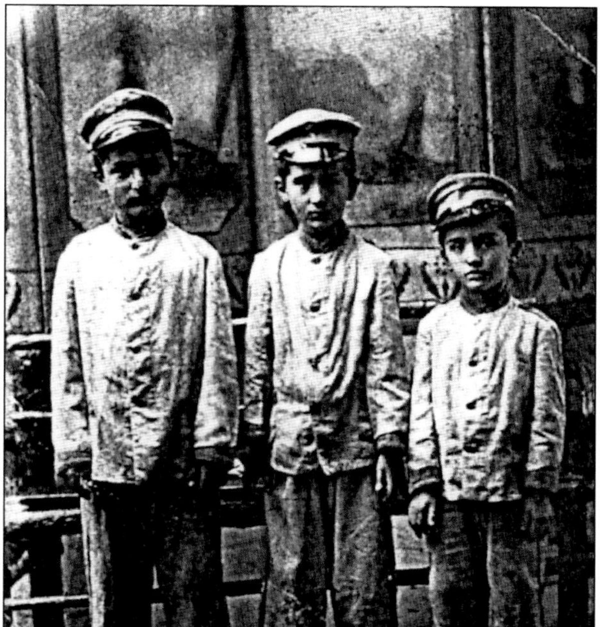

A wonderful photograph of Tony, Mike, and George Demitre in 1914.

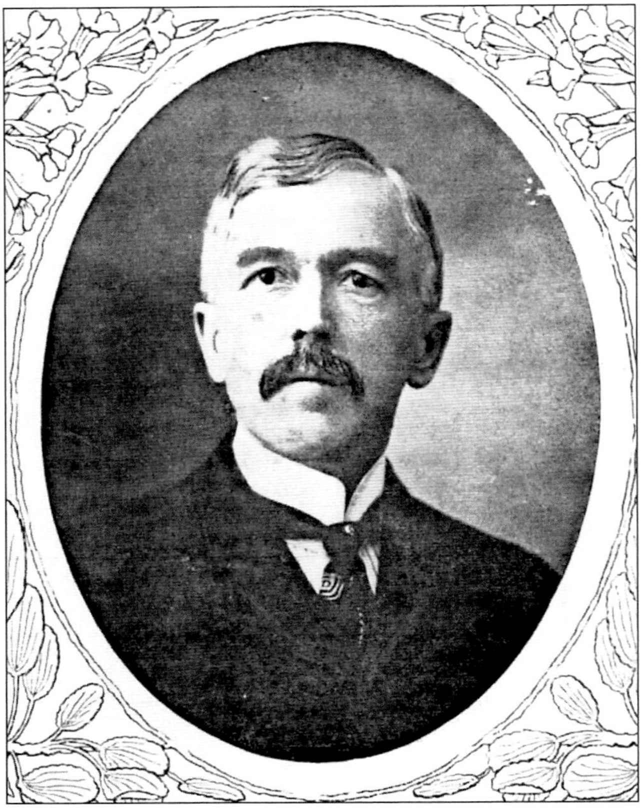

The islands did not only attract visitors from faraway destinations. Albert A. Cordwell was the mayor of Westbrook from 1893 to 1895. He served as a Republican in the Maine Legislature from 1901 to 1904, and in later years was cashier and paymaster at S.D. Warren Co.

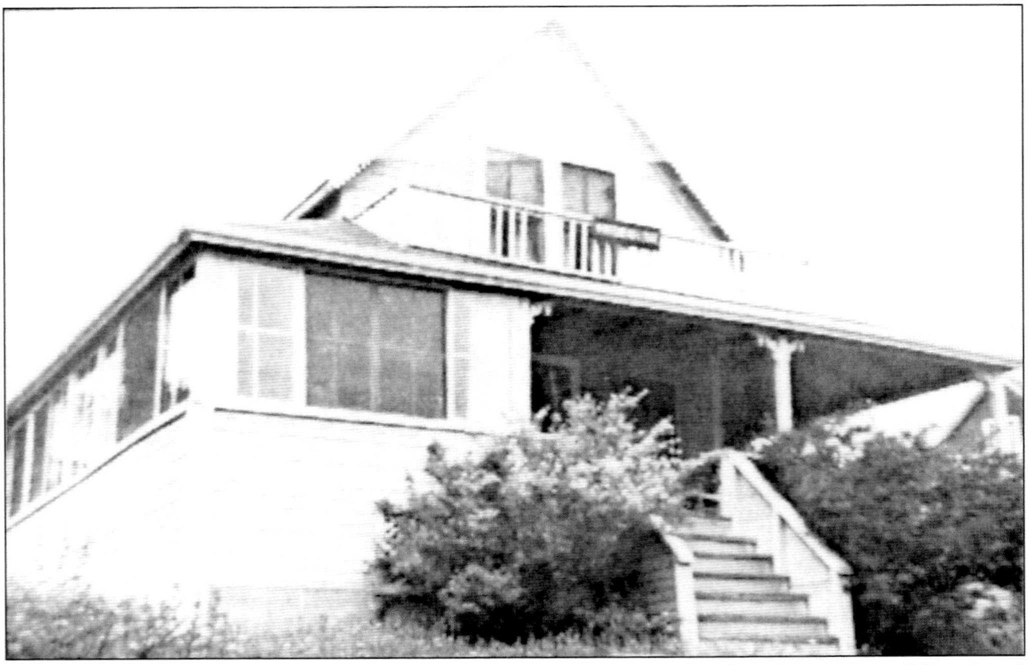

This is Albert Cordwell's summer home on Peaks Island. He built it himself on Whitehead Street, and from its windows the family could enjoy spectacular views of Cushing Island's Whitehead profile.

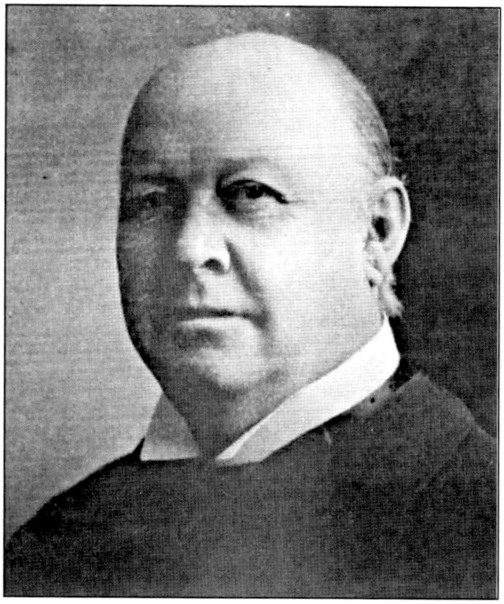

A 1899 photograph of Thomas Brackett Reed. He was a regular and notable summer visitor.

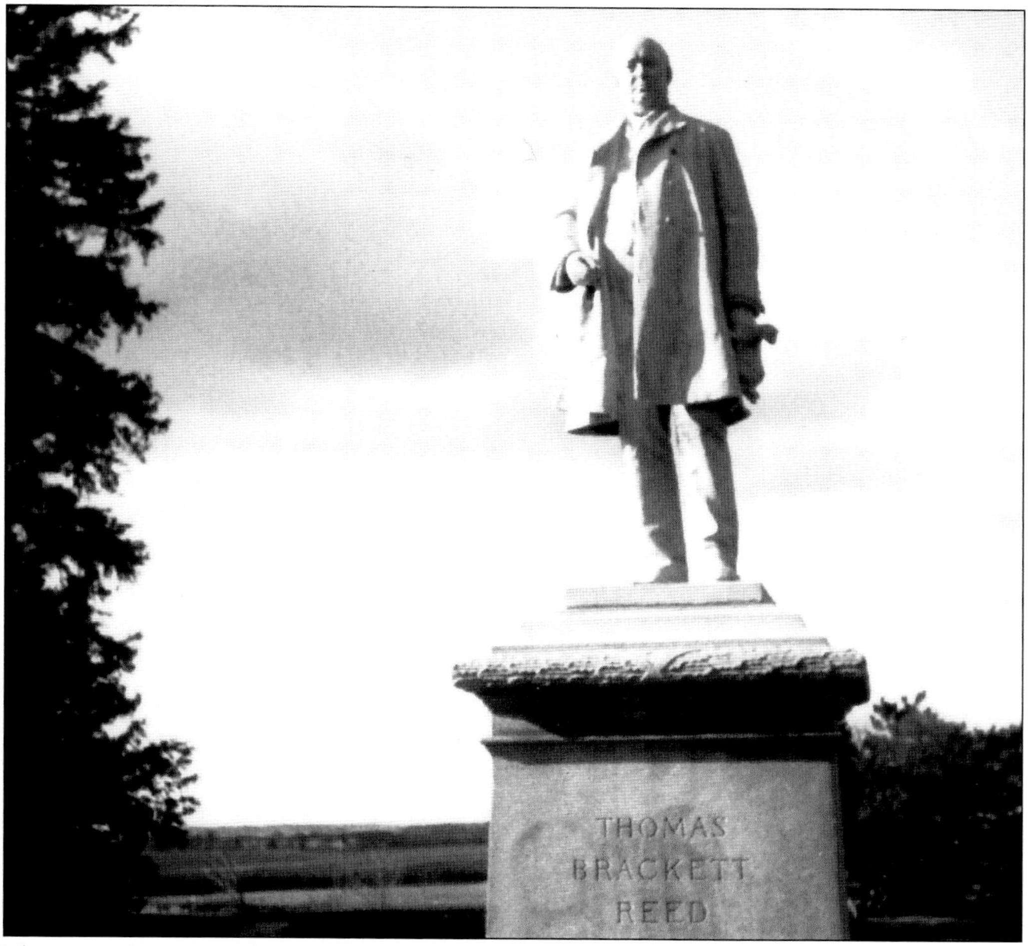

This statue honoring Thomas Brackett Reed is located on Portland's western promenade.

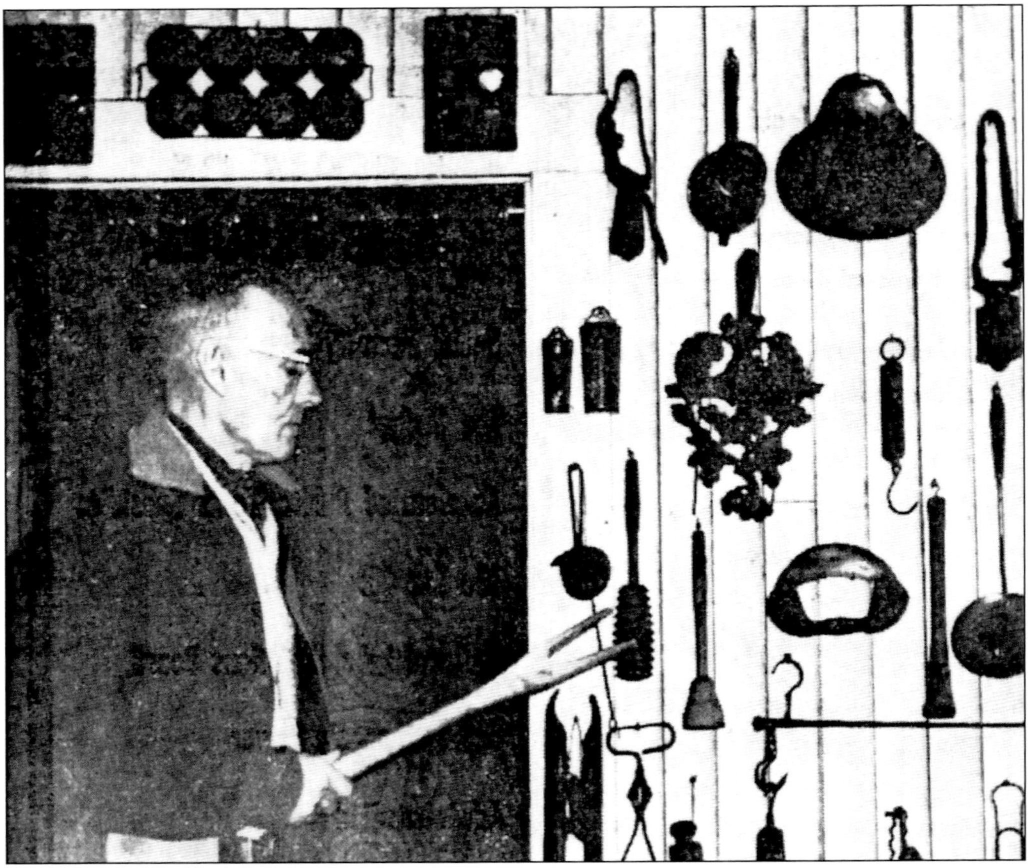

Malcolm Leete, an antique collector and a delightful host and conversationalist, displays a few of his holdings. How many can you identify?

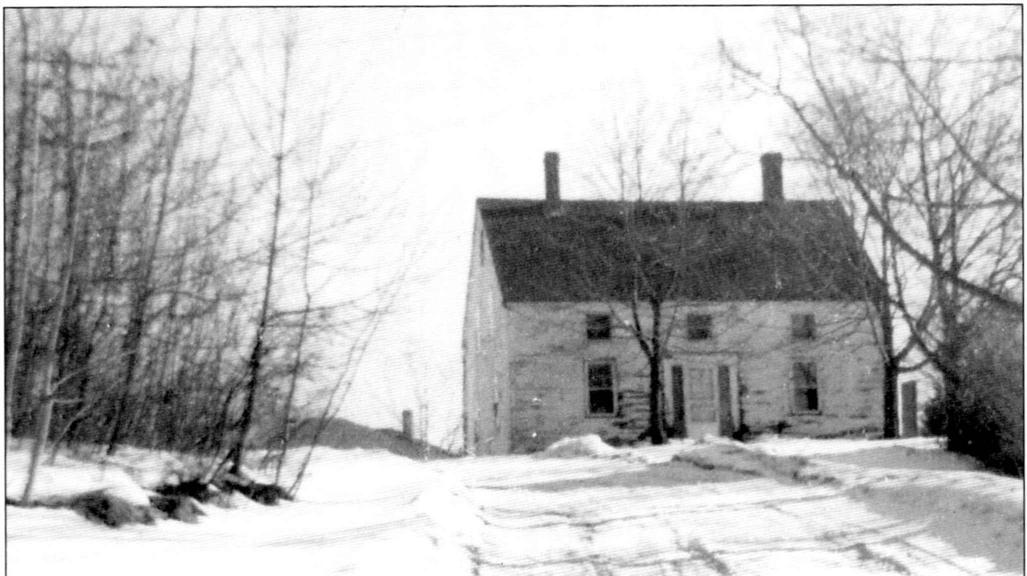

The old Brackett homestead where he displayed his treasures.

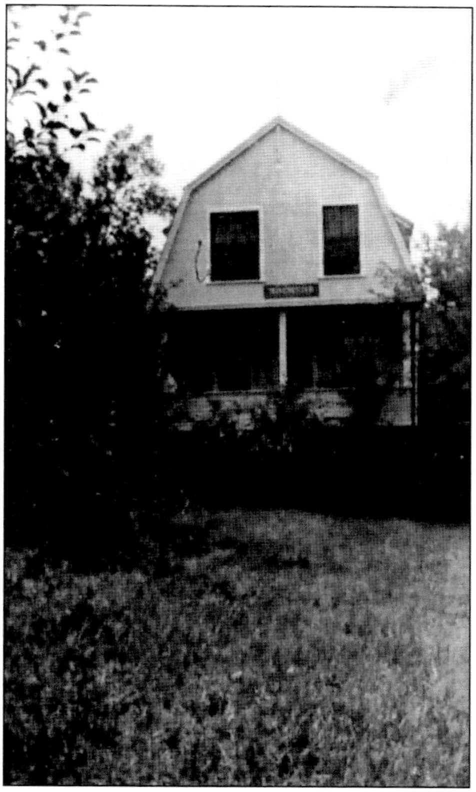

The "Winchester," a cozy home.

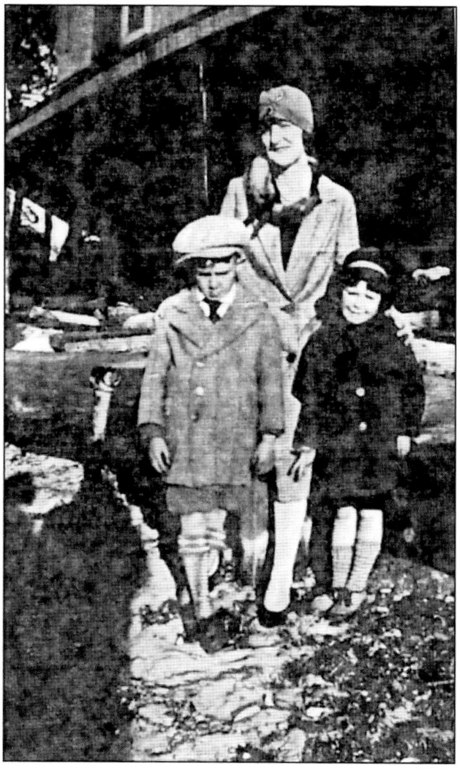

Pictured in front of the "Winchester" in the 1920s are Bea Munn and her children, Phil and Gloria. Bea was a telephone operator on Peaks Island.

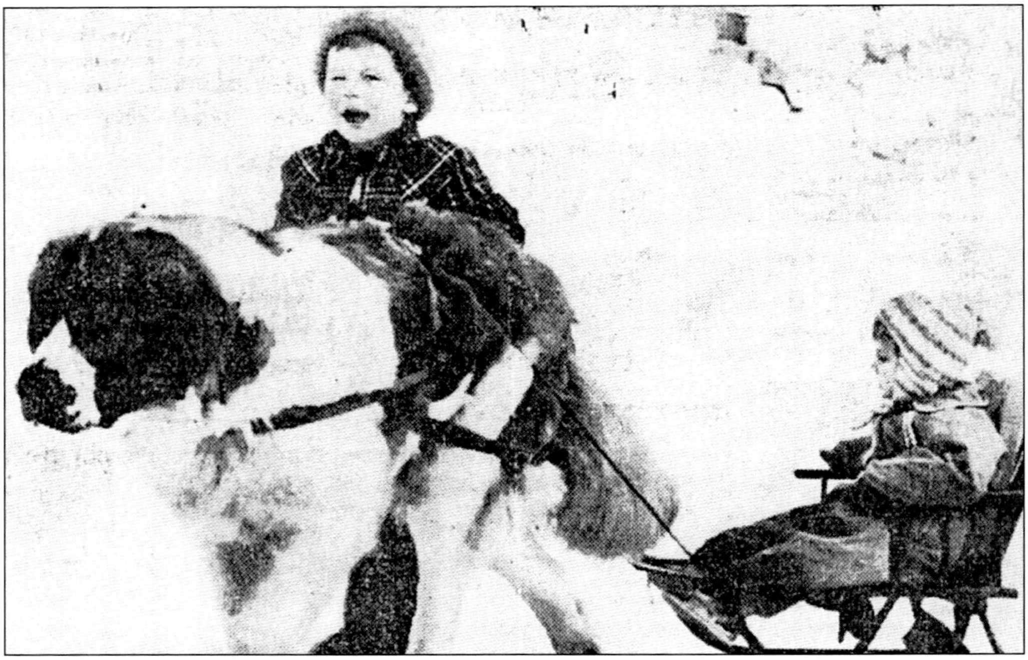

This photograph of an adventurous local trio, Philip Laughlin, Gail Laughlin, and Boris the St. Bernard, seemed to capture the very essence of an idyllic childhood on the islands. It was sent far and wide via the Associated Press and *Stars and Stripes* (the newspaper of the Armed Forces). The children's family received reports of "sightings" from across the United States and even as far afield as Europe.

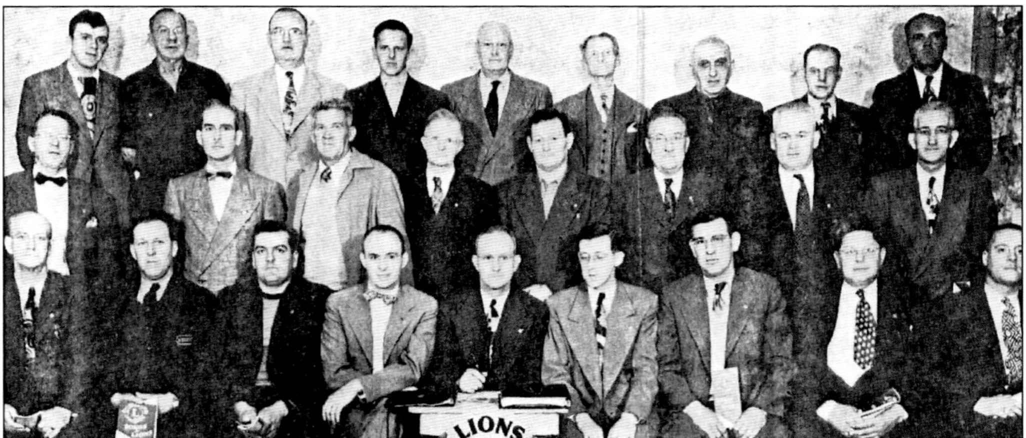

The charter members of the Peaks Island Lions Club in 1950. From left to right are: (front row) Phil Skillings, Elwin Valle, Clyde Goff, Tom Kirk, Arthur Smith, Robert Stephens (president), Raymond Boyle, Morrill Jones, and Robert McConniley; (middle row) Henry Hoar, Dr. Dearborn, Leslie MacVane, Ernest Elliot. Stanley Farmer, Floyd Austin, Cy Sinnott, and Richard Howland; (back row) Richard Hasson, Harold Clark, Dr. Raymond Sweeney, Roland Hoar, Dr. William Bryant, George Keenan, John Phillippi, Fred Stephenson, and Malcolm Murray.

Seven

Peaks Island Amusements

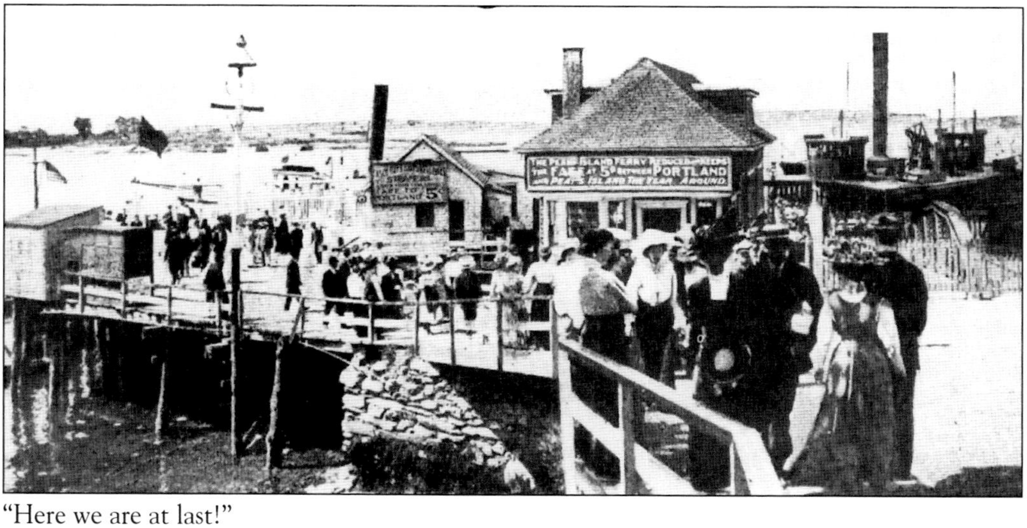

"Here we are at last!"

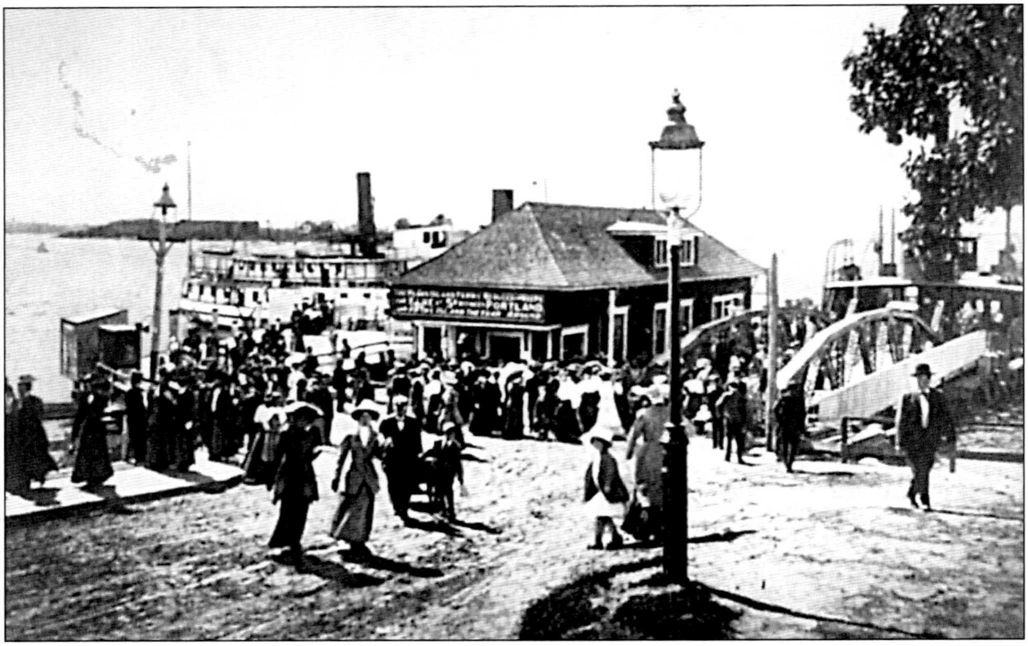

Here they come! Visitors from near and far, getting off at the Forest City landing, the busiest landing on Peaks Island. There is something magical about a trip across the water for an island vacation "away from it all."

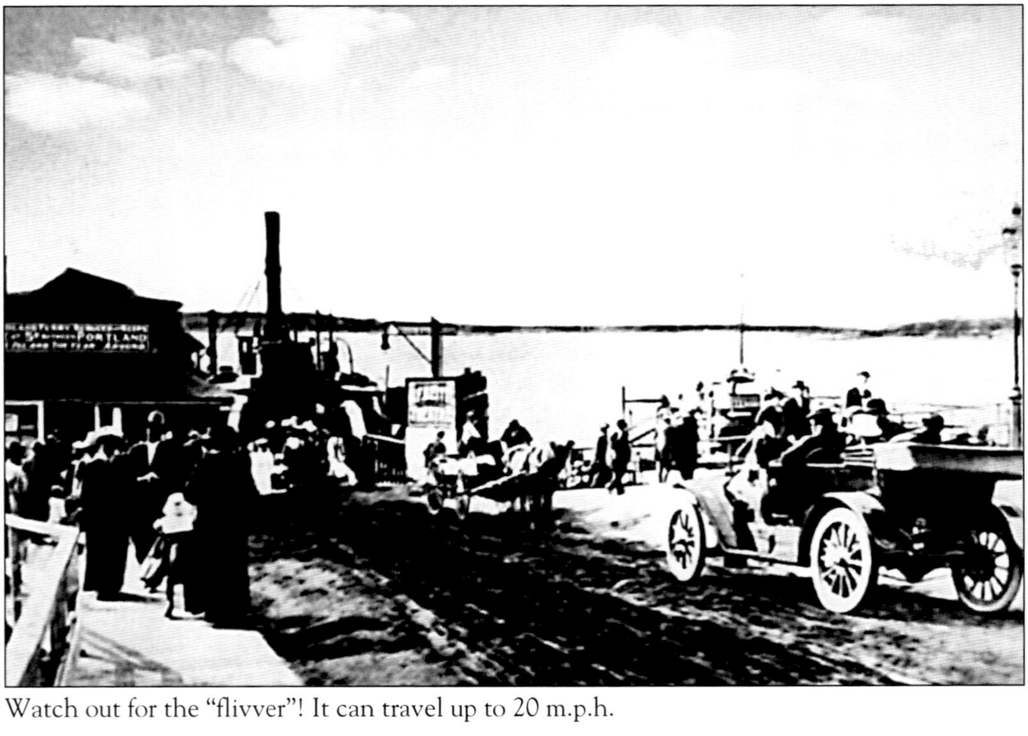

Watch out for the "flivver"! It can travel up to 20 m.p.h.

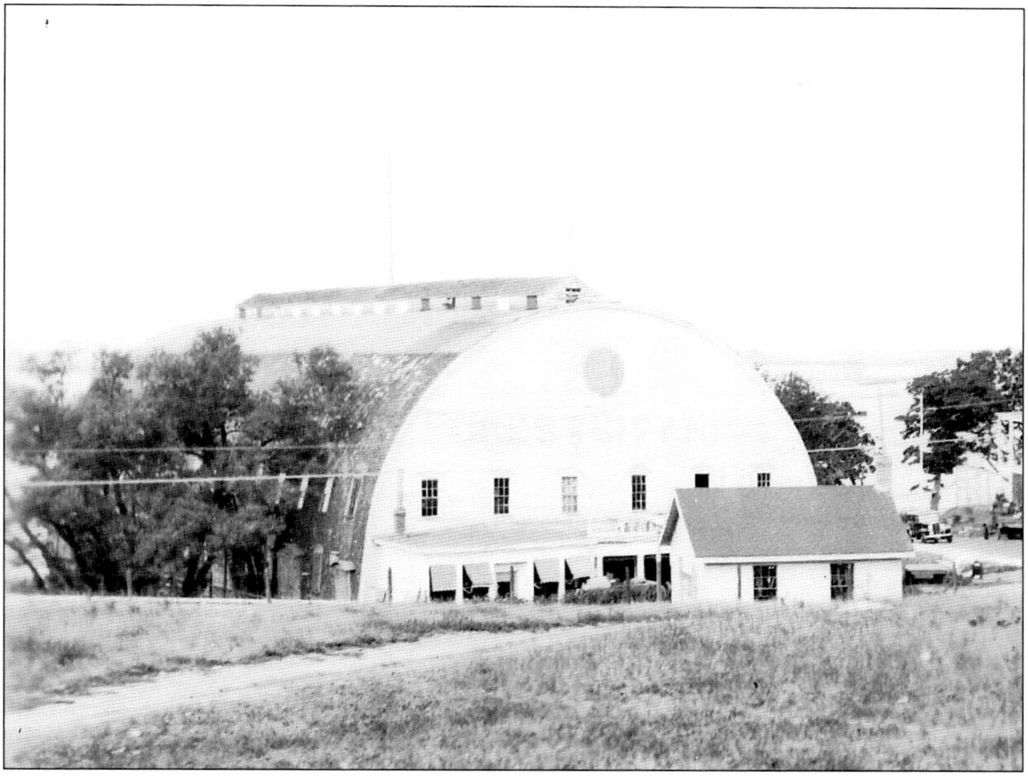

Skating's great—even in the summertime!

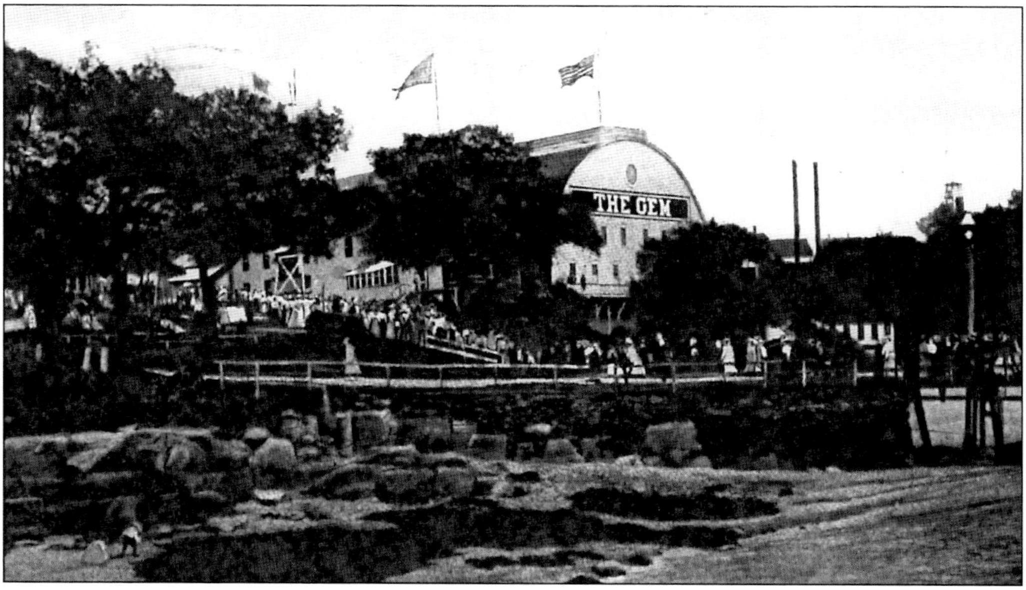

Later on the Gem Theatre offered movies and dancing at the same time. You could sway and cuddle in the darkness while watching a drama on the big screen—you could call this a double feature!

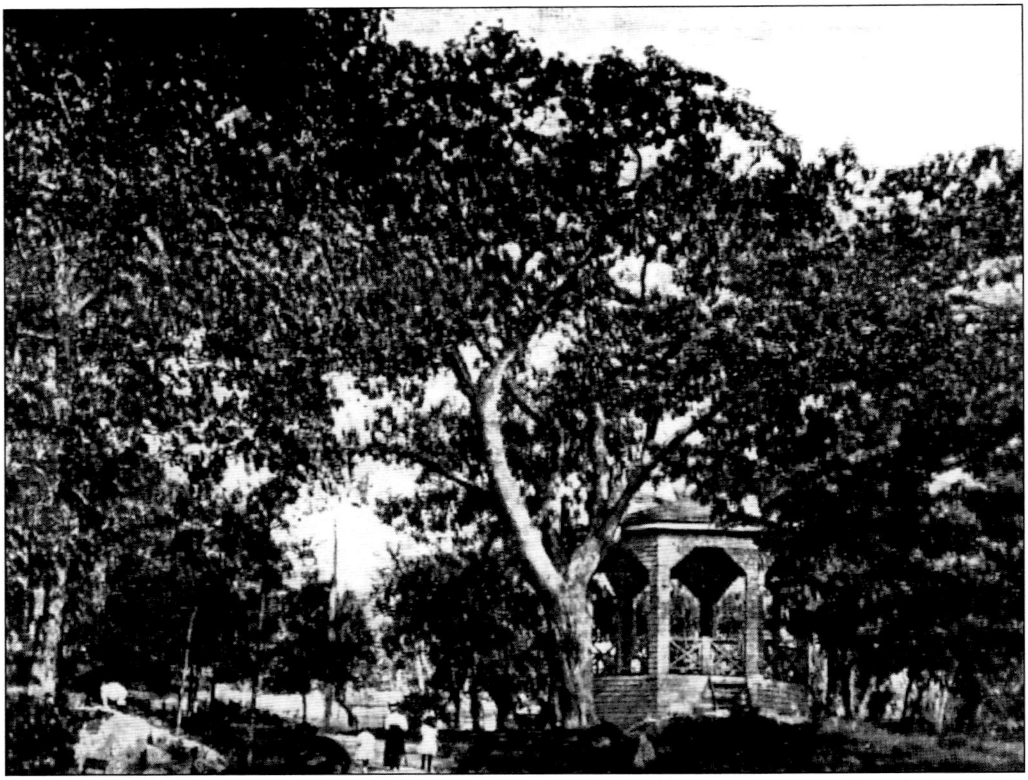

What's nicer than a concert in a bandstand on a summer afternoon? This postcard shows the bandstand at Greenwood Garden in the 1930s.

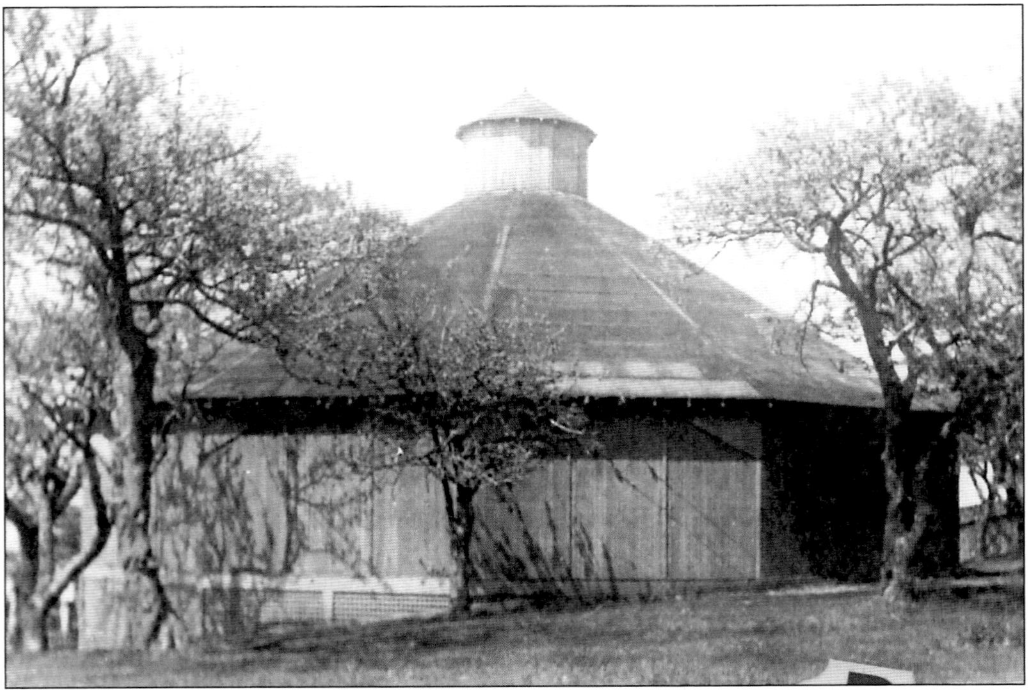

The back of the merry-go-round building at Greenwood Garden.

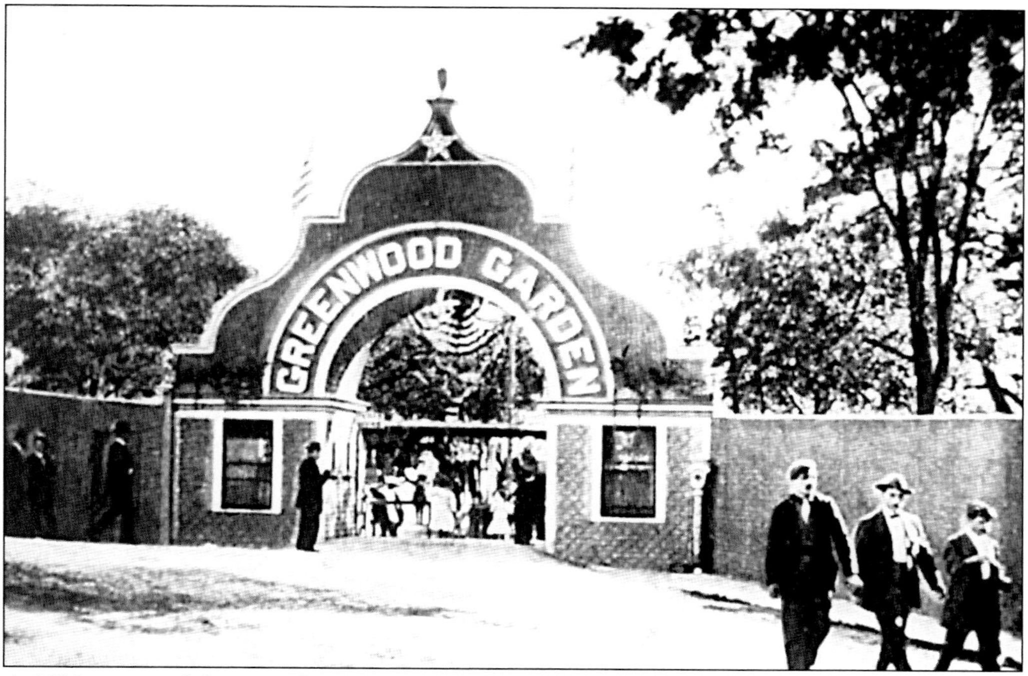

A 1920s postcard showing the entrance to Greenwood Garden.

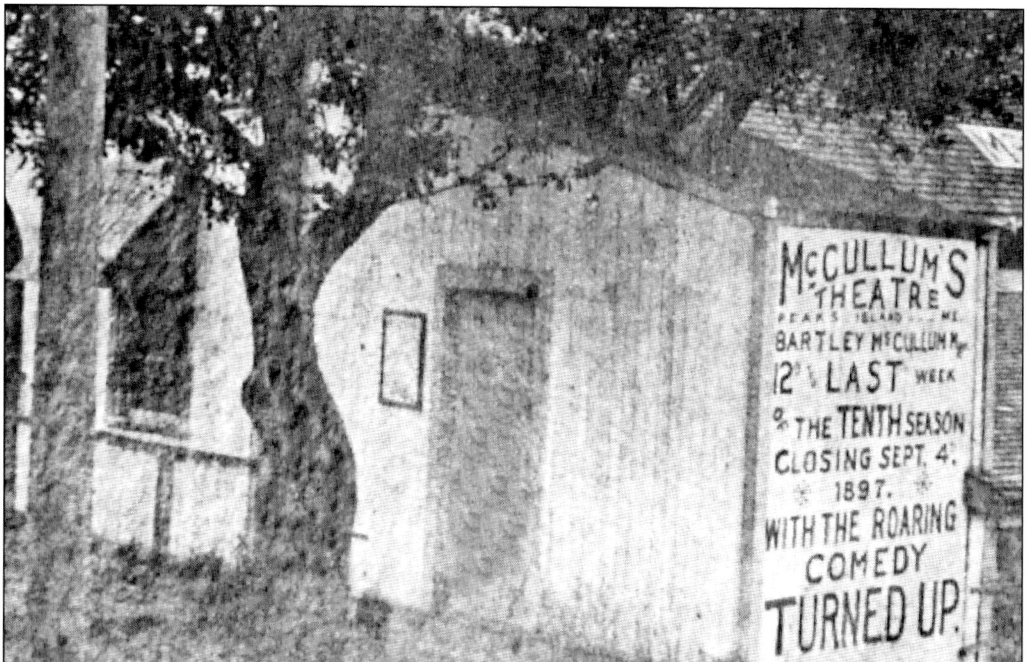

The theatre in Greenwood Garden began operation in 1887 and finally closed in 1953. Many well-known Broadway performers—among them, Miriam Hopkins, Sylvia Sidney, Rod Steiger, and Diana Barrymore—starred in such favorites as *A Streetcar Named Desire* and *Pygmalion* during the summer season. Other actors and actresses tested their talent here then went on to fame and fortune in the cities.

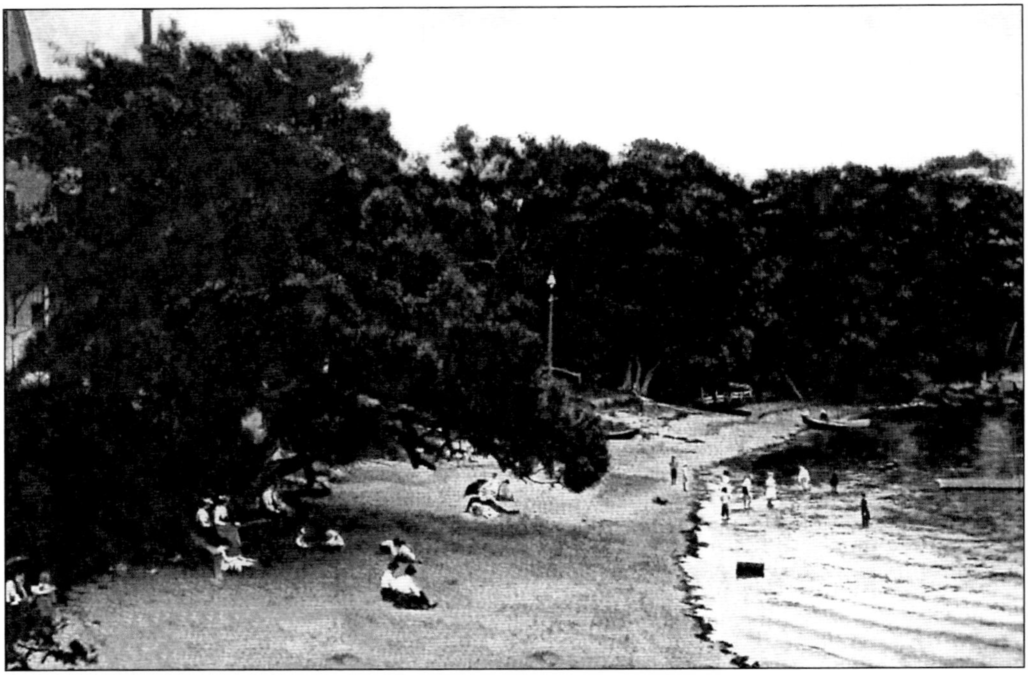

Who can resist a shoreline?

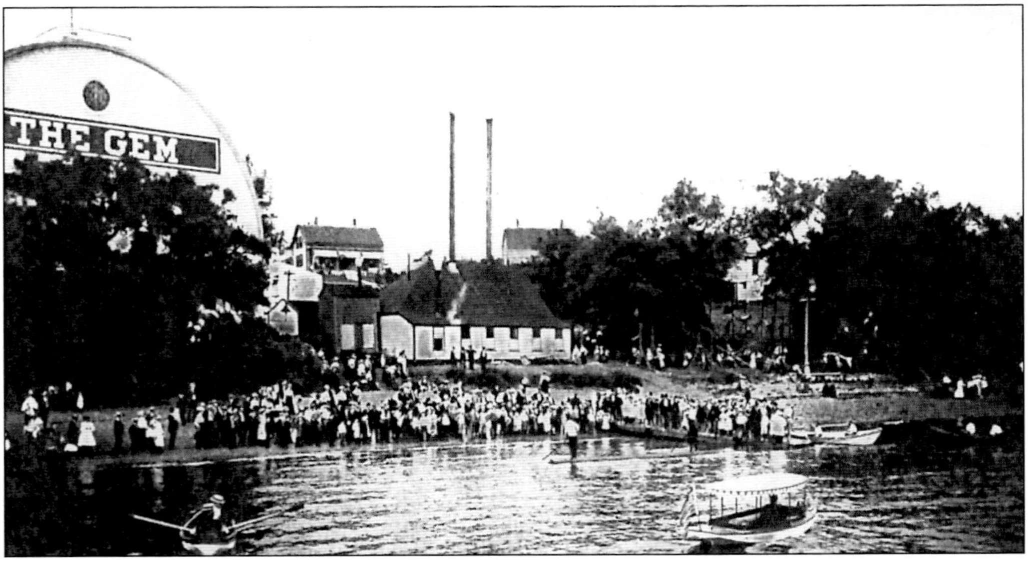

The crowds get ready to watch the boat races.

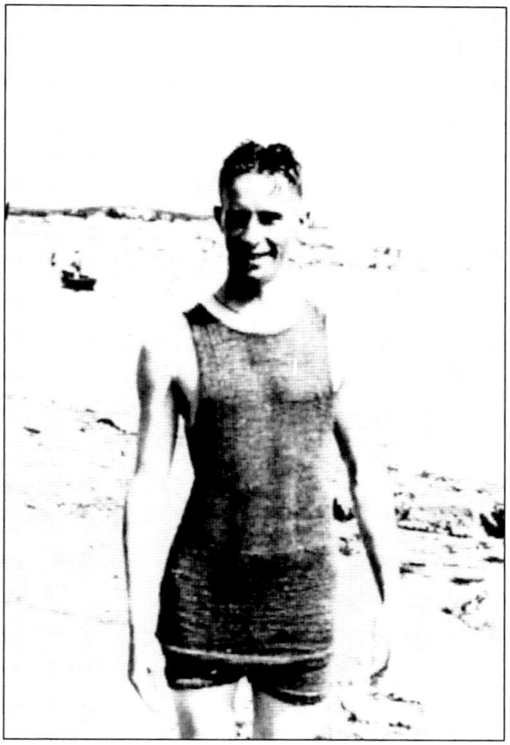

Come on in—the water's great!

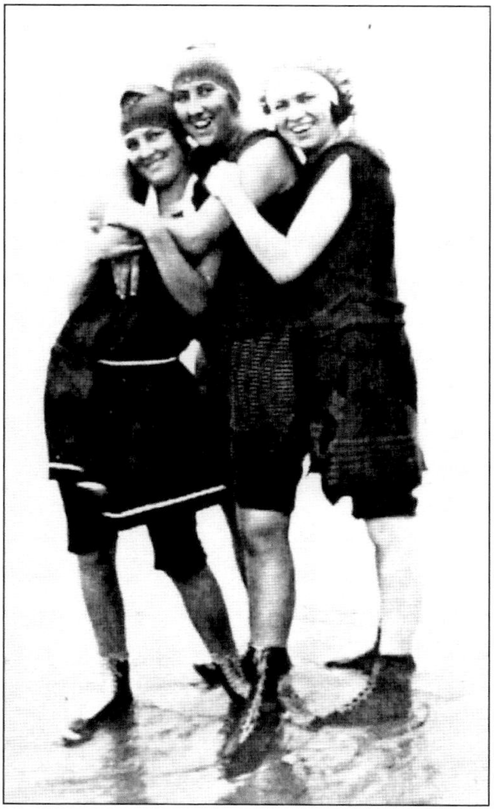

Bathing beauties.

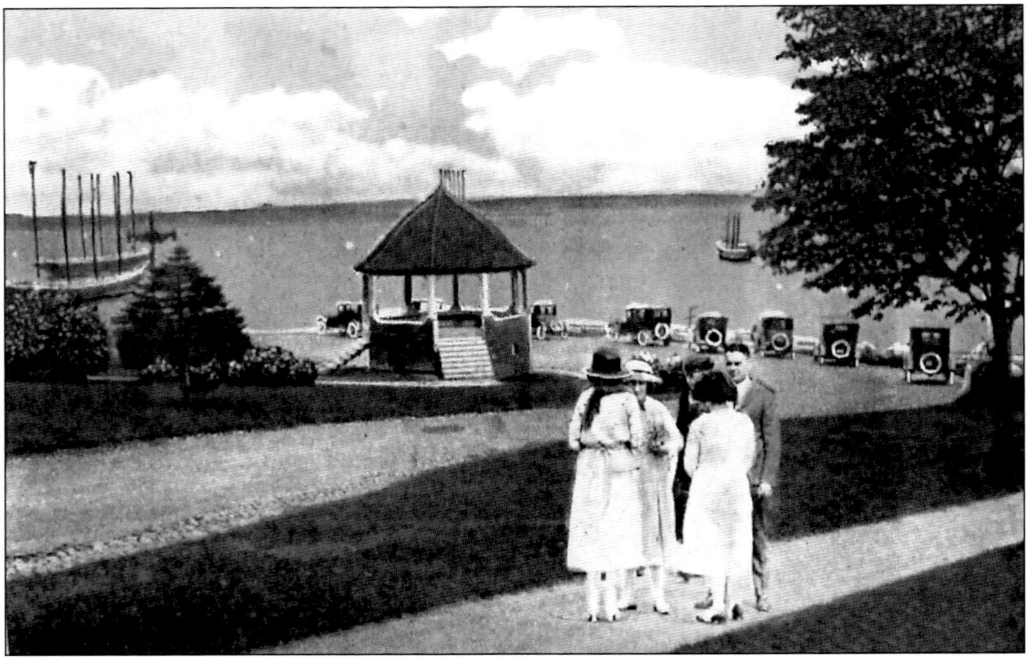

Some folks look out to the islands—a view from Fort Allen Park in Portland in the 1920s.

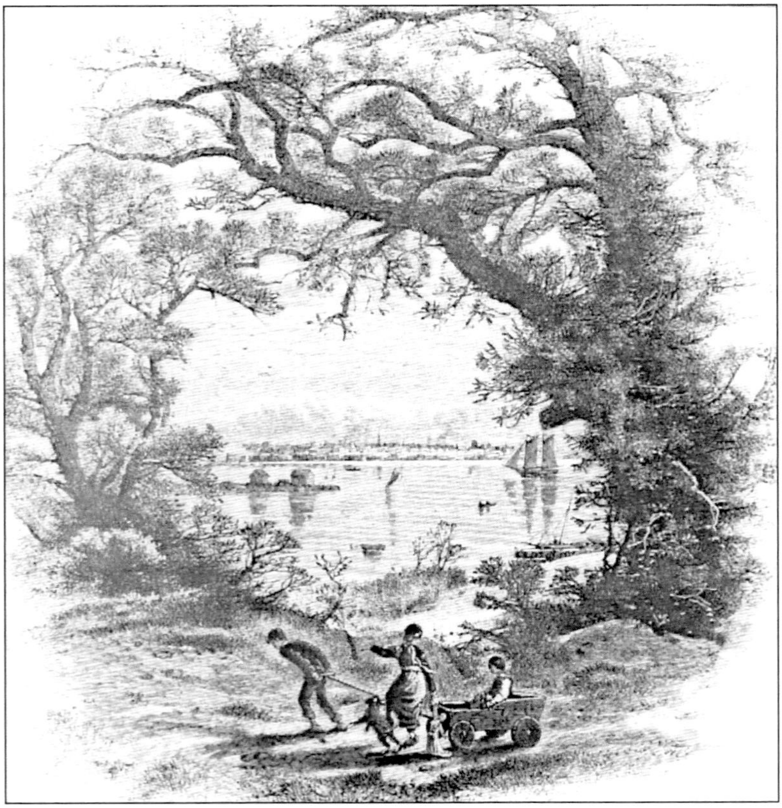

Others look over to "the main" in this delightful late-nineteenth century engraving.

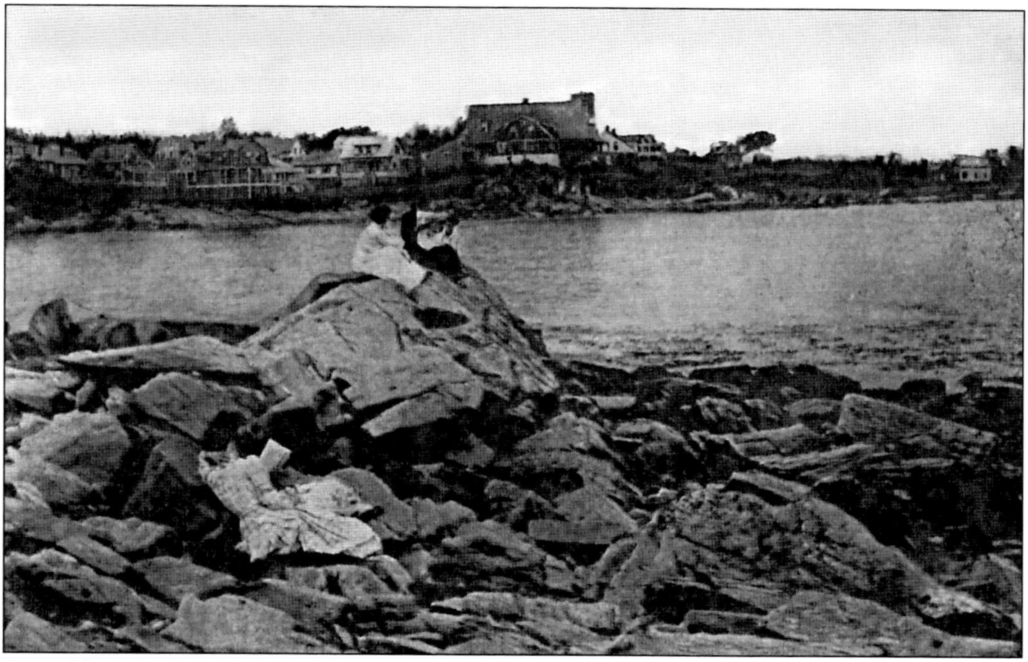
Some like peace and quiet.

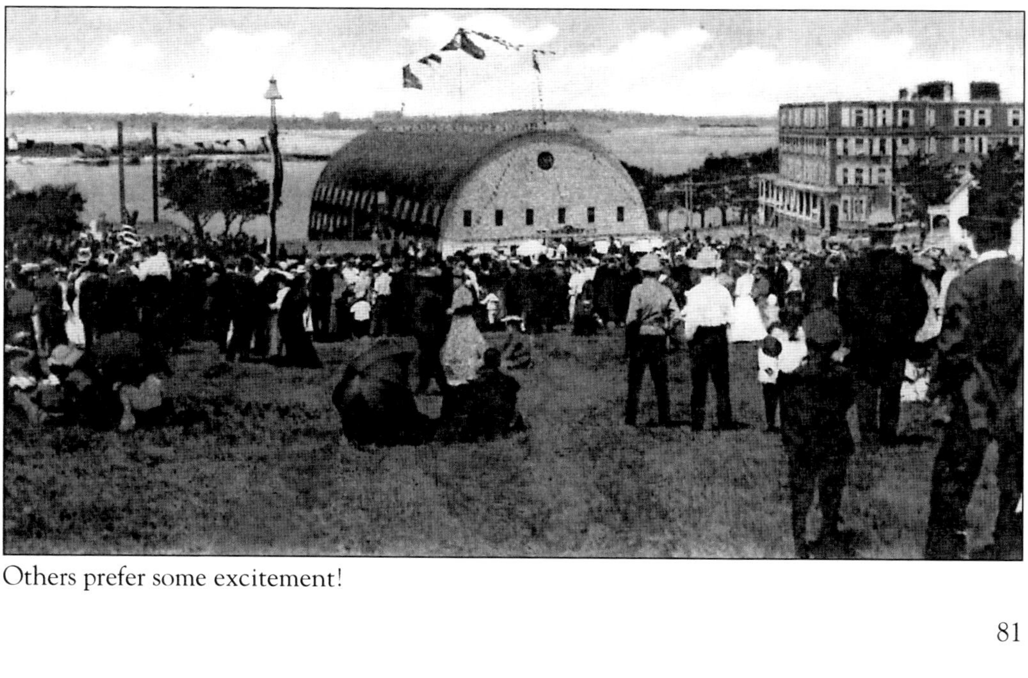
Others prefer some excitement!

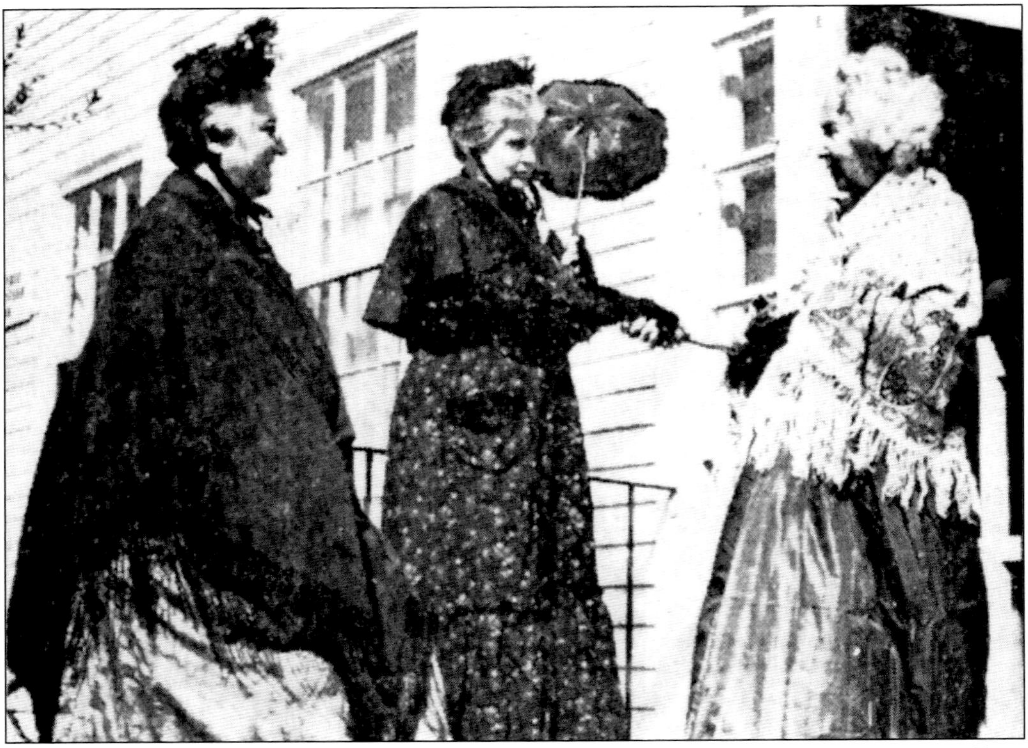

Never too old to play "dress-up," teachers Virginia Brackett and Beatrice Thompson call on Jessie Trefethen.

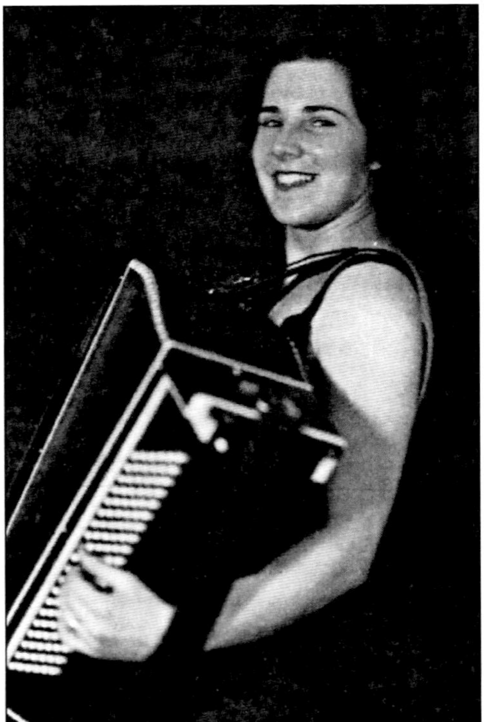

Janice Sullivan, professional musician, livens things up!

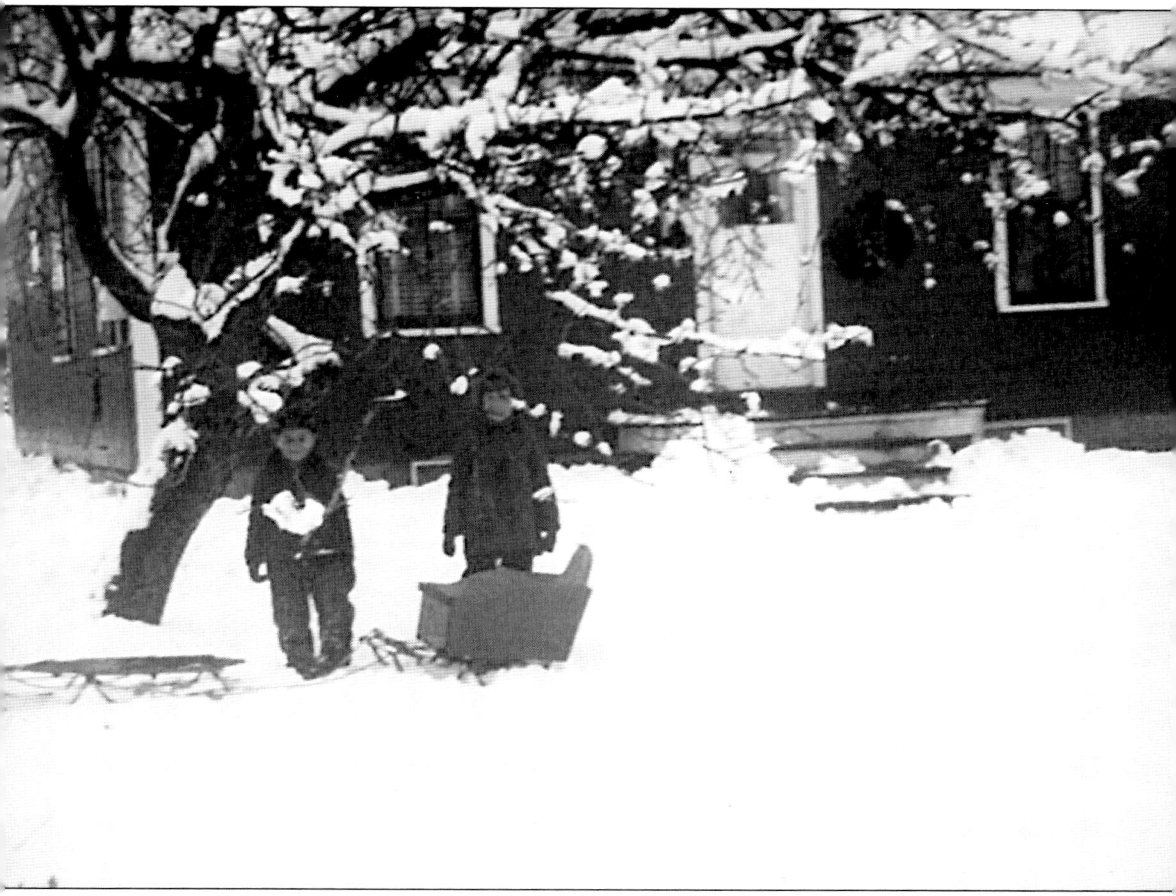
Even winter is fun on Peaks Island.

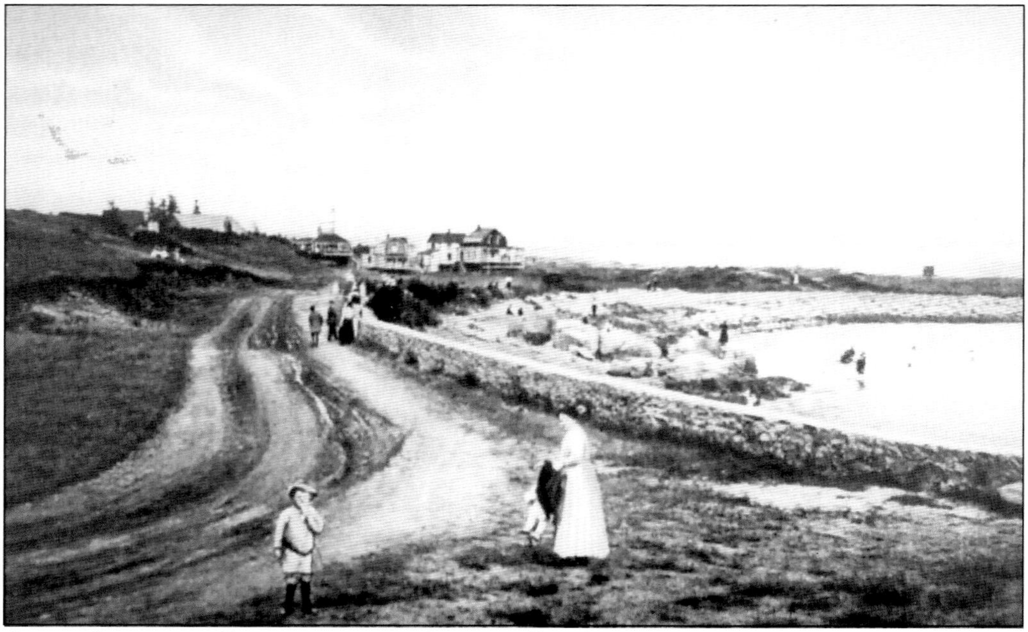

On an afternoon walk you can rest on the sea wall and watch people swimming in the cove.

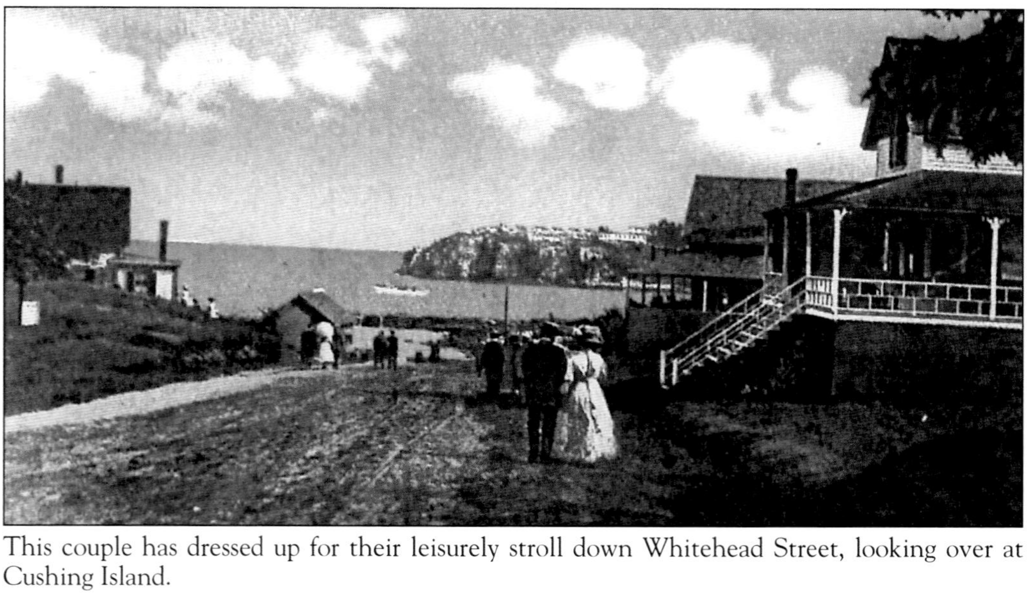

This couple has dressed up for their leisurely stroll down Whitehead Street, looking over at Cushing Island.

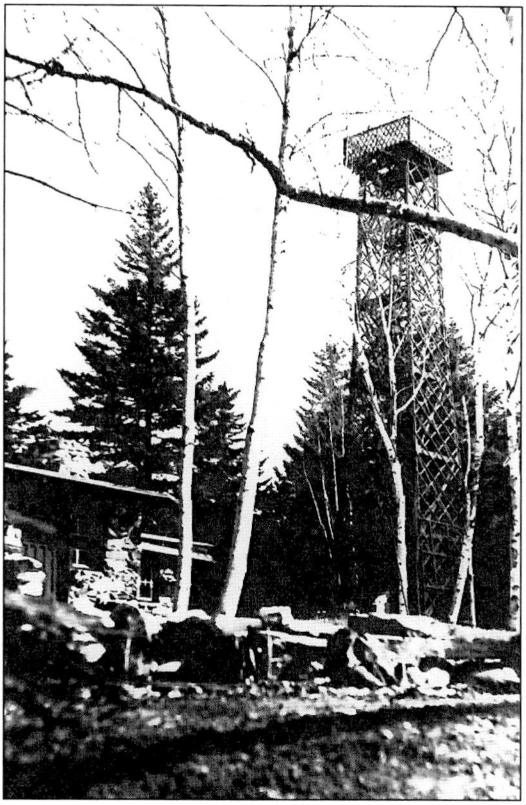

The observation tower—fun to climb up and look around.

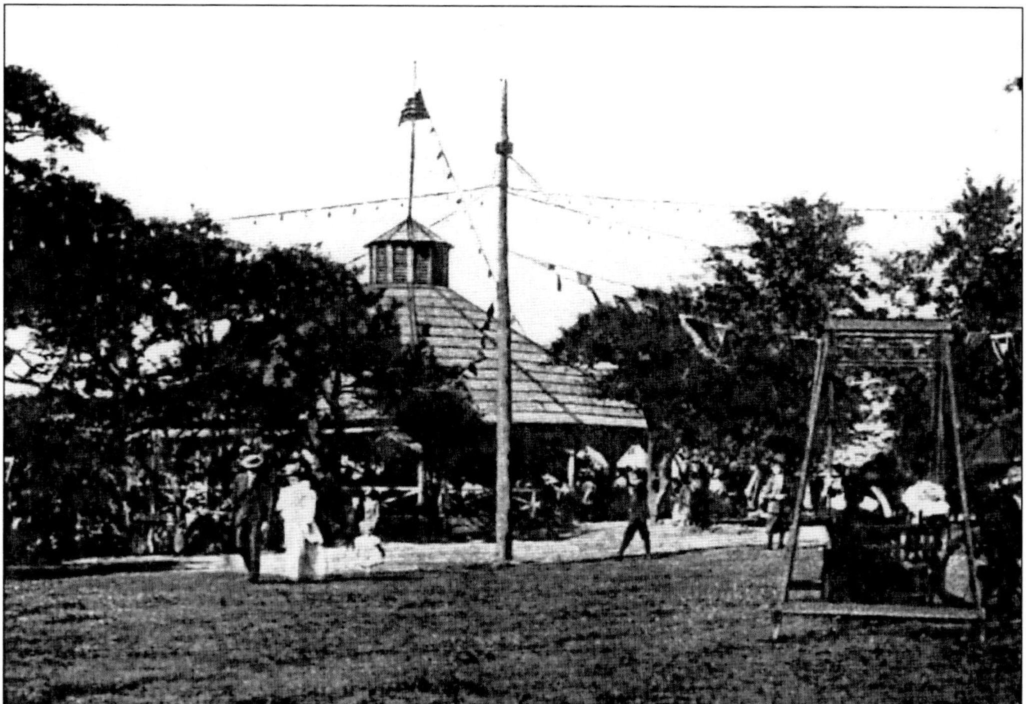

More attractions in Greenwood Garden—the merry-go-round and a romantic swing.

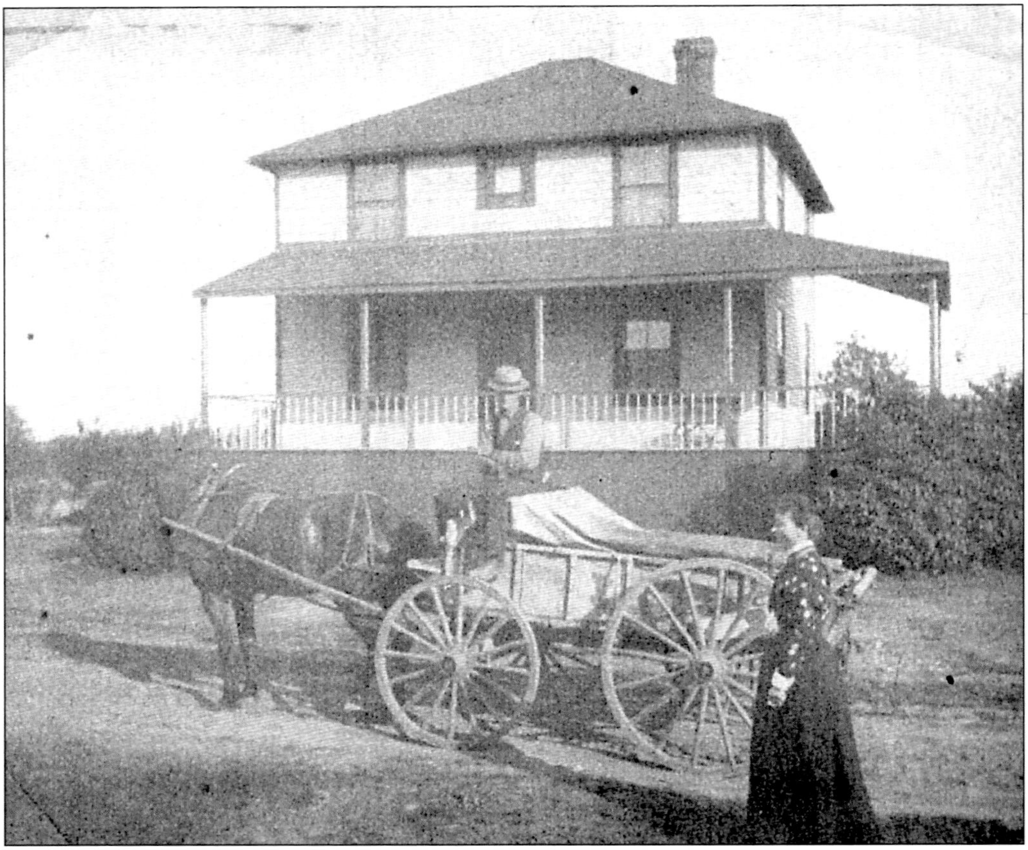

Kate Crocker stopping to buy fresh produce coming from Mr. Blackman's farm on the back shore.

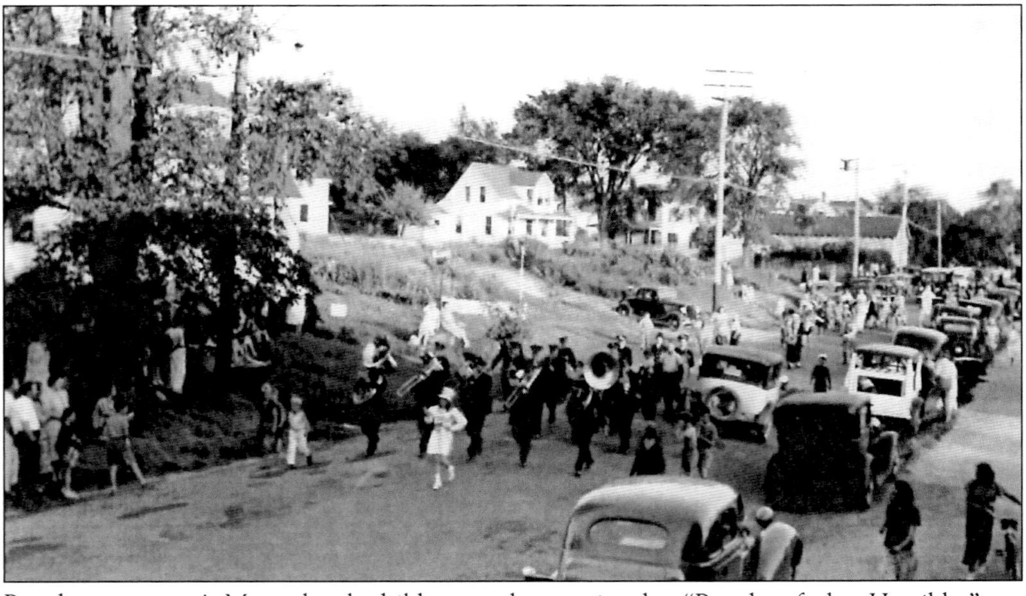

Parades are great! Many local children took part in the "Parade of the Horribles" on July 4, 1939.

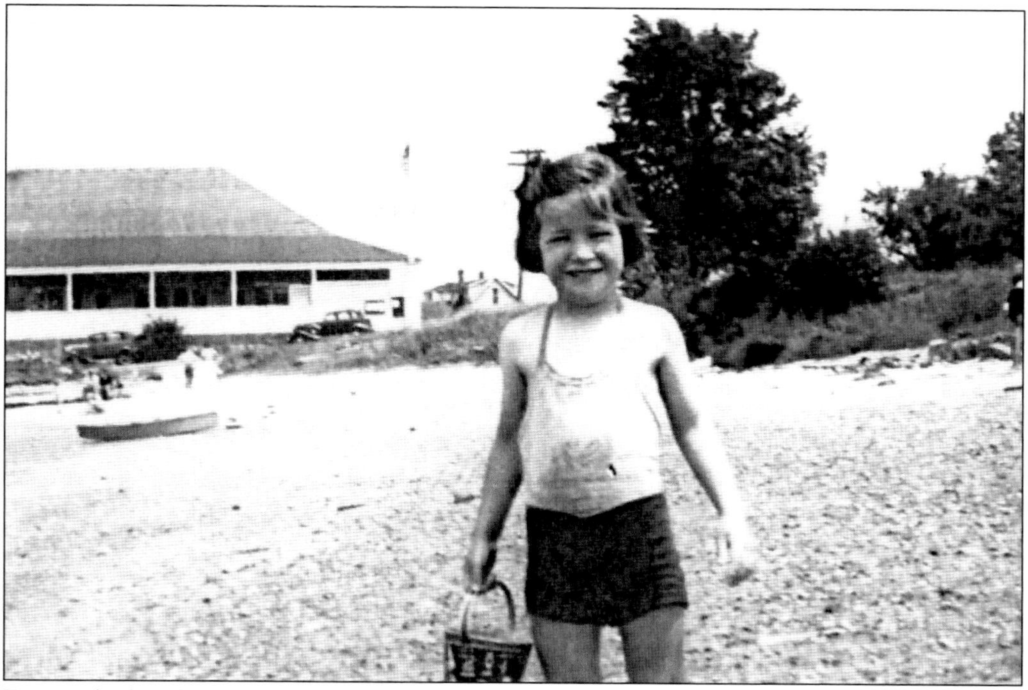
Fun on the beach near the Trefethen clubhouse and landing.

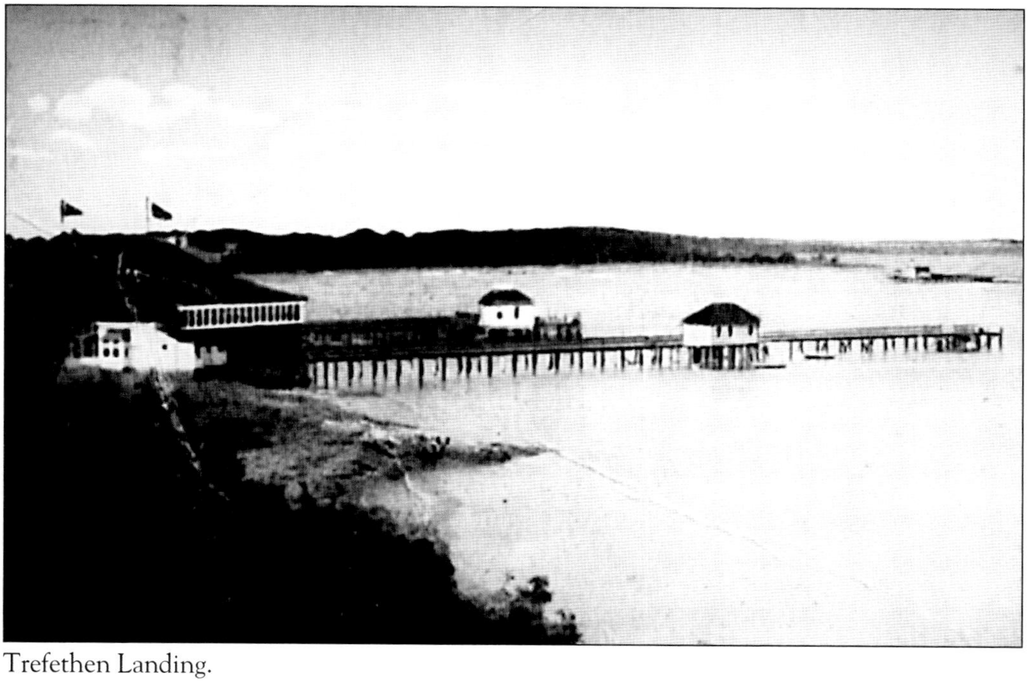
Trefethen Landing.

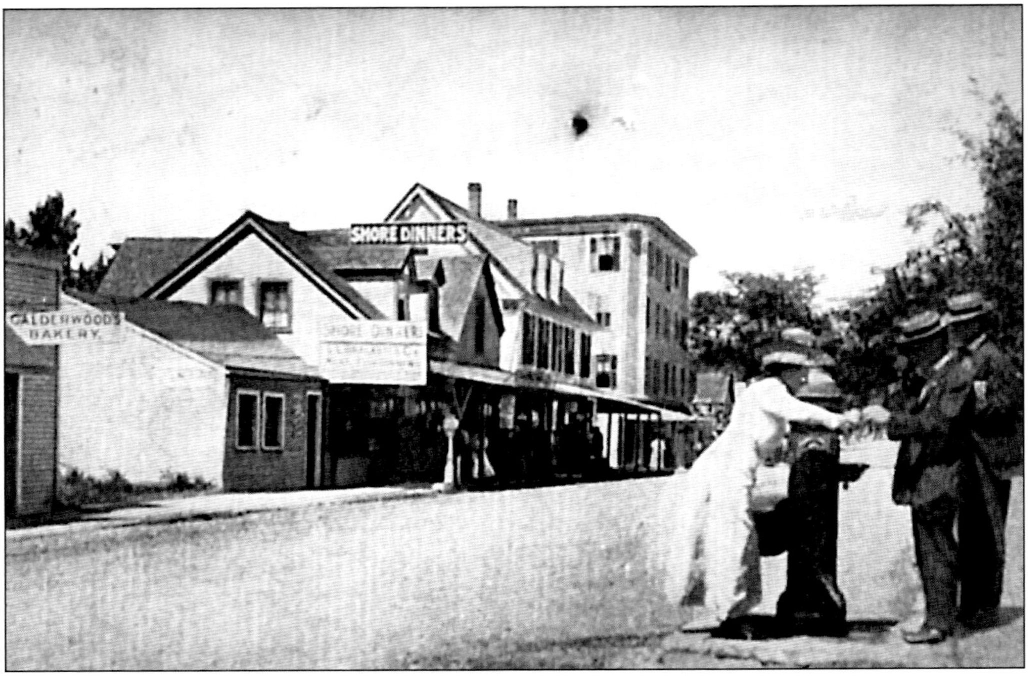

A show at one of the theatres could be followed by a grand "Shore Dinner."

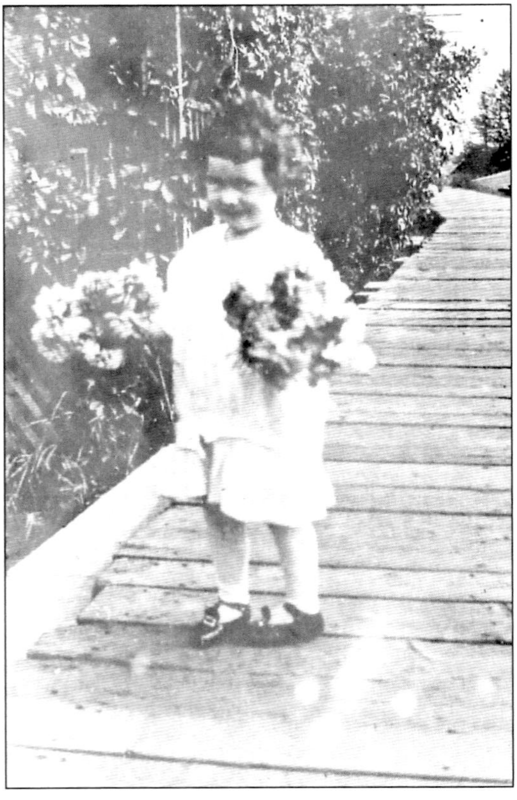

Peaks Island was, and still is, a wonderful place for children. On sunny days you could play outside from dawn until dusk, and on rainy days you could play indoors and look at the ocean or "take a trip" with the stereoptican.

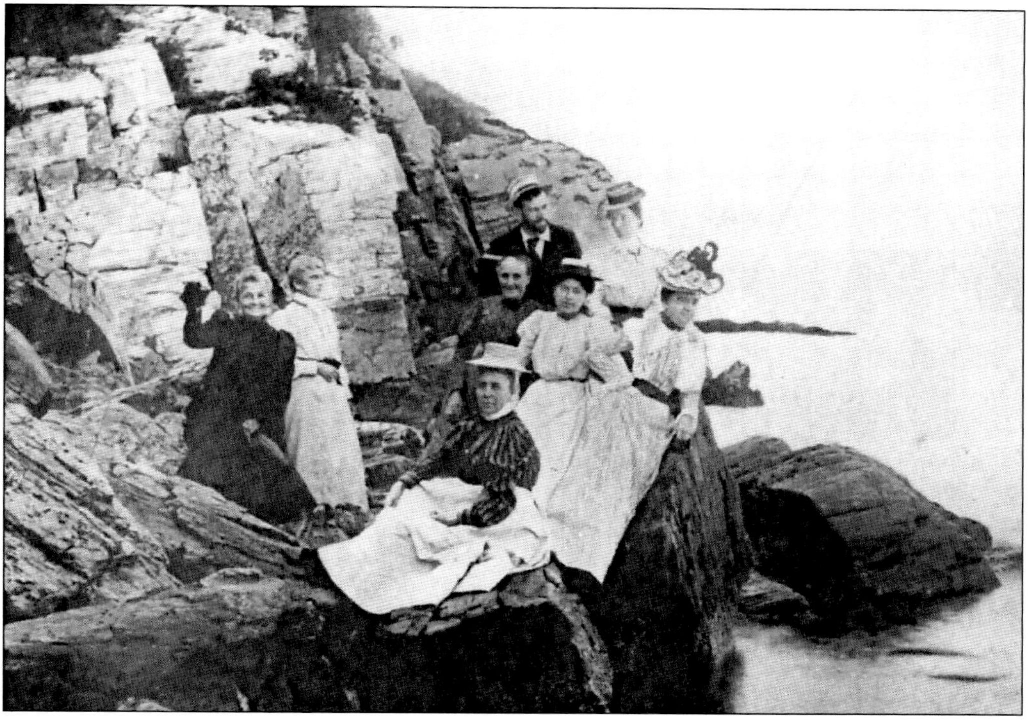

A Victorian group relaxing on the rocks.

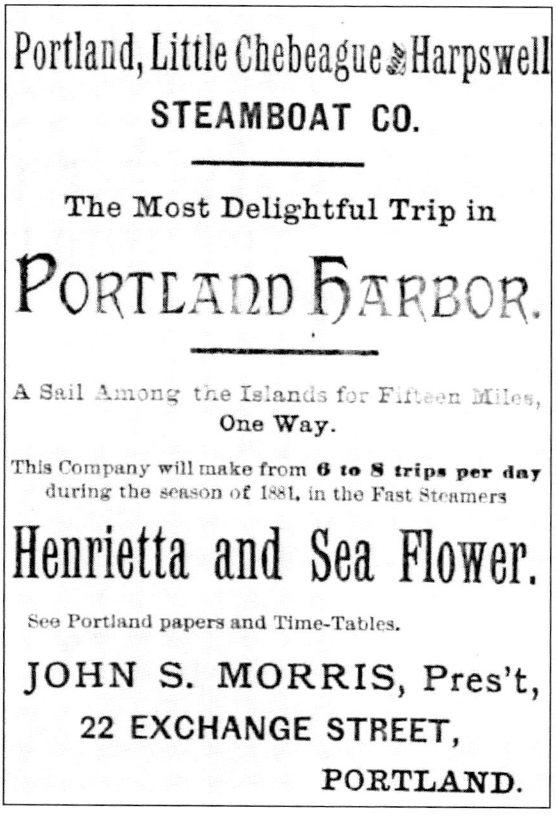

When visitors arrived this was the first thing they wanted to do.

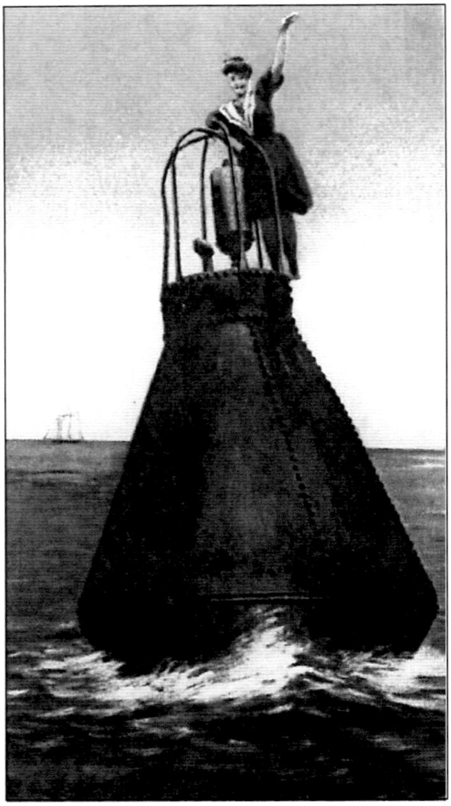

A great place for surf-watching!

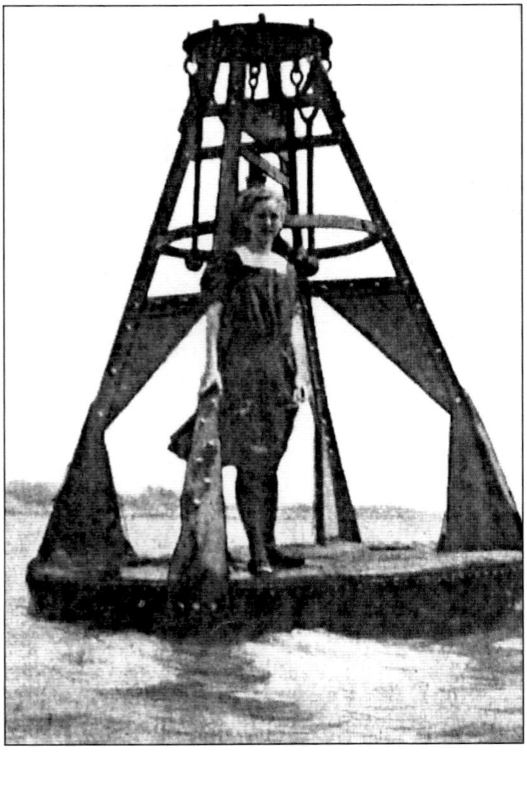

A strange hobby for the more adventurous.

Eight

Wartimes

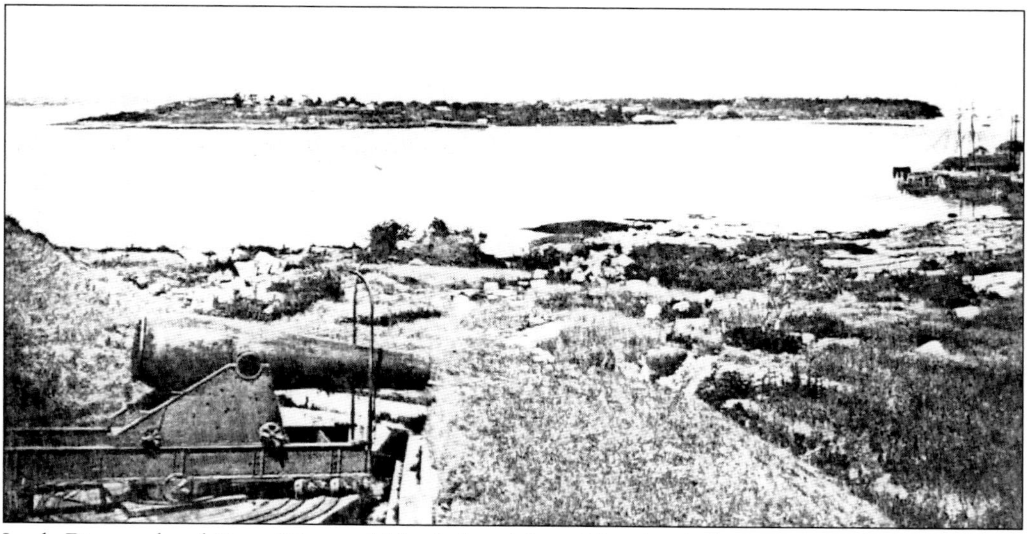

Little Diamond and Great Diamond Islands from House Island with the cannon in the foreground.

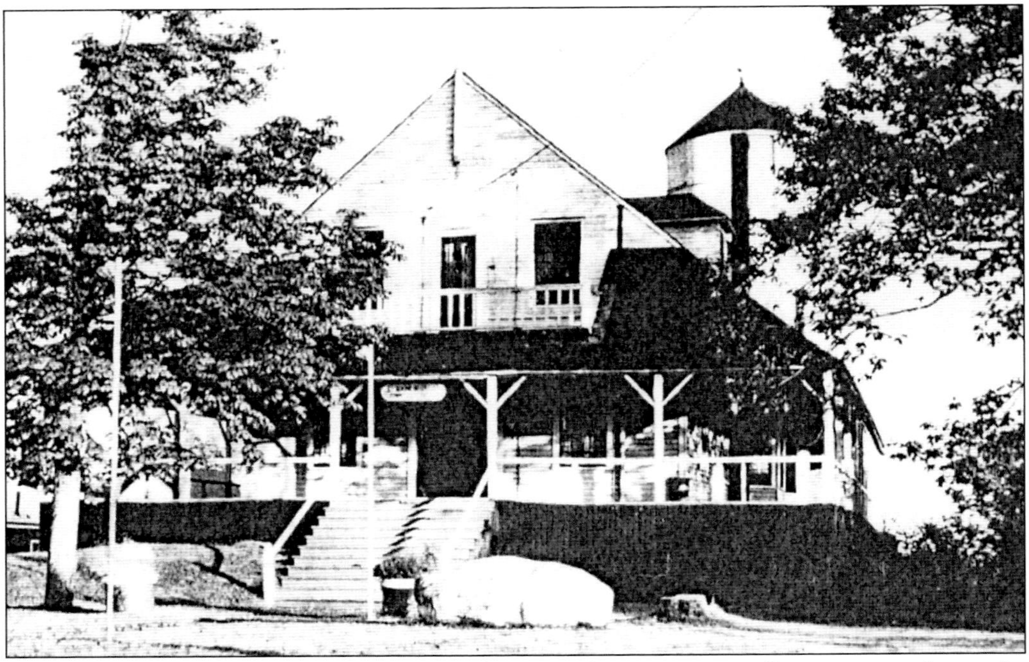

The Fifth Maine Regimental Building. Built in 1885, it was originally a vacation home for veterans and their families. It is now used for summer programs, meetings, fairs, dinners, dances, and weddings. It has a breathtaking view from the open porch in back.

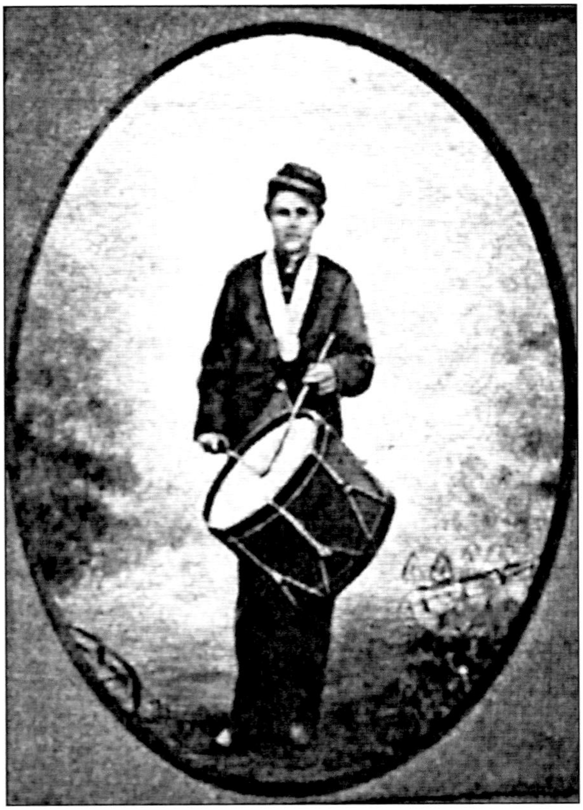

This painting of a drummer boy hangs in the office of the Fifth Maine Regimental Building. Drummer boys could once enlist at the age of twelve, and their main duty was to sound out orders given.

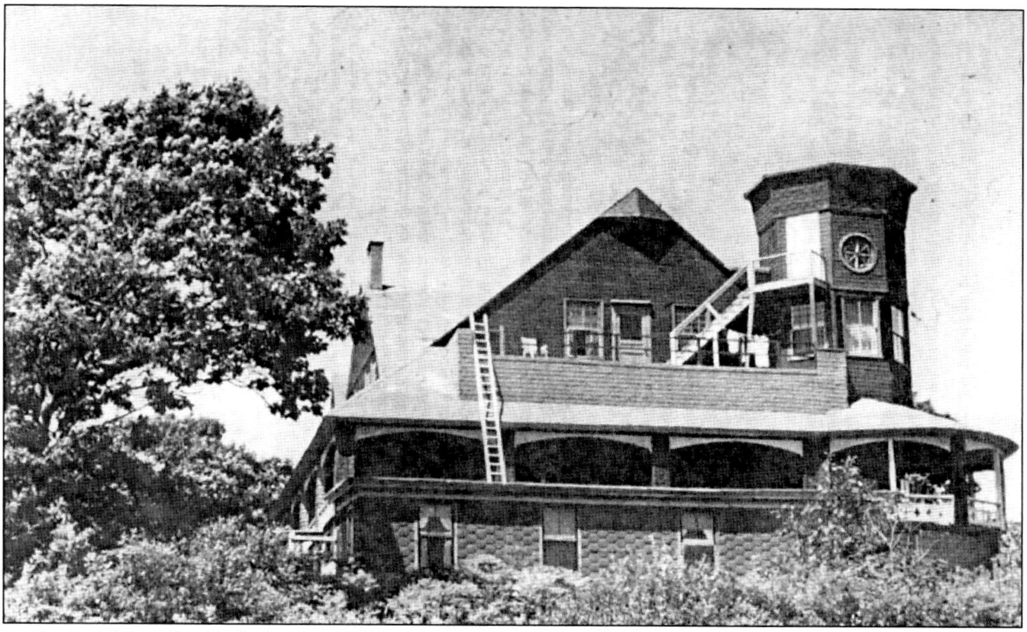

Built in 1888, the Eighth Maine Regimental Building was used by visiting veterans. It is now open to recommended guests during the summer season.

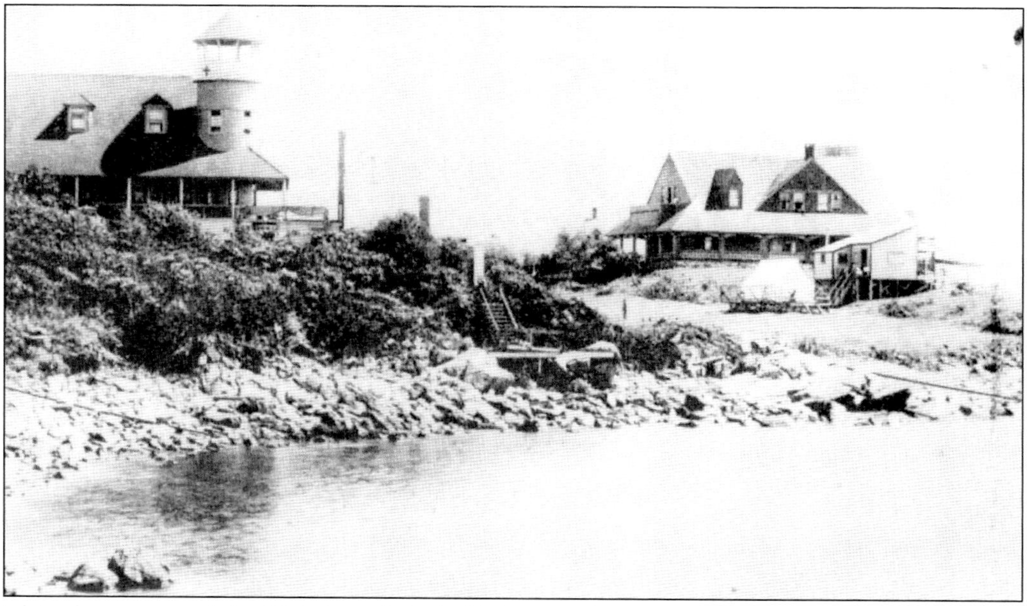

This photograph of the Eighth and the Fifth Maine Regimental Buildings shows their idyllic waterside location.

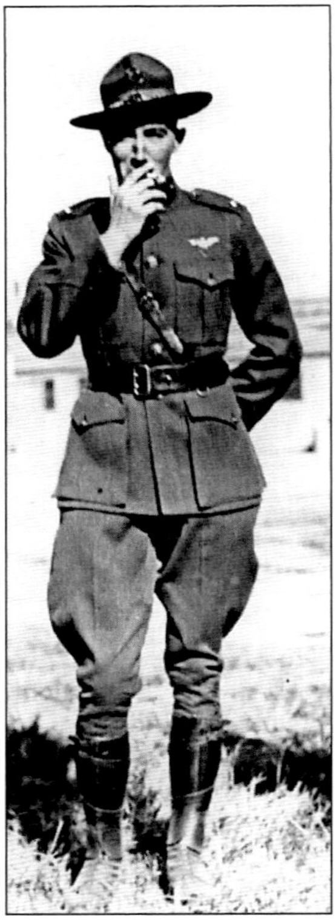

The Earl-MacVane American Legion Post was named for the two brave servicemen shown here. This is Earl Randall, who was lost in a plane crash during World War I.

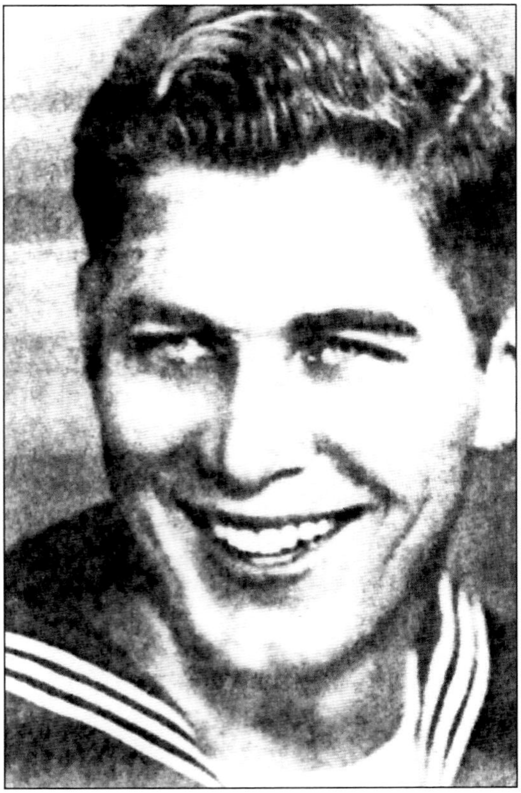

Arthur MacVane was in the US Navy. He was lost at sea on a submarine during World War II.

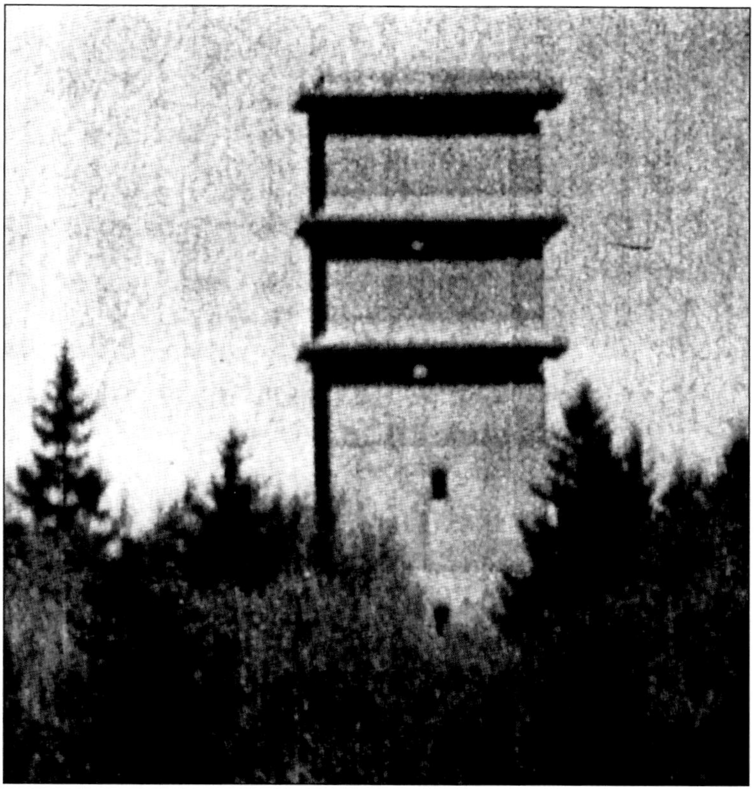

During World War II, steel nets were placed between some islands to prevent entrance by enemy submarines. The gates would be opened for US ships after they produced identification. This photograph shows one of the observation towers on Peaks Island.

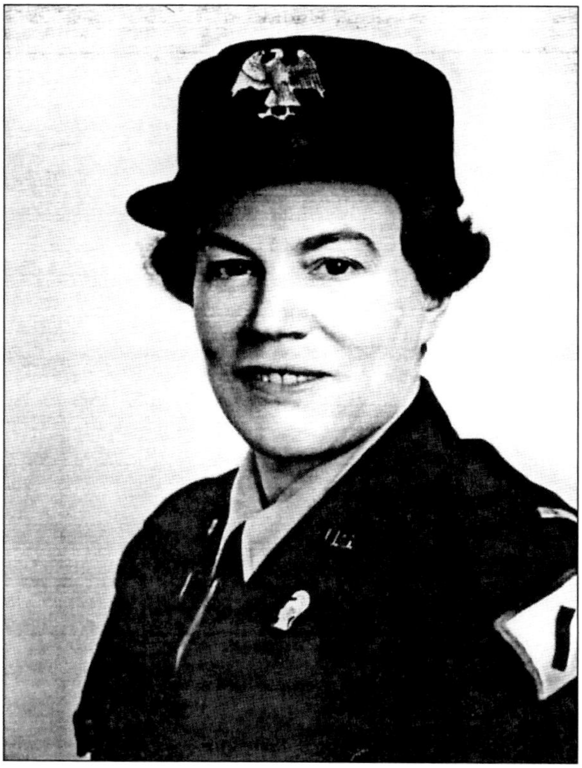

Margaret Randall, the first woman from Peaks Island to serve in uniform during World War II.

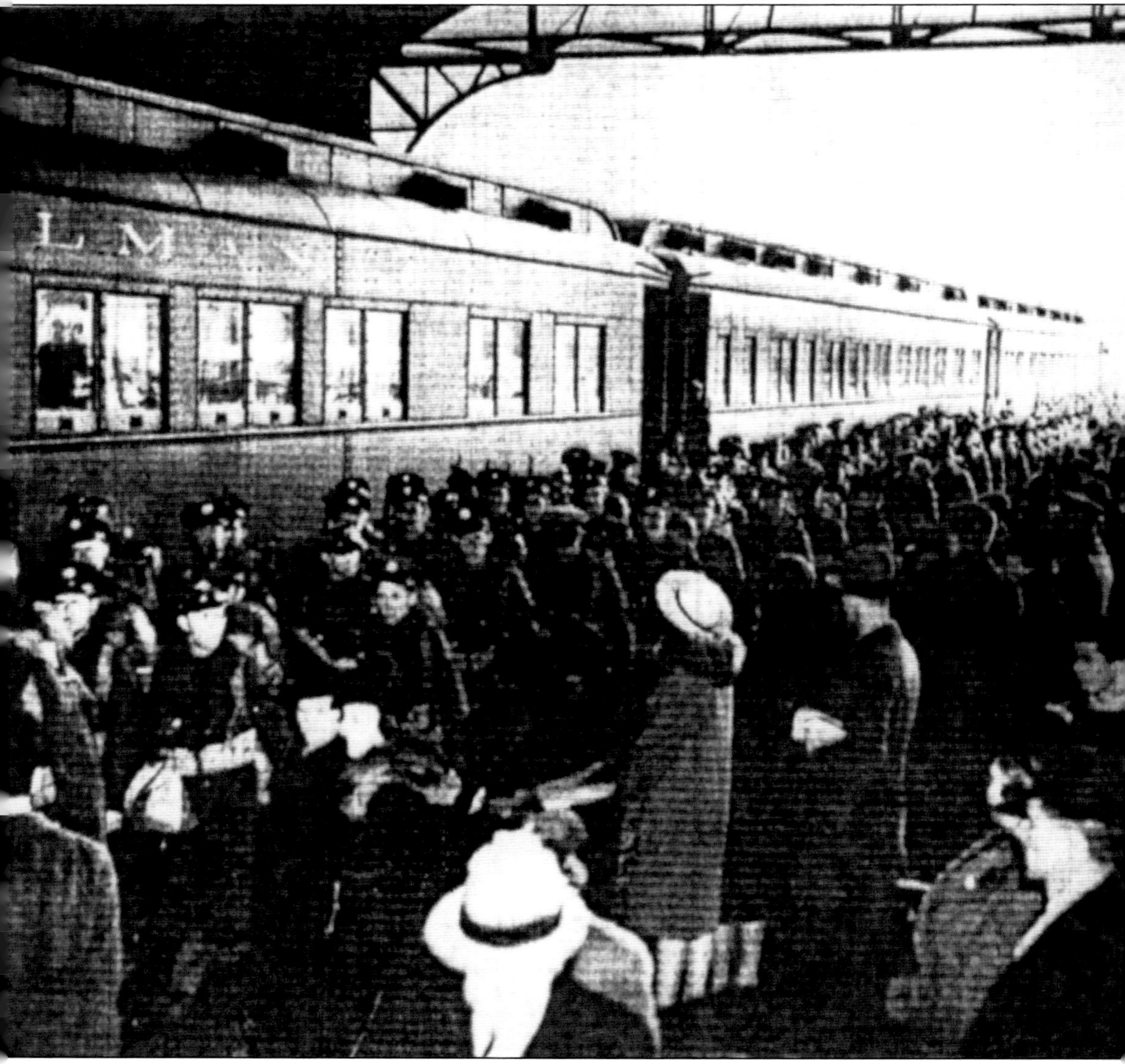

Seeing the island boys off at Union Station in Portland in the early years of World War II. There was definately tension in the air as those leaving and those staying wondered what lay ahead. But the closeness of island life provided a strength for all—for those that left and those that stayed behind. The beauty of island living is perhaps the way that people stick together through the good times and the bad.

Nine

House Island

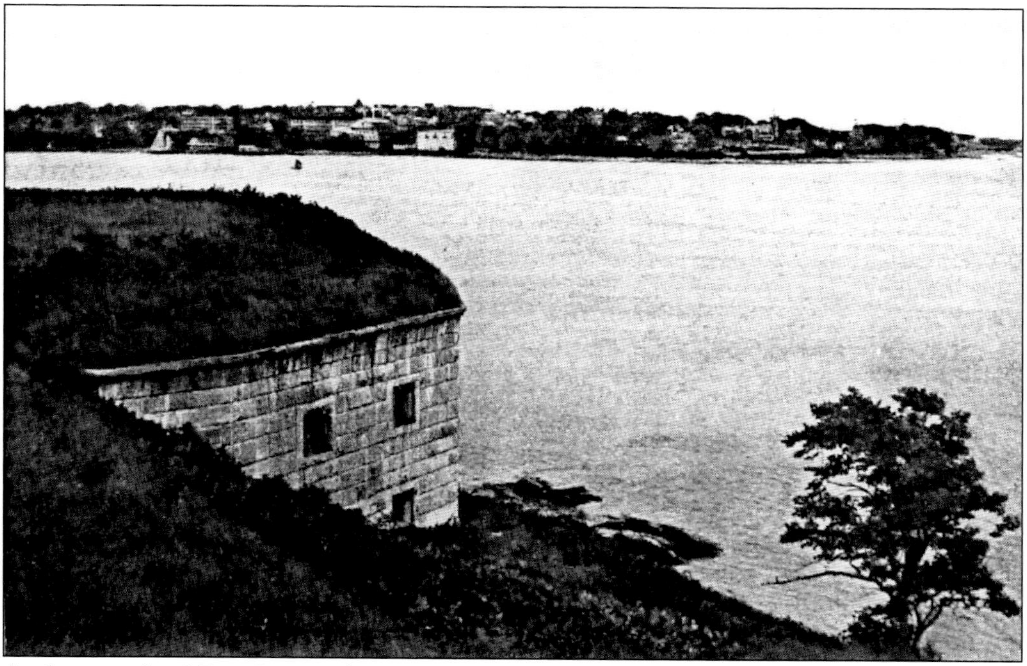

A photograph of Fort Scammel on House Island with Peaks Island in the background. Fort Scammel was built in 1809.

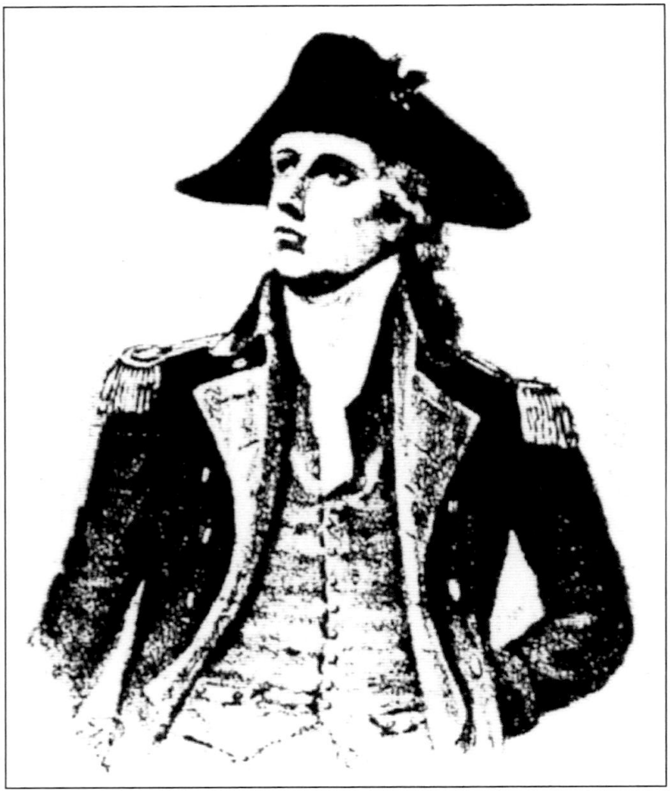

Colonel Alexander Scammel was an officer of the Revolutionary War.

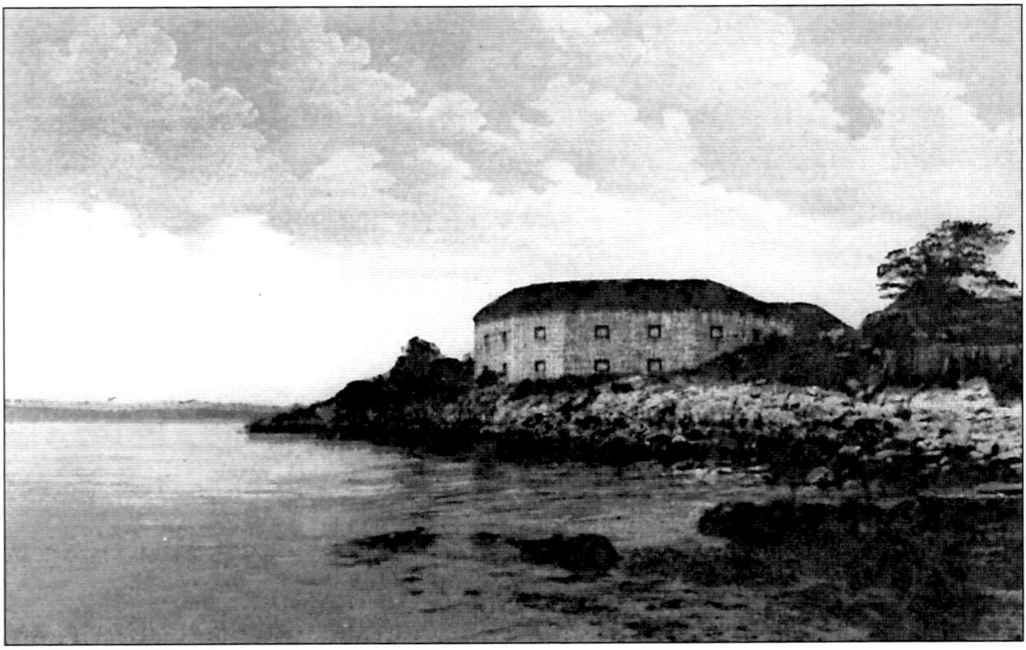

Another view of the imposing and sturdy Fort Scammel.

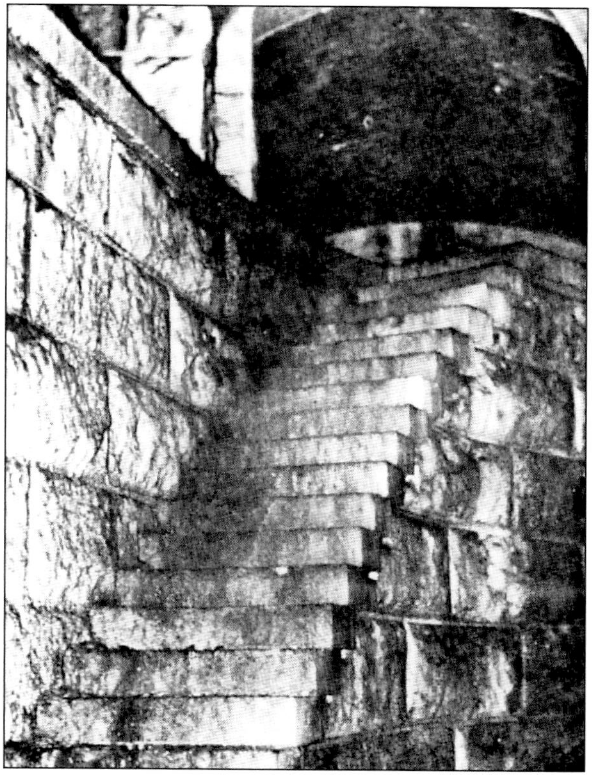

Stairs to the underground chambers. Mystery and history pervades these passages. What was life like here?

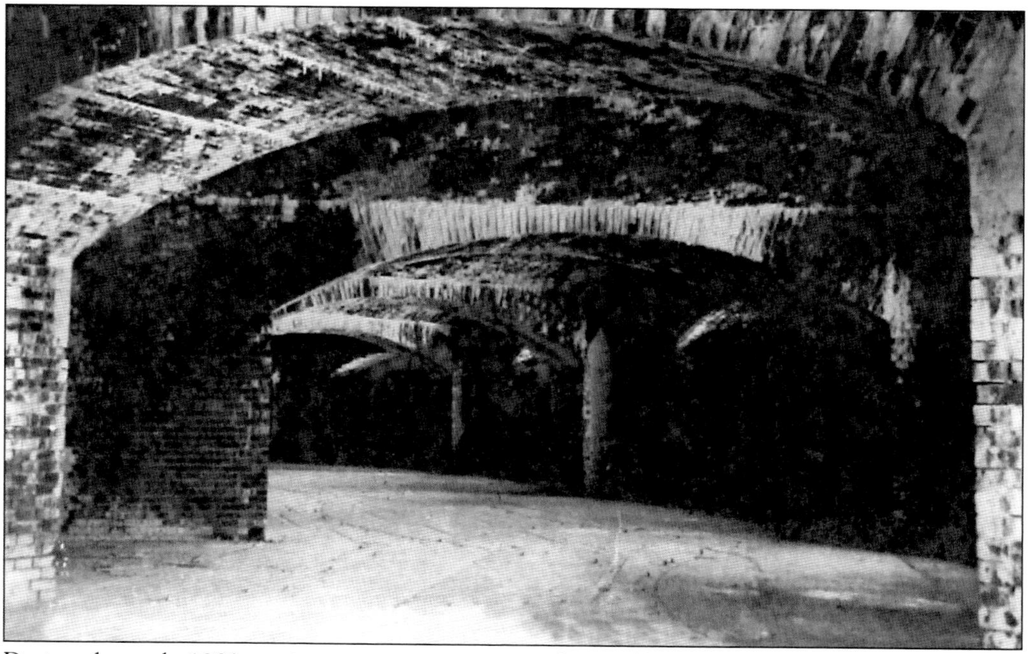

During the early 1900s an immigration station was located here—like a miniature Ellis Island. On summer Sundays neighboring Peaks Islanders would row over to entertain the immigrants.

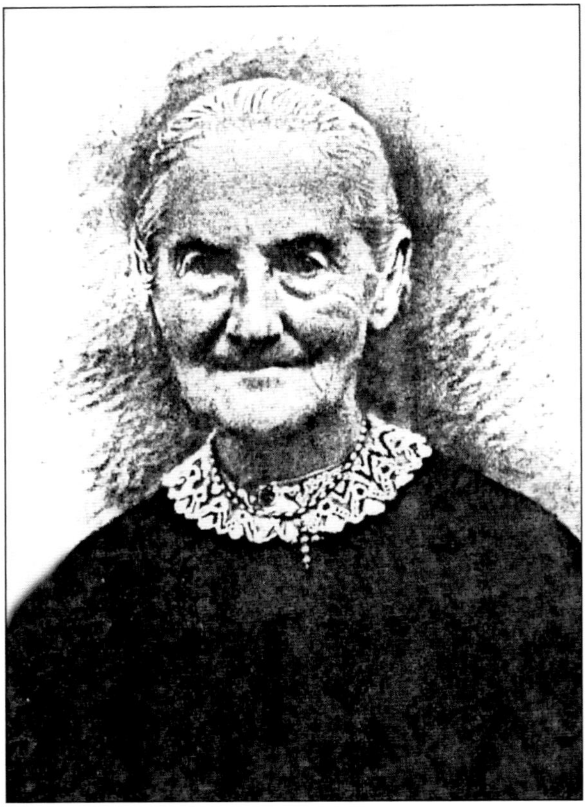

Mary (Polly) Thompson (1795–1880), a well-remembered resident of House Island.

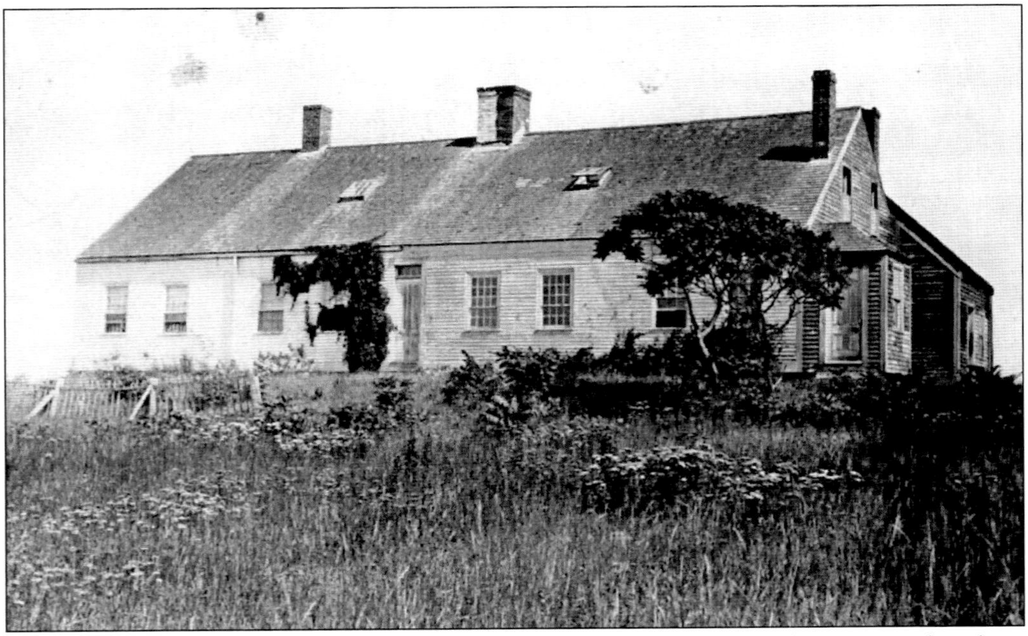

The smallest of the inhabited islands was never a pleasure spot, but more of a year-round working community. The first house was built around 1880.

Ten

Cushing Island

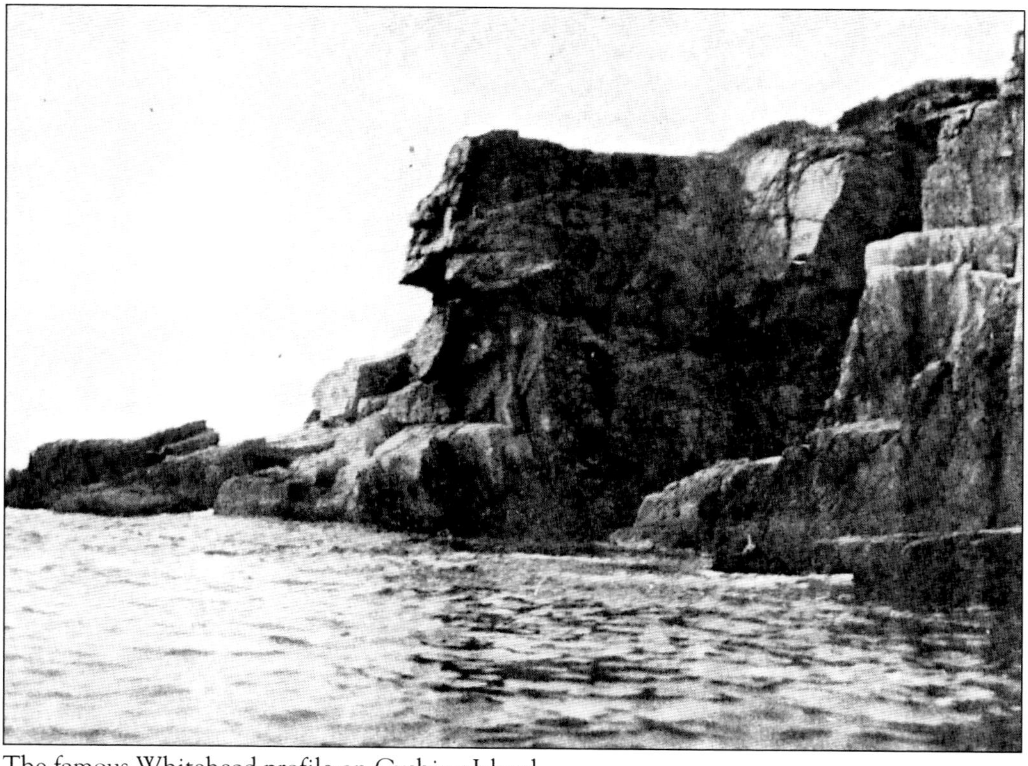

The famous Whitehead profile on Cushing Island.

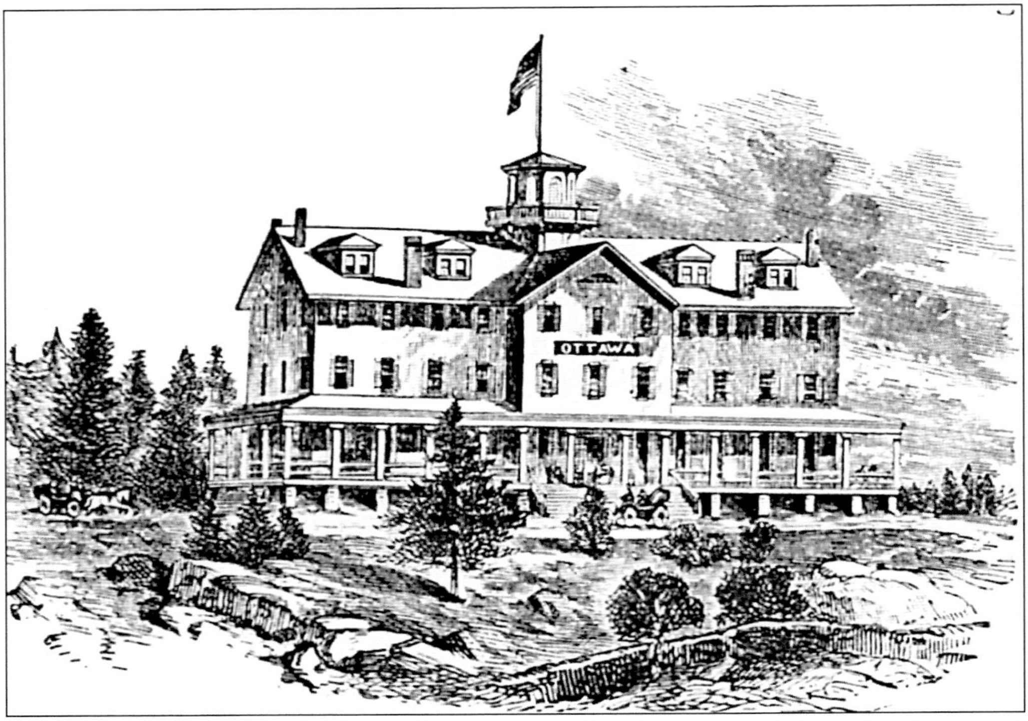

Ottawa House, the showplace of Casco Bay, catered to Canadian visitors. It burned to the ground, was rebuilt, and destroyed by fire a second time due to a total lack of firefighting equipment.

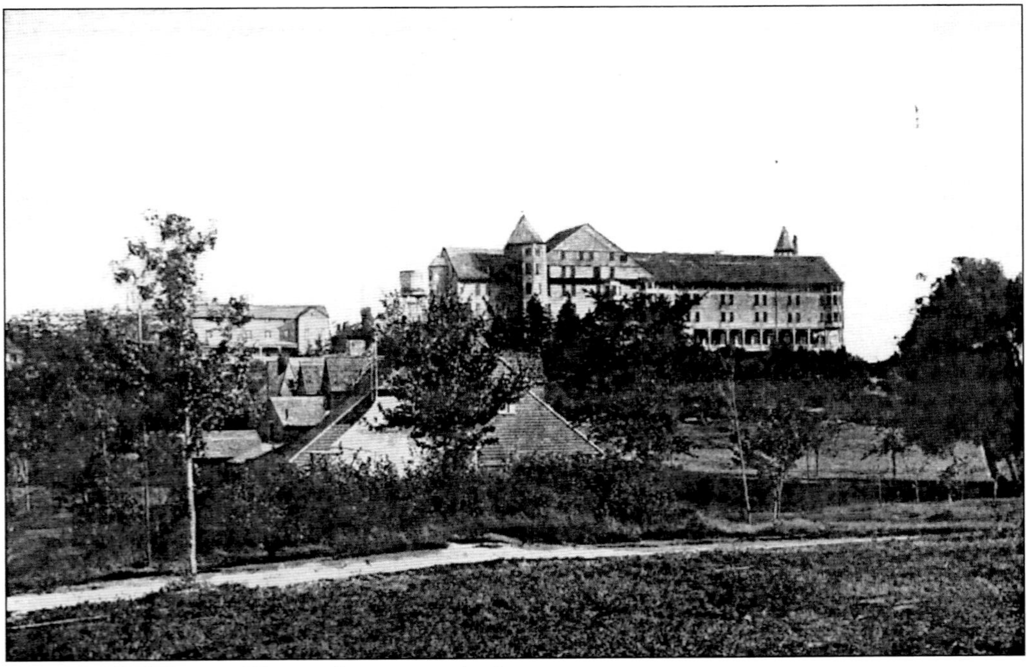

A postcard of Ottawa House after it was rebuilt.

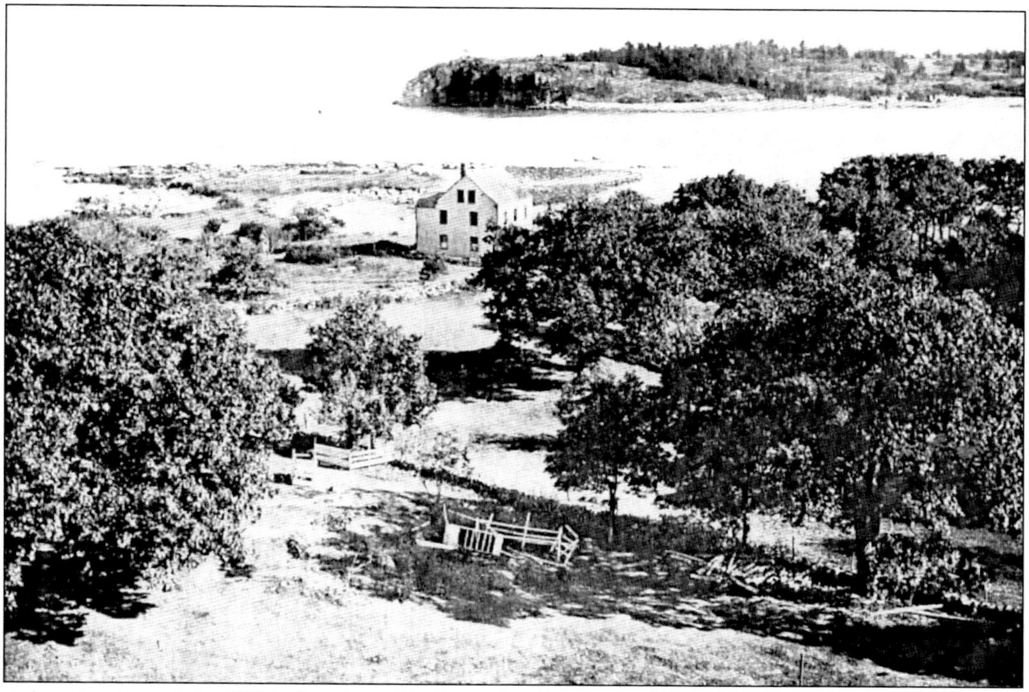

A lovely view of the Whitehead profile from the Greenwood Garden observatory.

Many of the cottages on Cushing and the Diamond Islands were designed by the famous architect, Dortegos. Cottages on Peaks Island in particular have been given some intriguing and endearing names over the years, such as "Big Enough," "Camp Comfort," "Oak Rest," "Uncle Tom's Cabin," "Bide-a-Wee," "Sans Souci," "Dozen in One," "Camp Lookout," and "Lift the Latch."

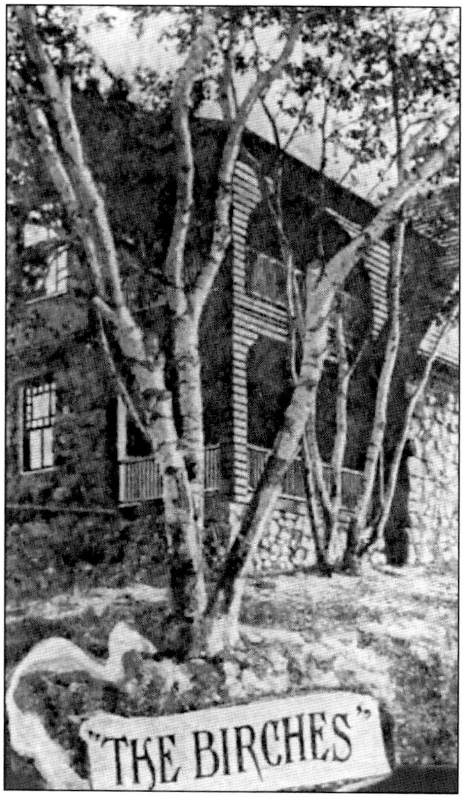

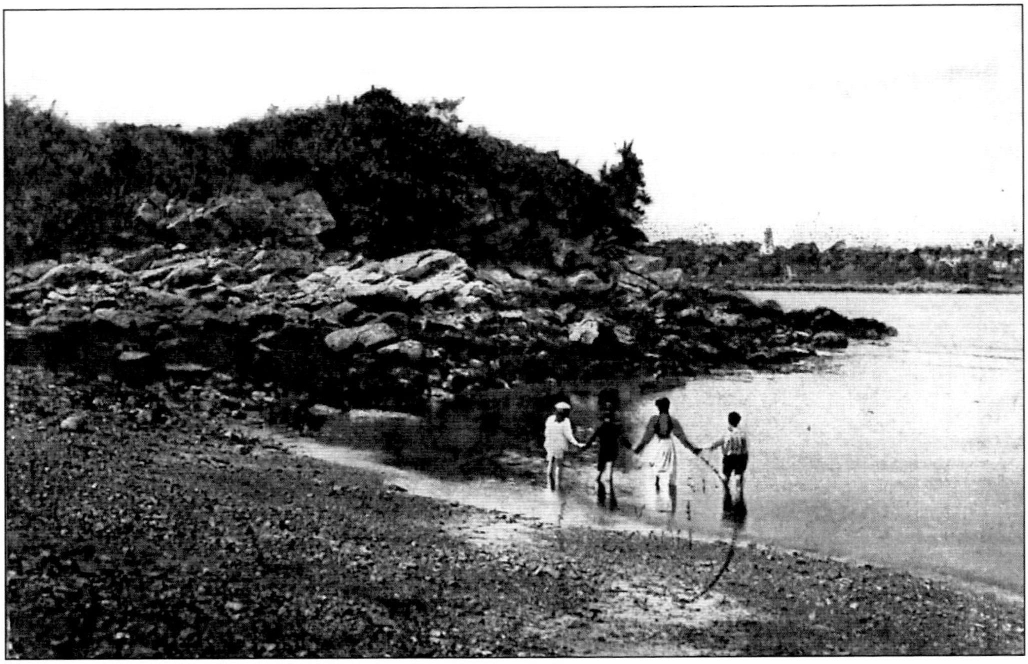

Children enjoying the surf in Spring Cove.

Cushing's Point with Fort Scammel in the distance.

Eleven

Little Diamond Island

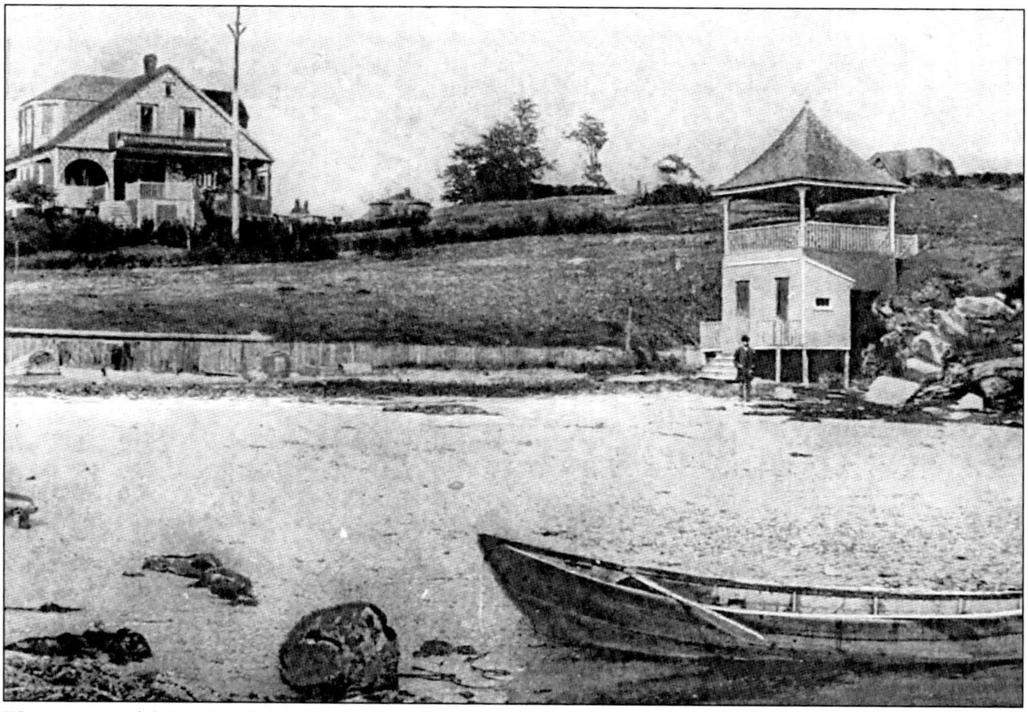

"Sonnenstrahl," A.M. Smith's summer home on Little Diamond Island on a lovely day.

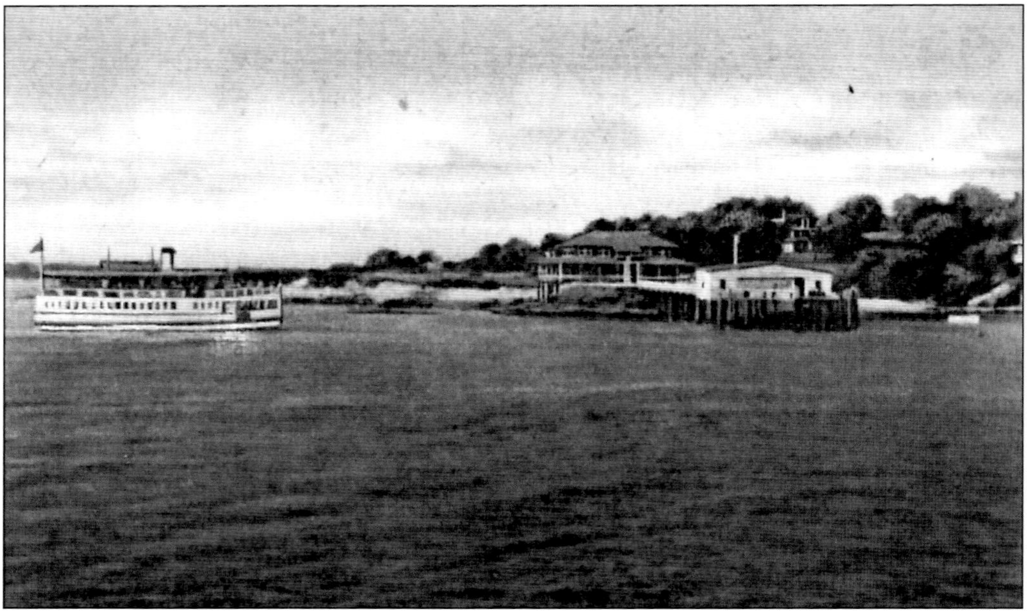

The steamer *Gurnet* approaching Little Diamond Island wharf.

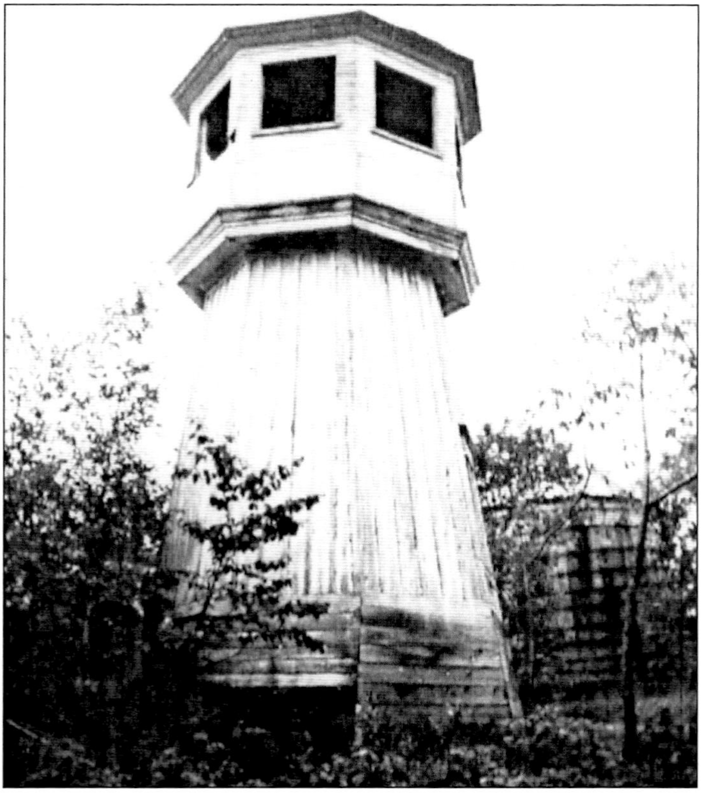

The old Breakwater Lighthouse. The tower of the lighthouse was moved to the island in the 1870s. To the right is the original water storage tank.

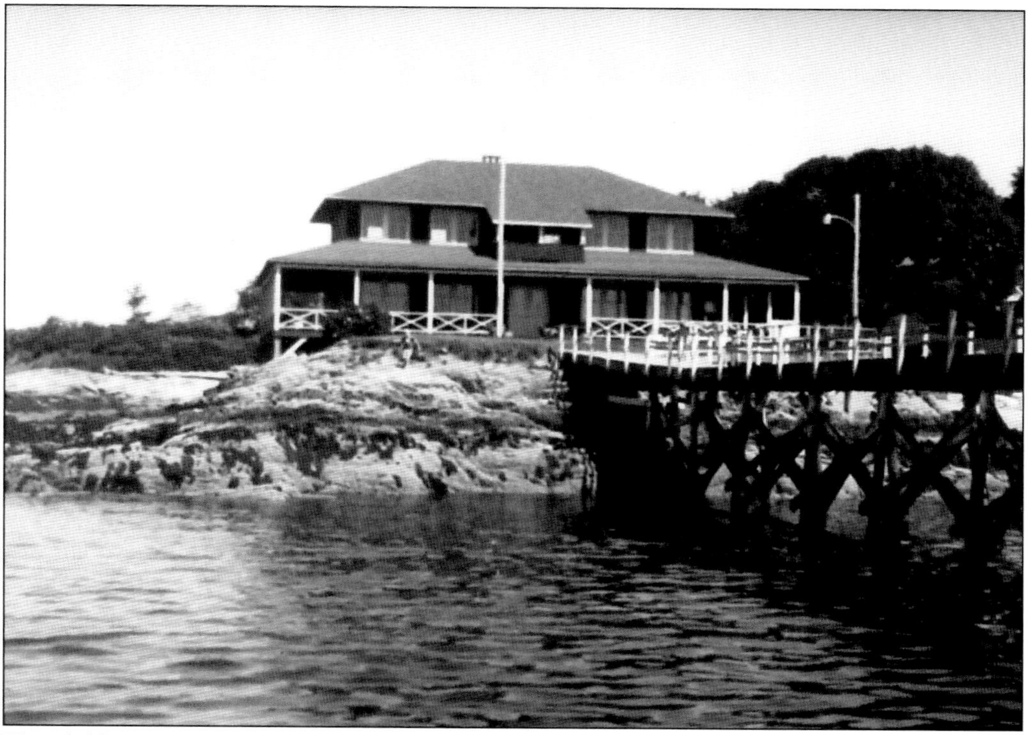

The clubhouse at the new wharf in 1908.

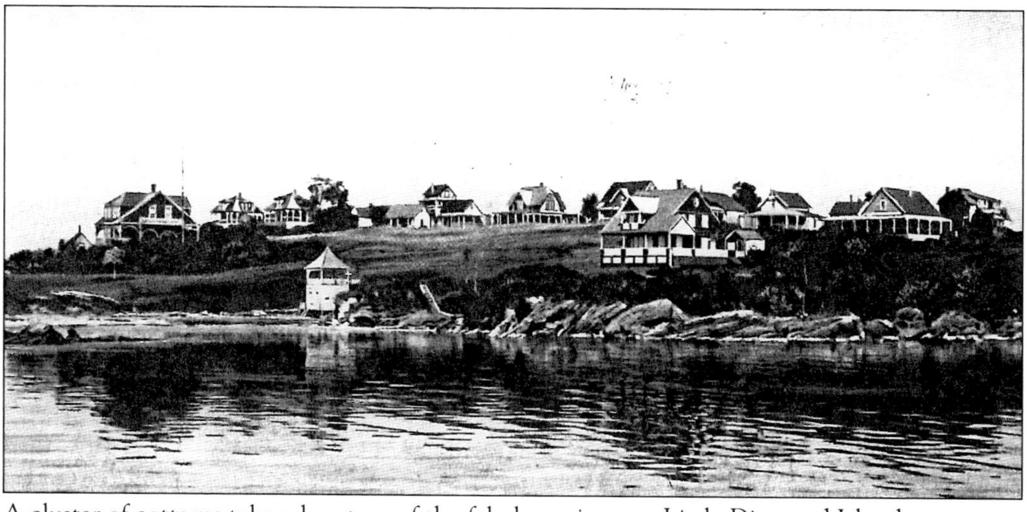

A cluster of cottages take advantage of the fabulous views on Little Diamond Island.

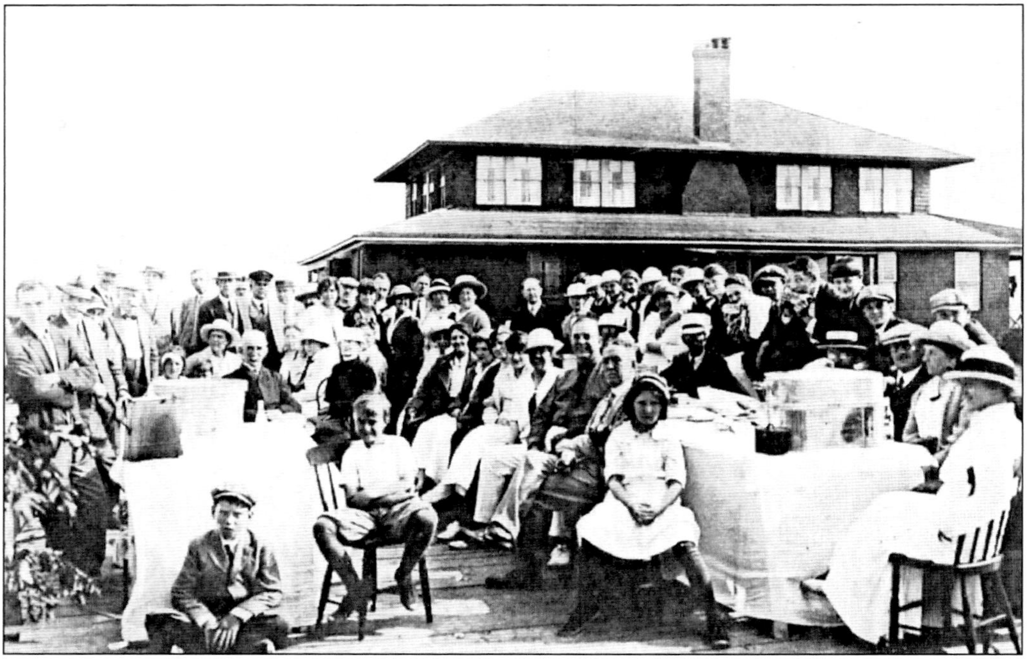

A huge summer party was thrown by Mr. Smith at his home on Little Diamond Island. It looks as if everyone has dressed up for the occasion.

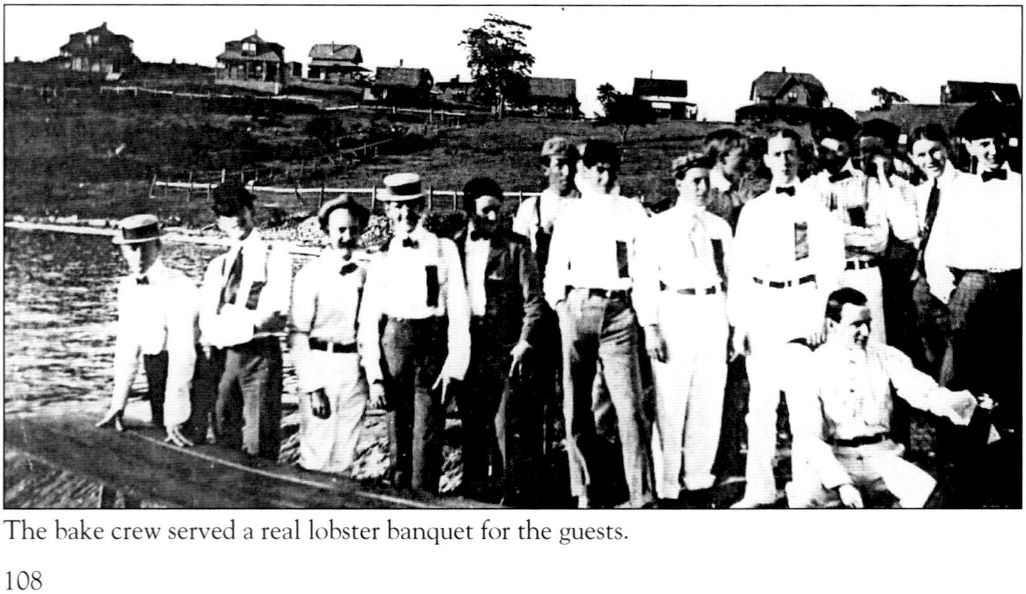

The bake crew served a real lobster banquet for the guests.

Twelve

Great Diamond Island

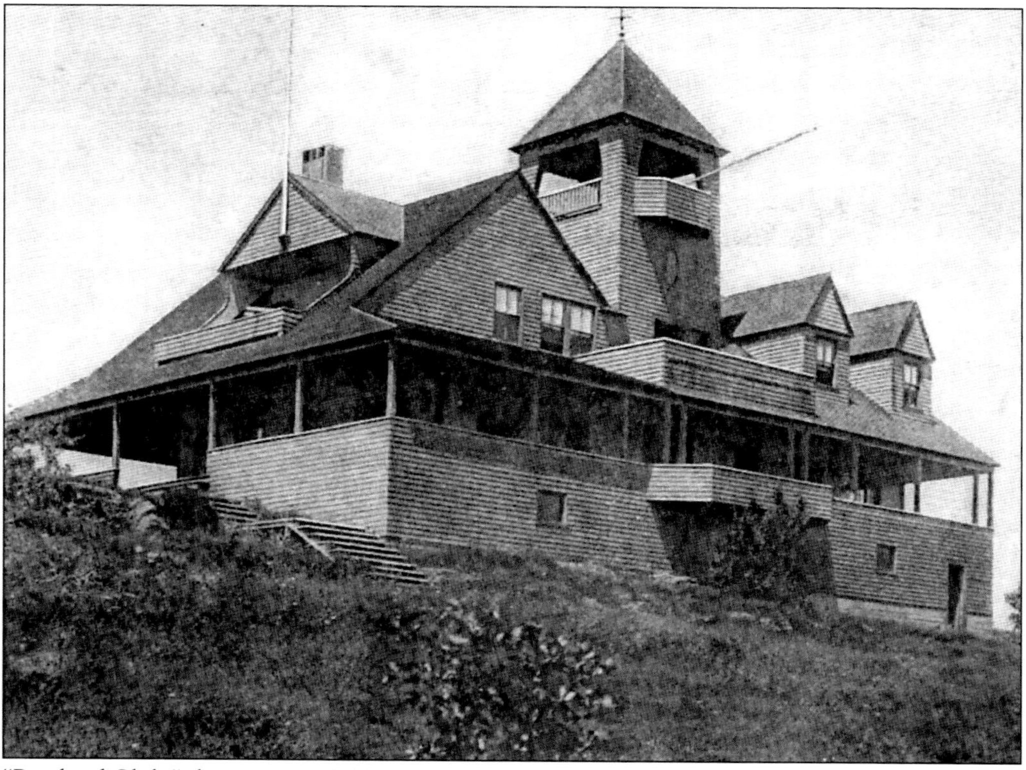

"Portland Club," the summer clubhouse, was the center of all activity on Great Diamond Island. It was designed by the famous architect, John Calvin Stevens, and completed in 1888. The two Diamond Islands are connected by a sandbar which is traversable at low tide. The islands were originally called Hog Islands.

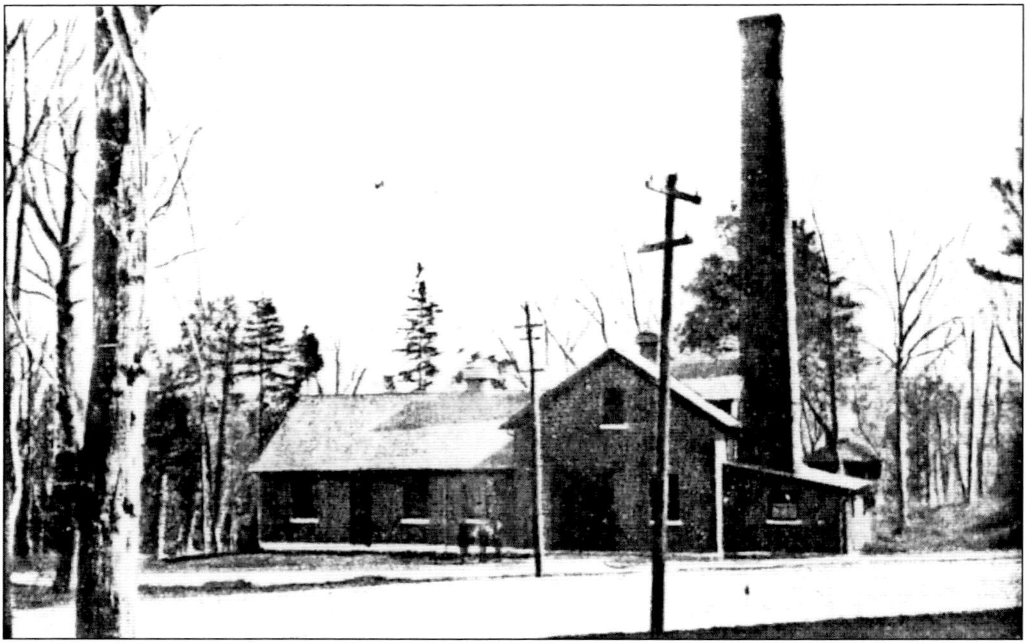

A reservation was built to defend the harbor and nearby islands during World Wars I and II. This postcard shows the pumping station at Fort McKinley.

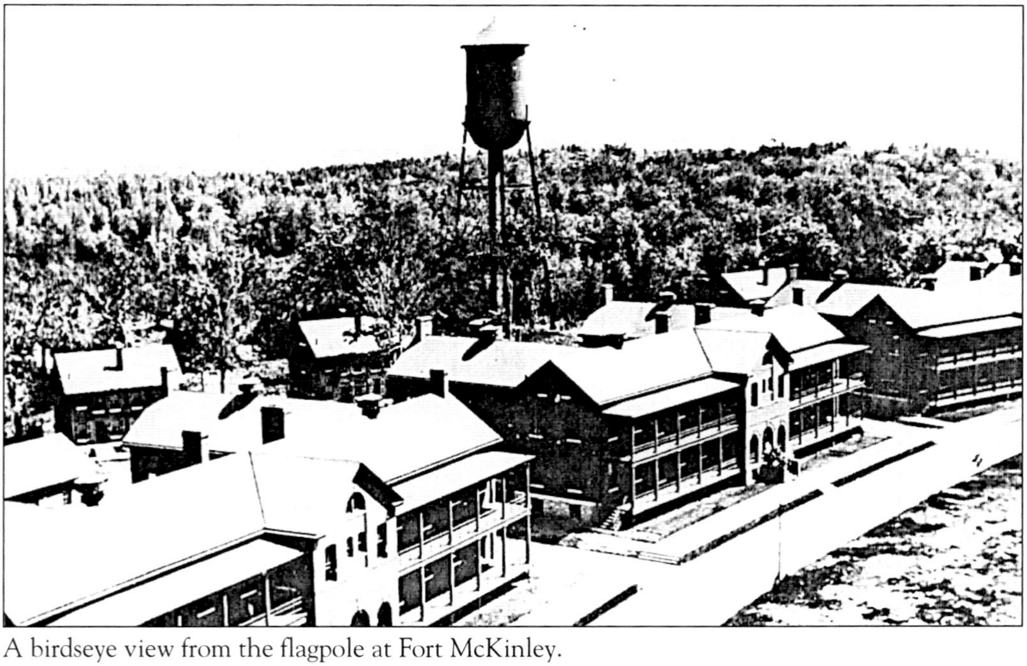

A birdseye view from the flagpole at Fort McKinley.

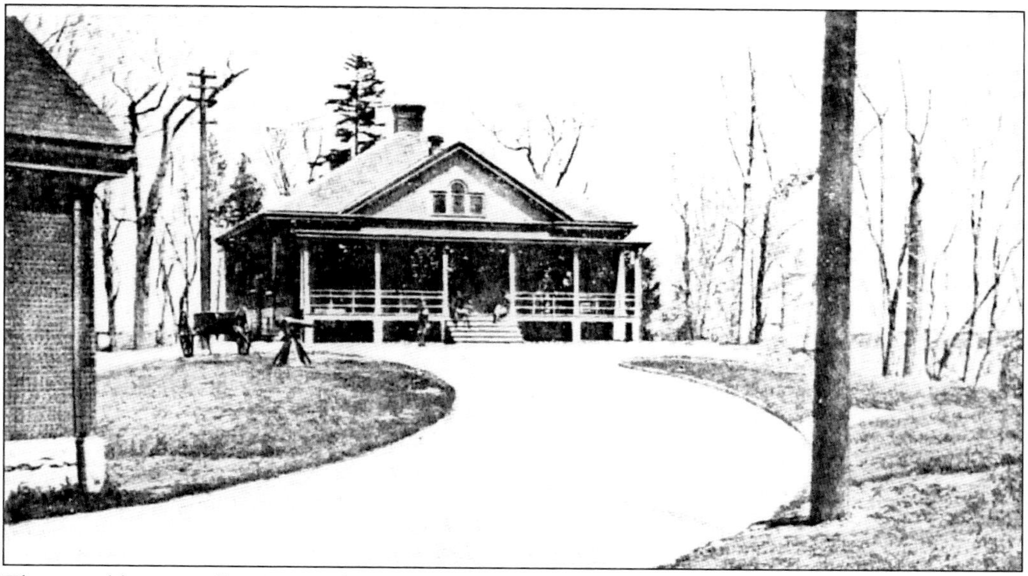

The guard house at Fort McKinley.

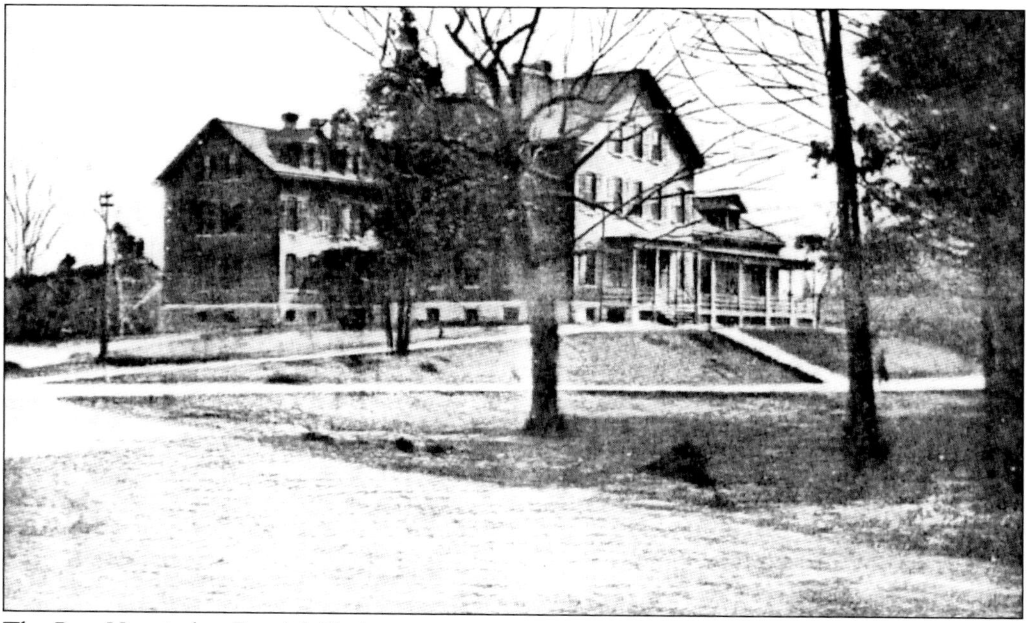

The Post Hospital at Fort McKinley.

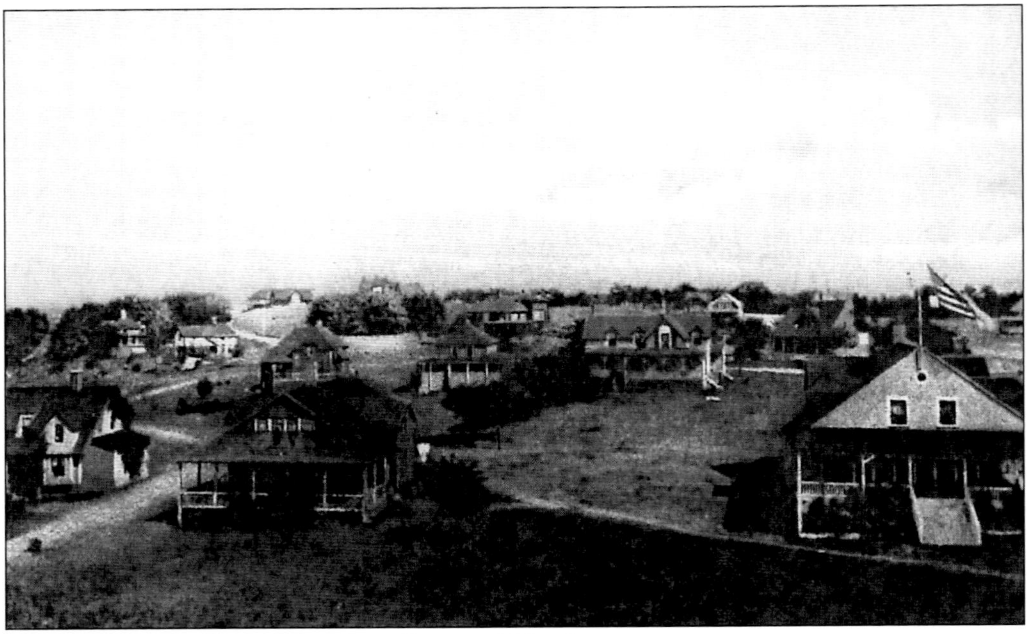

A selection of the cottages on Great Diamond Island.

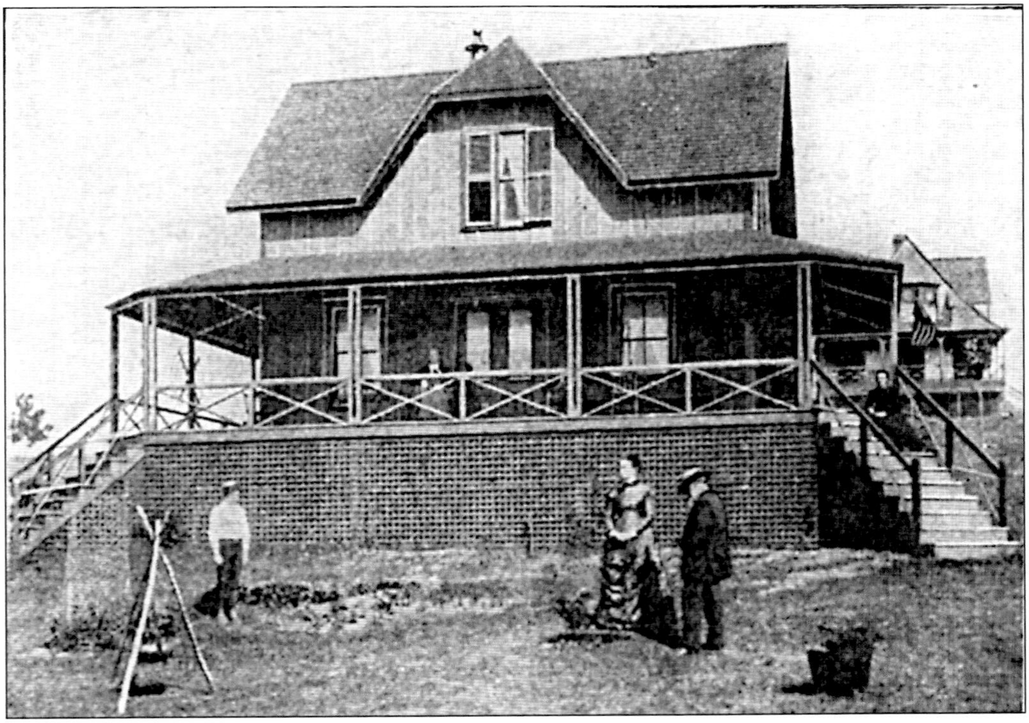

Cooking outdoors in the yard of George H. Libby's summer cottage.

Thirteen
Long Island

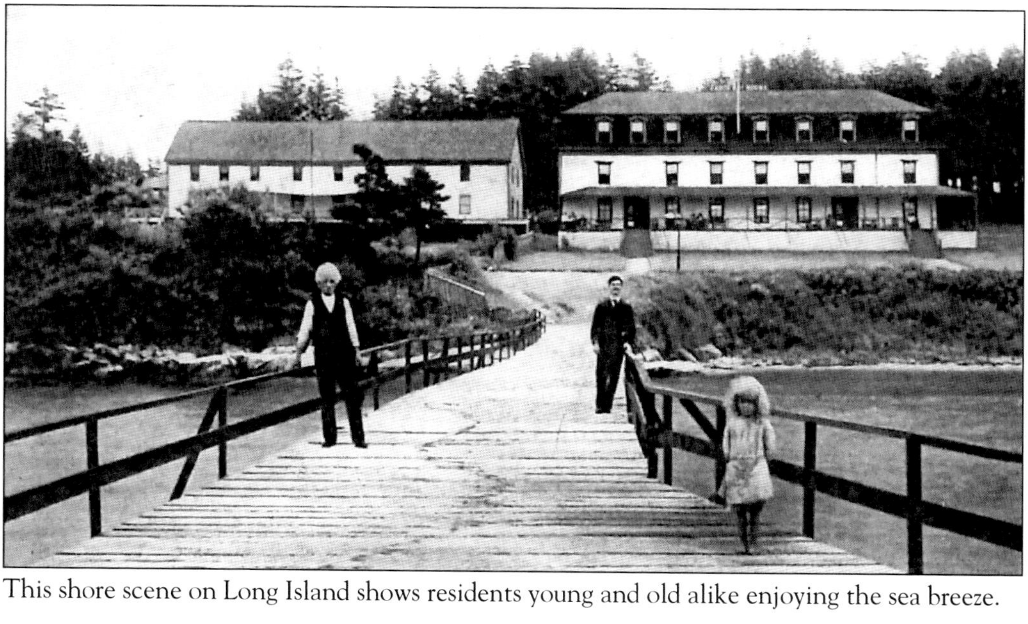

This shore scene on Long Island shows residents young and old alike enjoying the sea breeze.

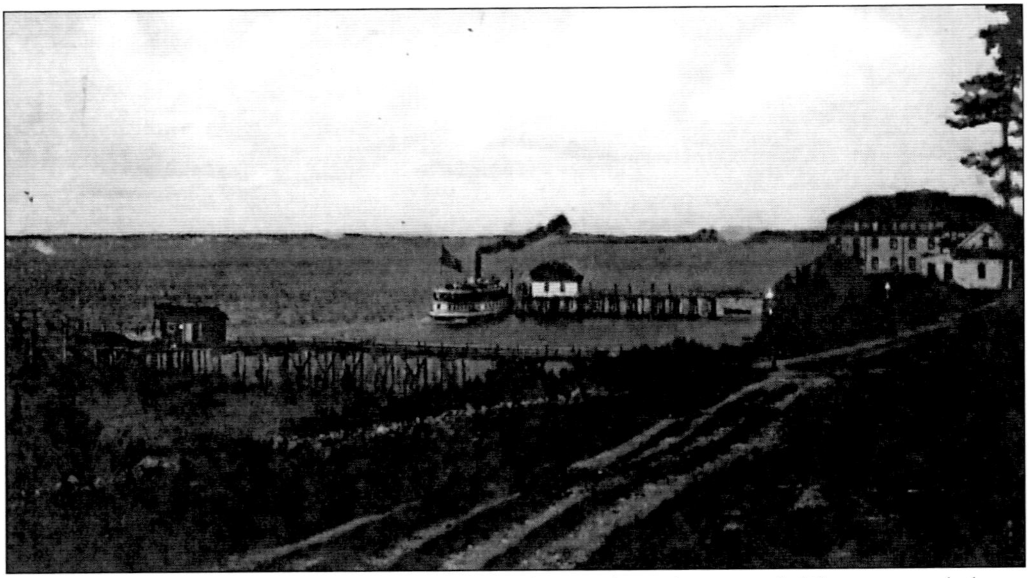

Long Island was so long that three different wharves have been used. This postcard shows Doughty's and Ponce's Landings.

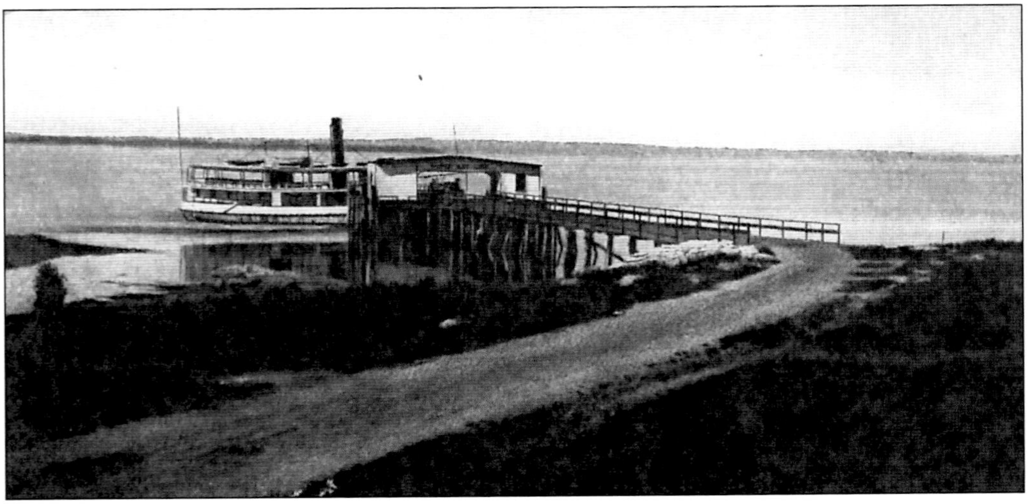

Doughty's Landing.

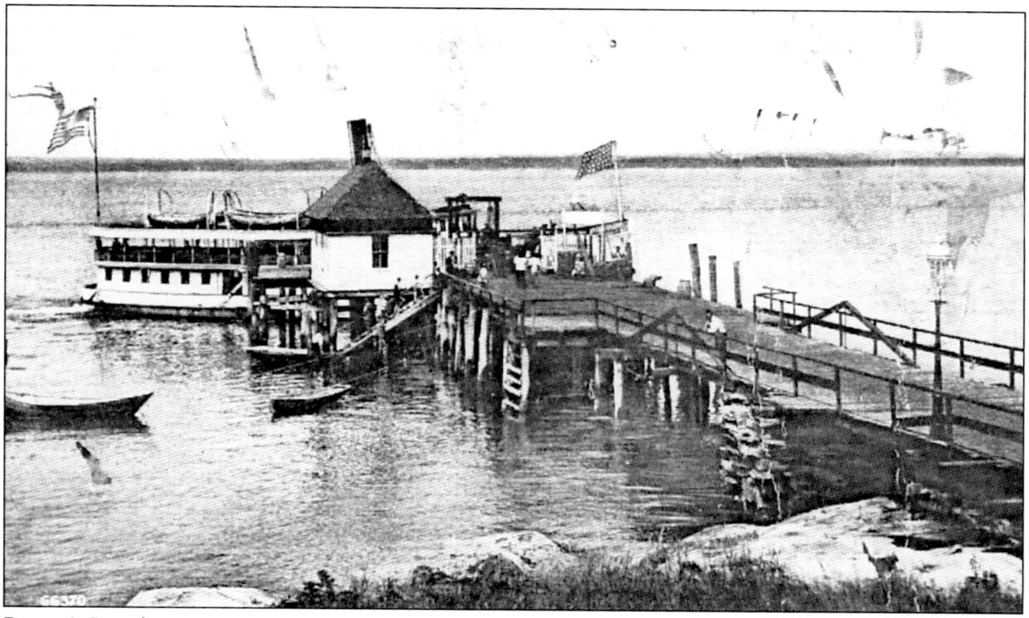

Ponce's Landing.

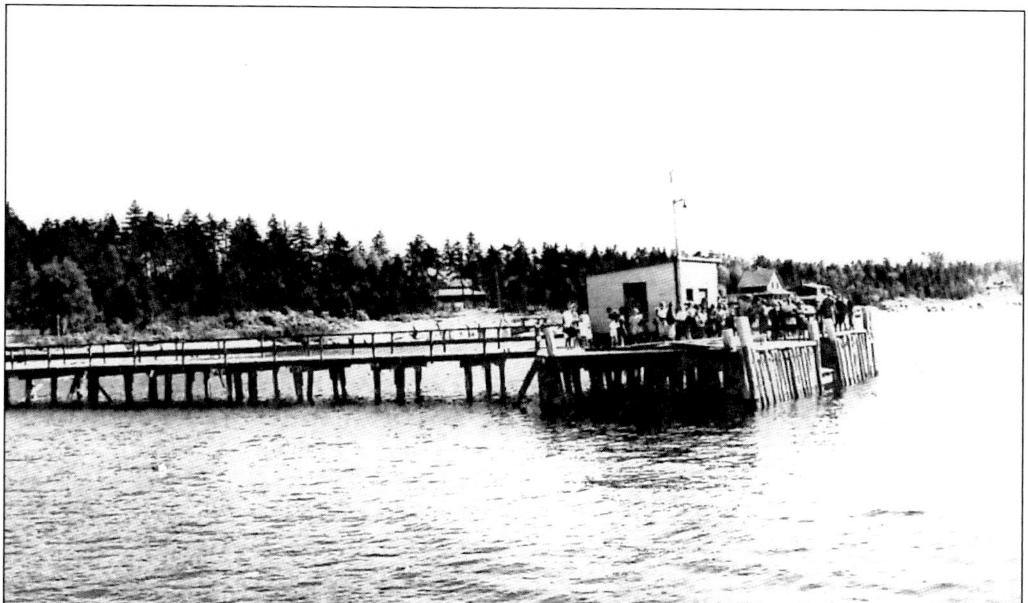

Boat's late again! Doughty's Landing, crowded with passengers awaiting the boat. Living on an island makes you aware that time schedules cannot be maintained too strictly where the weather and the ocean are involved.

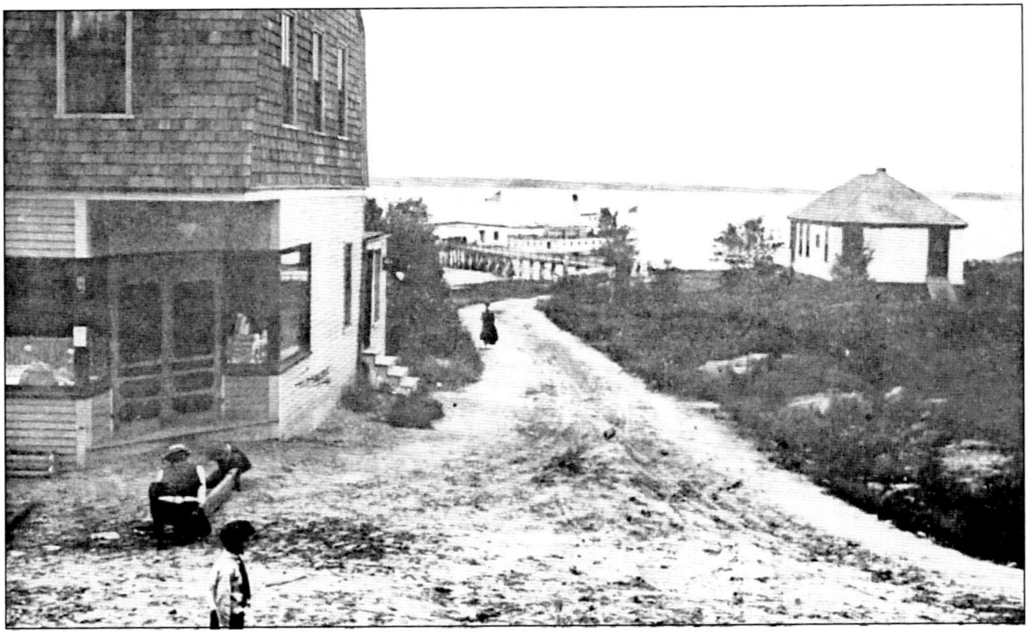

She'd better hurry or she'll miss the boat!

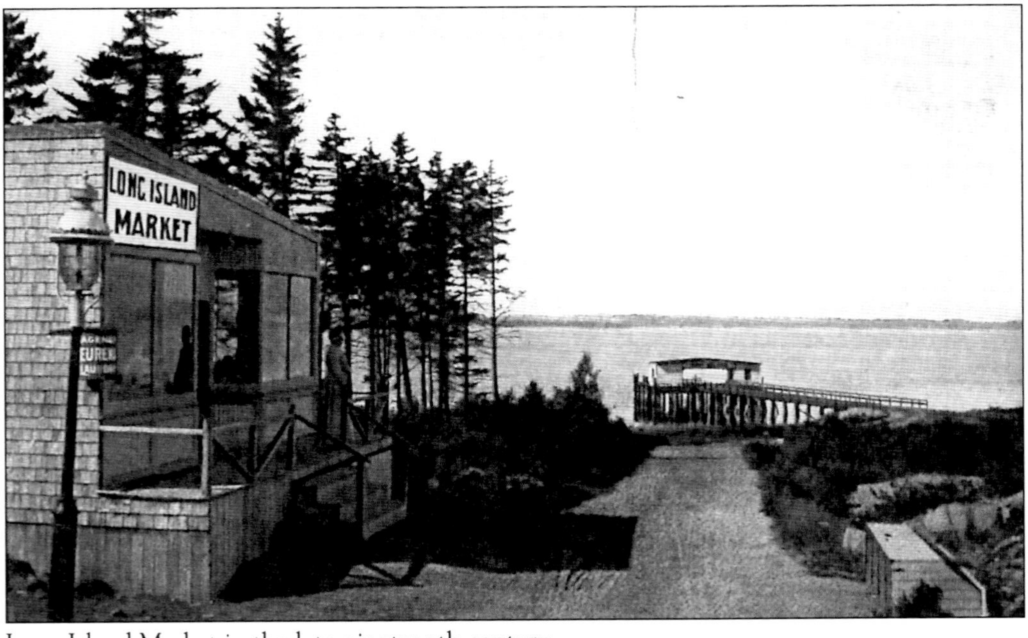

Long Island Market in the late nineteenth century.

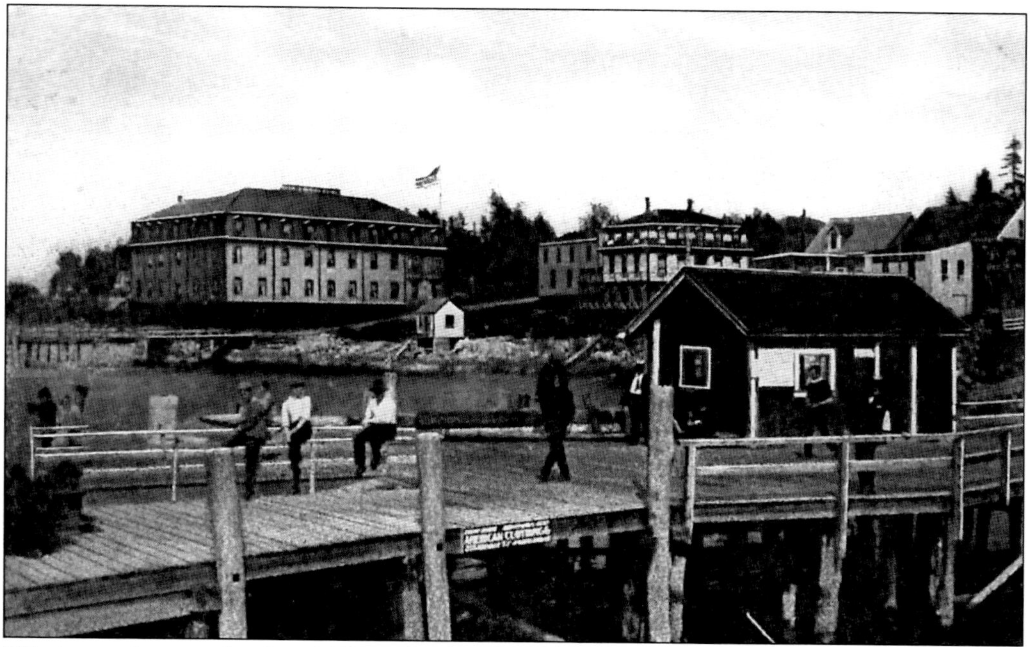

Who's coming on the boat? The wharf and waterfront on Long Island, with some of the prominent old buildings in the background.

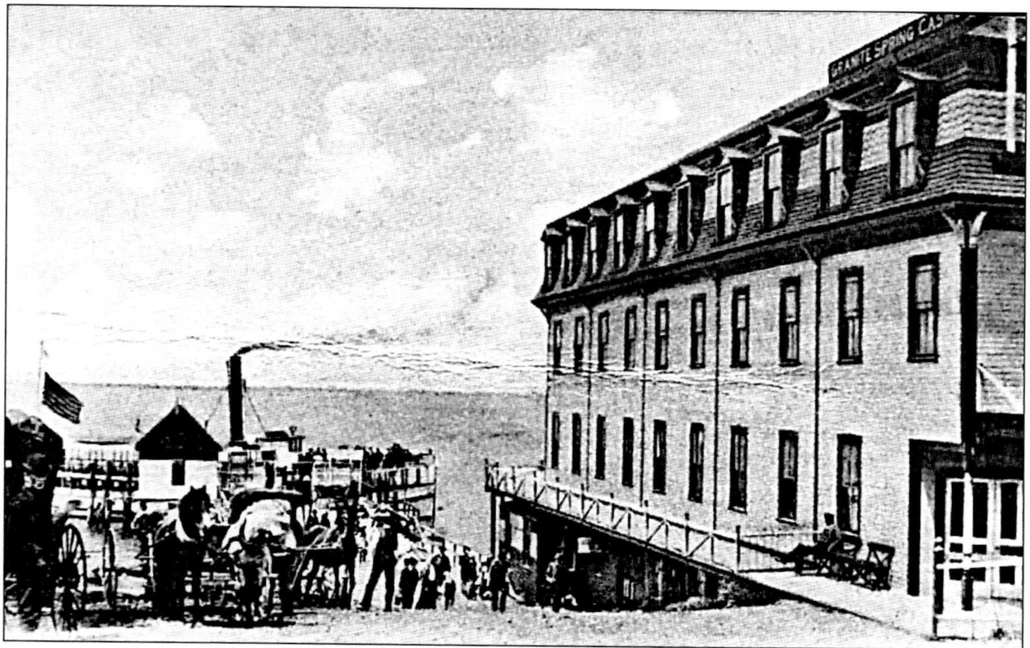

Hustle and bustle around the steamboat landing on Long Island.

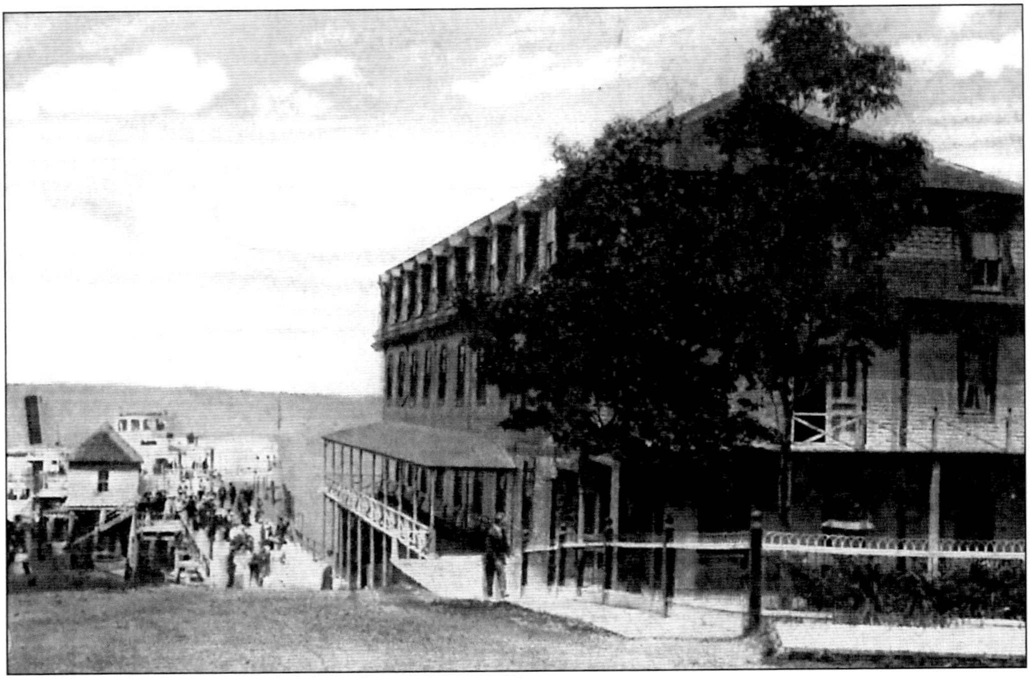
The New Granite Spring Hotel at Ponce's Landing.

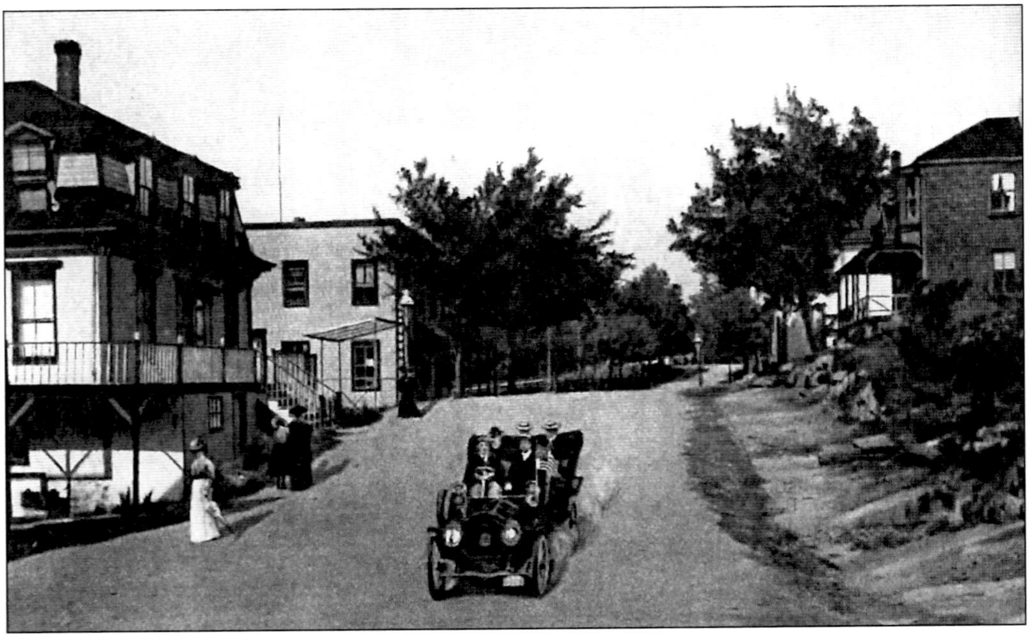
A Long Island street scene.

Fourteen

Chebeague Island

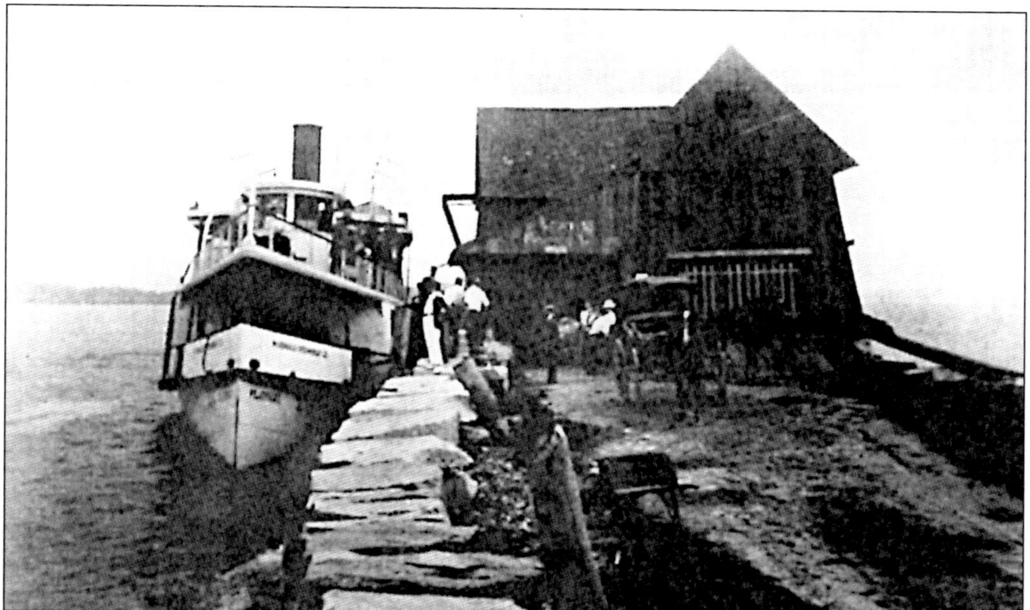

The *Pejepscot* unloading passengers and freight at the Stone Wharf on the northeastern end of Chebeague Island.

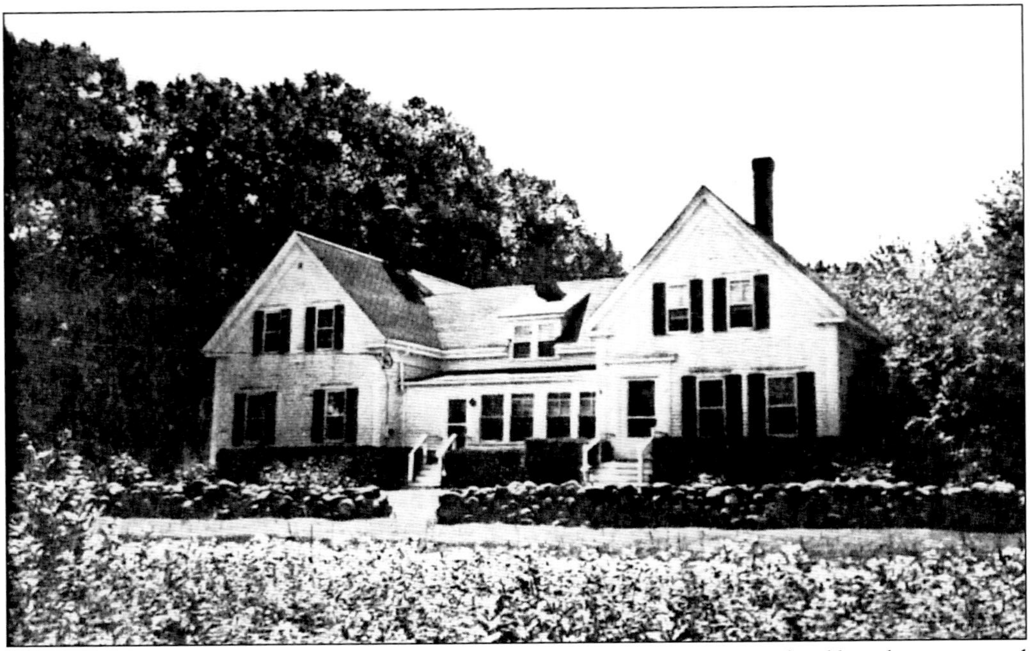

The McCall House. The owner of this Greek Revival home was an avid golfer who supported the creation of a golf course on the island.

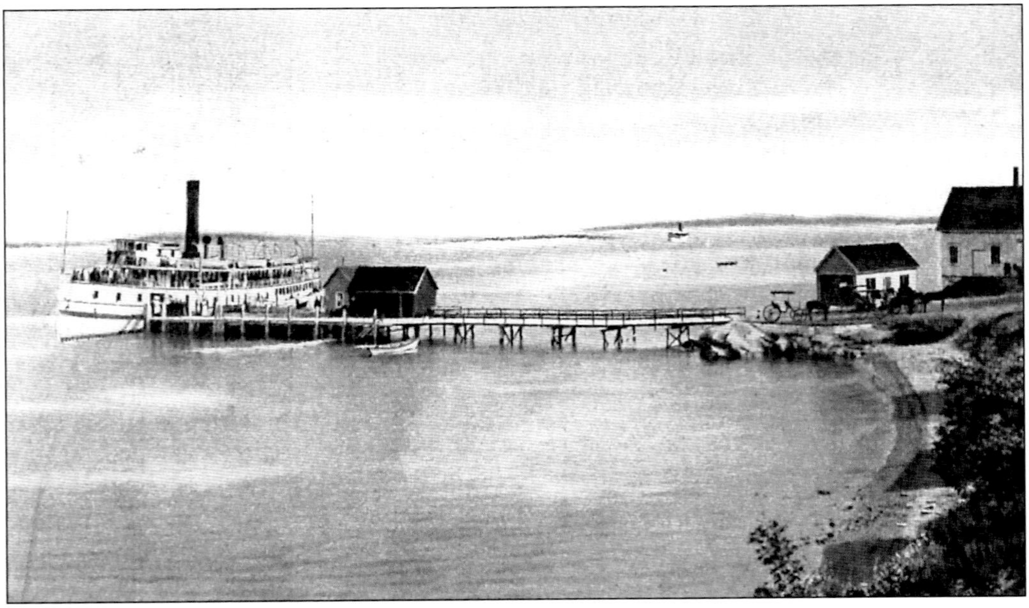

Littlefield's Landing.

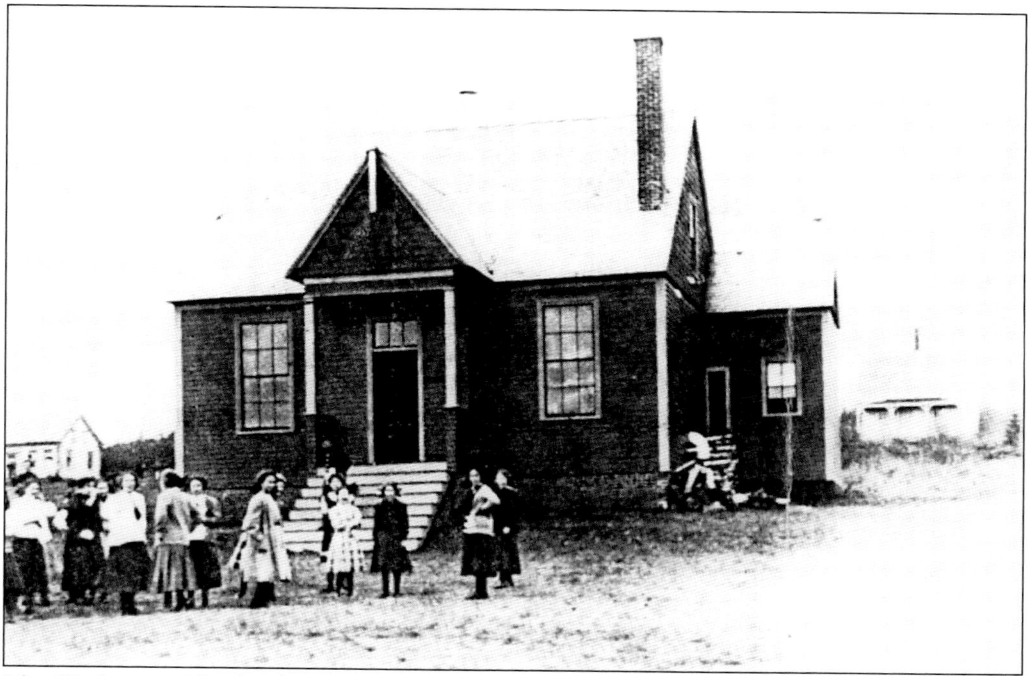

The Chebeague Island Schoolhouse in the late nineteenth century.

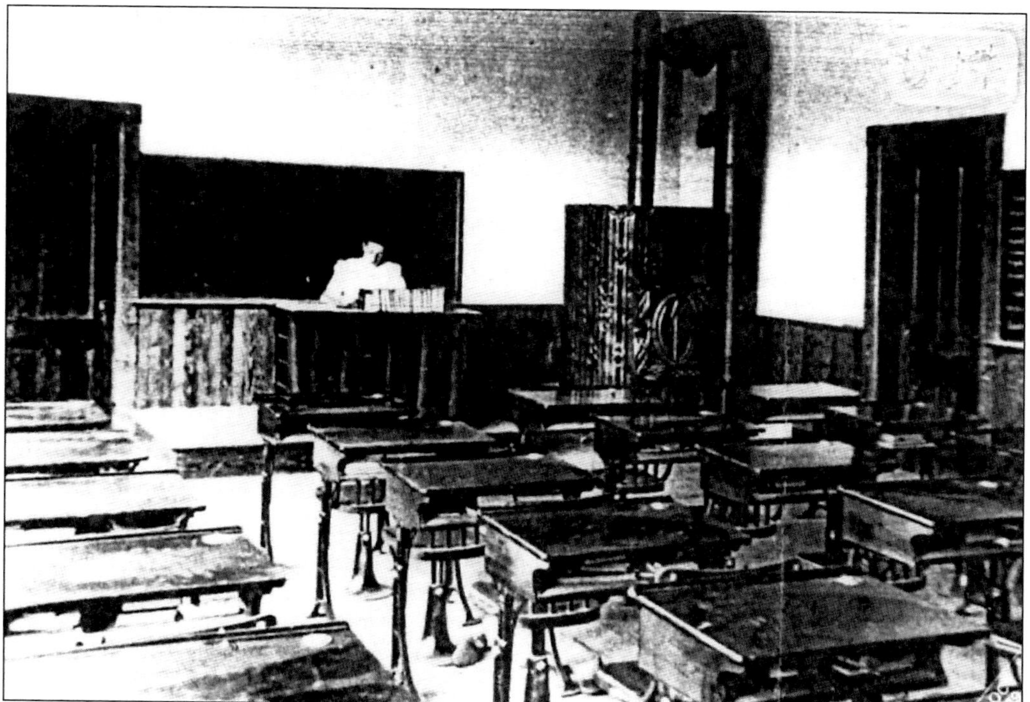

A Chebeague Island schoolteacher in the days when the only heating system was an enormous woodstove in the one-room school.

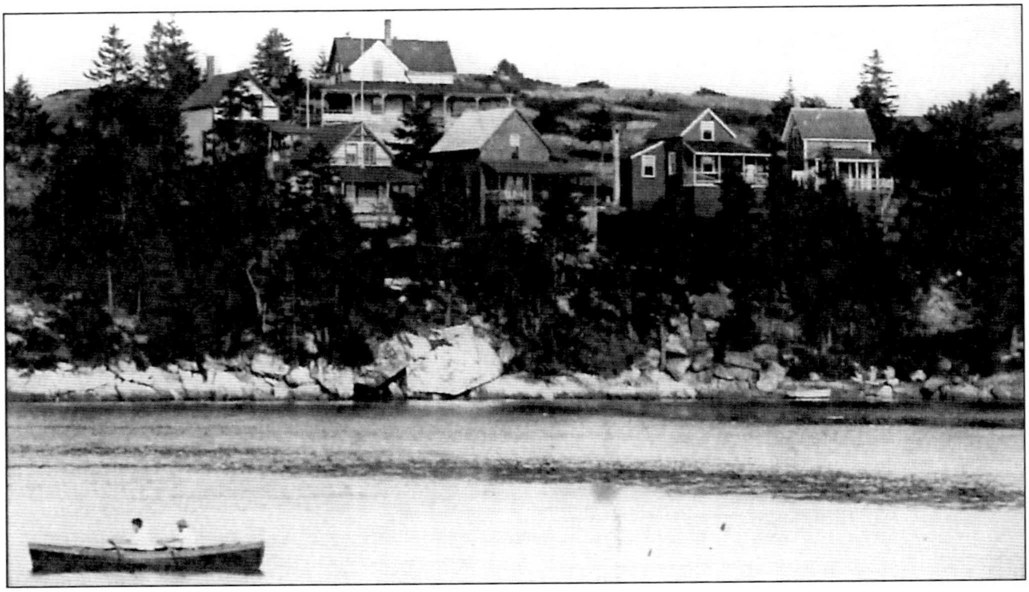

These homes have a lovely view all year round.

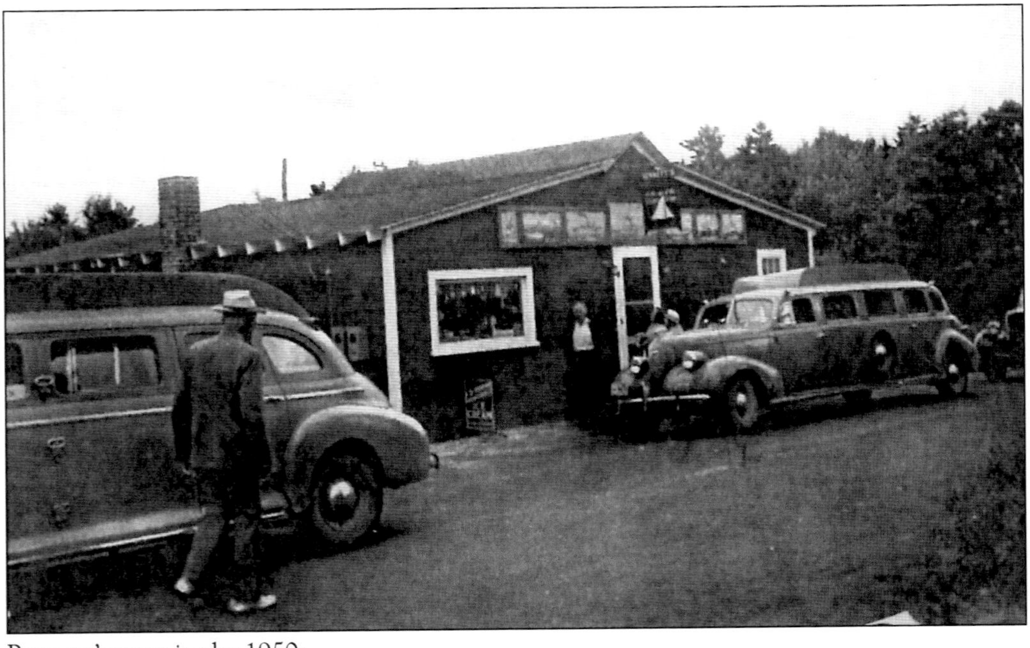

Bennett's store in the 1950s.

Fifteen
Cliff Island

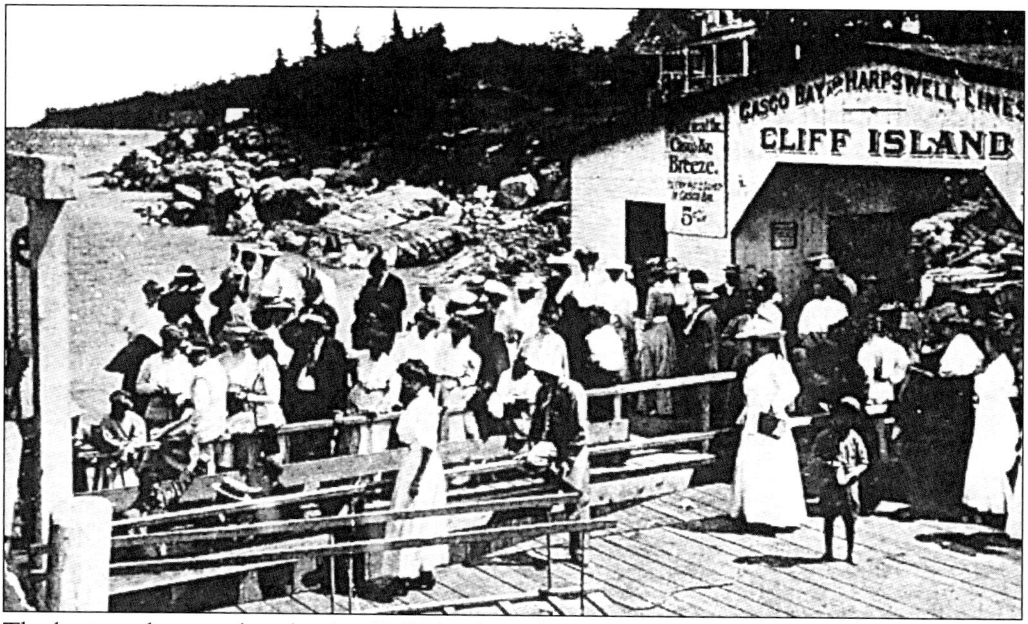

The busiest place on the island—Cliff Island Landing.

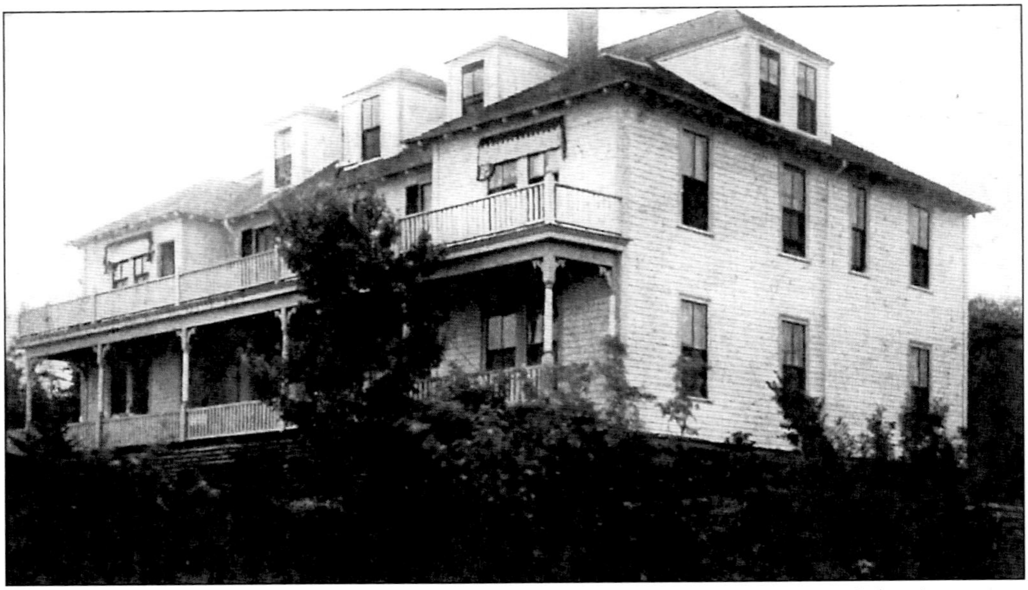

A picture from a 1906 postcard that was sent out to advertise the opening of the Aucocisco House. The proprietor was Walter A. Castner.

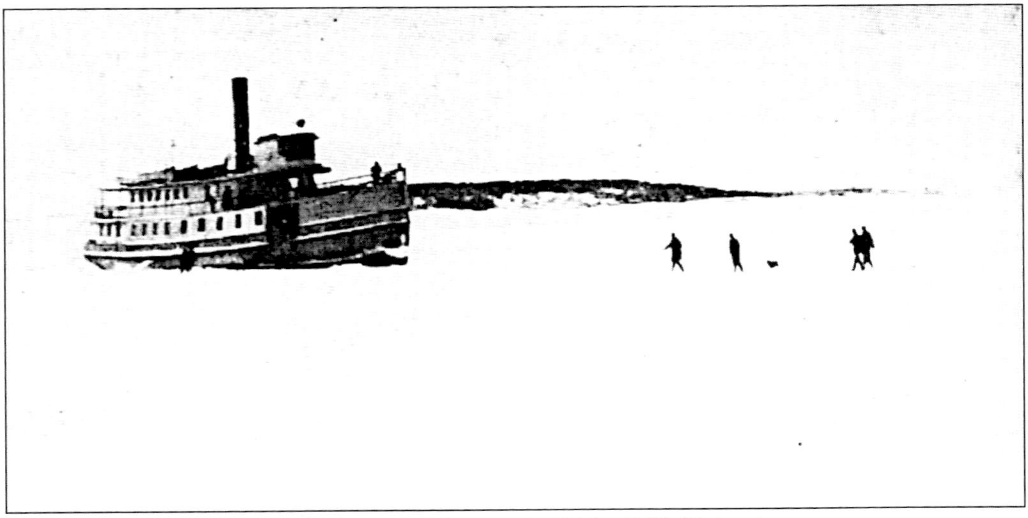

An amazing ice landing took place on February 1, 1918 off Cliff Island.

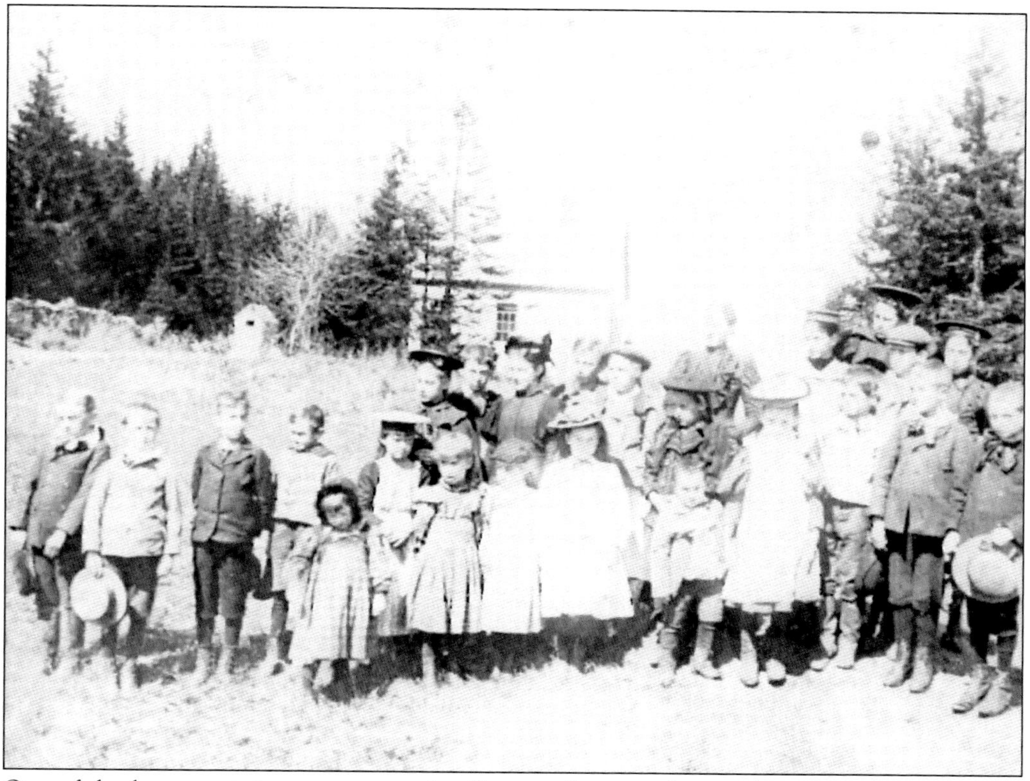

One of the last remaining one-room schoolhouses. Parents of its students have had to fight a long, drawn-out battle to keep it from being closed in the face of cutbacks.

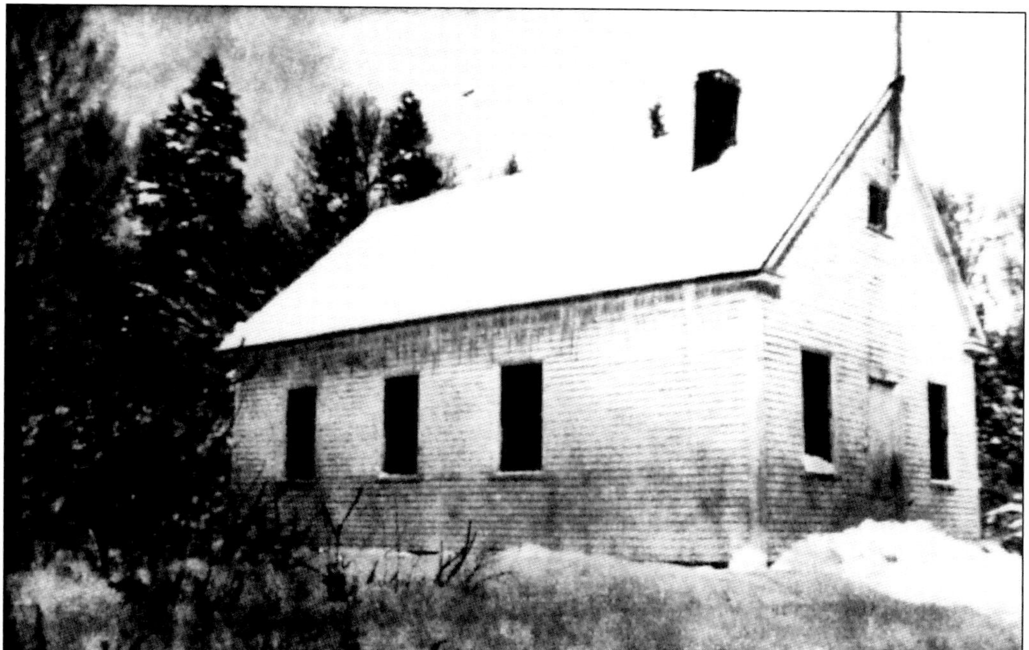

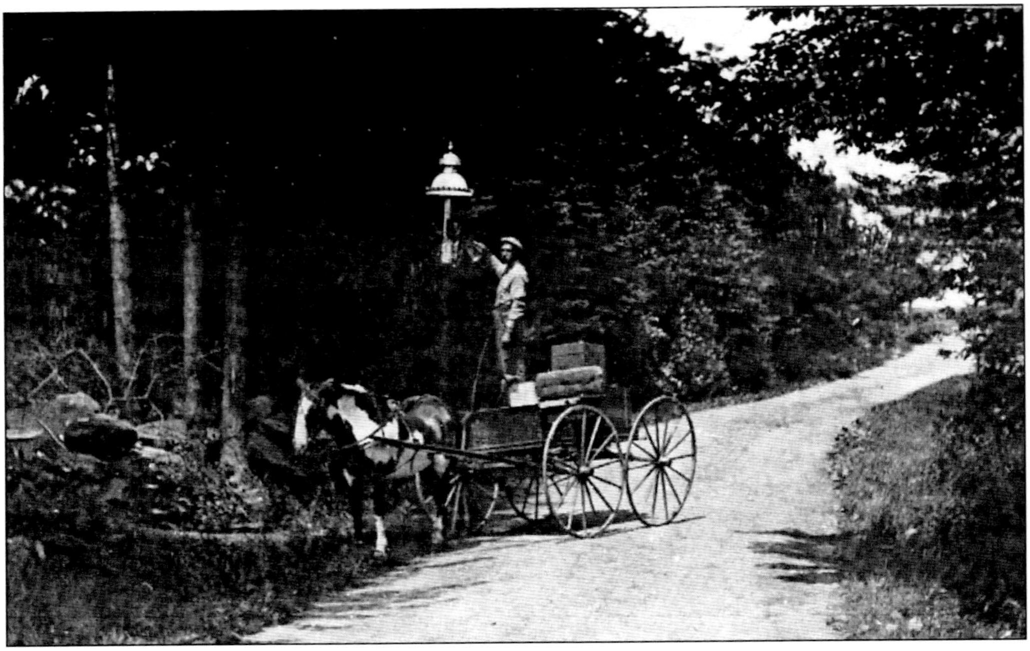

The old lamplighter on Cliff Island.

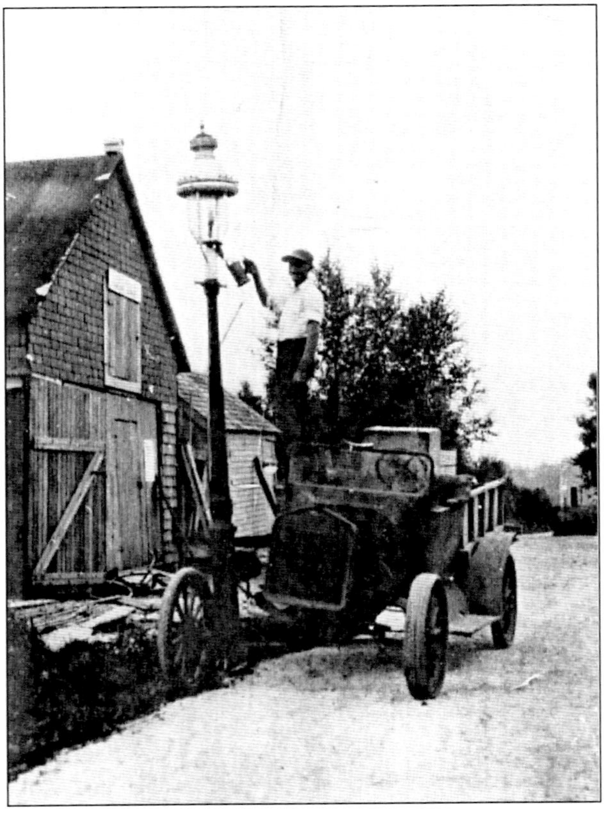

He probably made better time on his evening rounds in the "flivver."

Sixteen

Fort Gorges

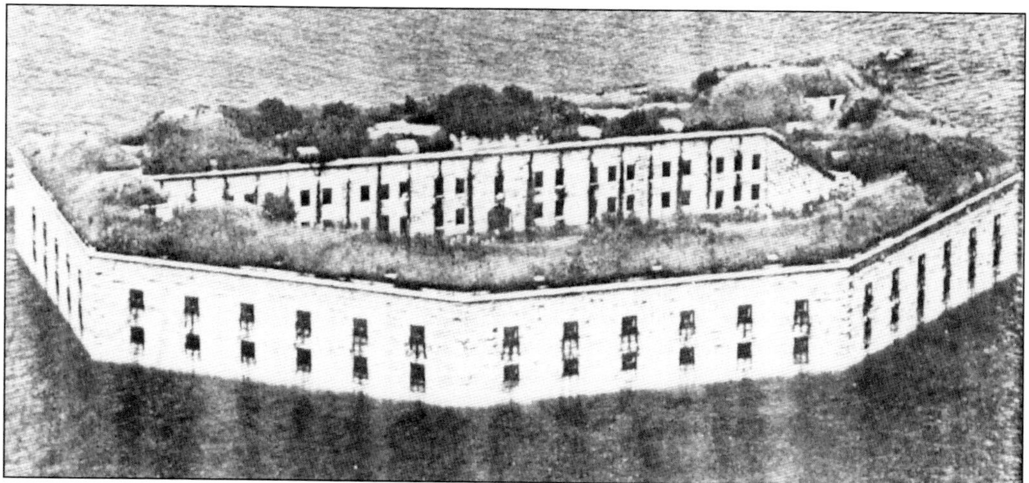

Fort Gorges, a vast granite fort, is the only major landmark in Maine named for Sir Ferdinando Gorges, the backer of the earliest discovery of Maine.

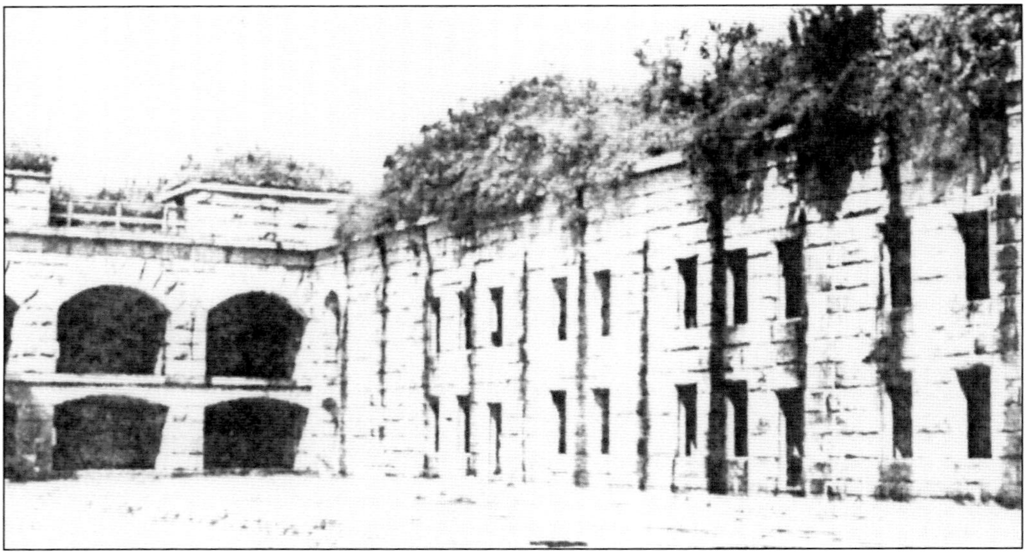

An interior of Fort Gorges.

Acknowledgments

To all who shared their knowledge and treasures with me, and especially to: Dick Adams, Bette Beane, Nancy Bartlett, Nancy Beebe, Eleanor Cushing, Starr Demitre, Marge and Richard Erico, Bob Foley, Dot and John Flynn, Bea Gulliver, Clint Graffam, Leatrice Hasson, Mary Haynes, Hal Hackett, Rick Hasson, Rev. Charles Hale, Martha Hamilton, Beth Harmon, Eileen Herrick, Nance Ivers, Mary Jaquith, Herman Littlejohn, Debbie Lucatores, Larry Legere, Marion Litchfield, Kevin MacIsaac, Doug MacVane, Pat MacGillicudy, Lynne Mills, Judy Morris, Editha Nelson, Kathy Newell, Virginia Paton, Steve Pedersen, Betty Sterling, Earl Shettleworth, Jan Sullivan, Gloria Nilsen Stackhouse, Sister Rosina, Kay Taylor, Johanna Von Tilling, Helen Verraci-Fana, Lorinda Volls, Gladys Whitten, Maggie Watson, and Gloria Zotos.